ACCLAIM FOR

LORRAINE BRACCO'S

On the Couch

"Pulling no punches, Bracco addresses all."

—*Contra Costa Times*

"Few details are spared in this wrenching personal account."

—*Los Angeles Times*

"This honest and captivating autobiography is just right for summer reading, and fans of *The Sopranos* will not want to miss her page-turner. This is an unflinching look at the realities of fame and fortune from a woman who went to the heights, fell, and is now back on top."

—*Inside Bay Area*

"Best known for playing the famously untalkative Dr. Melfi on TV's *The Sopranos,* Bracco opens up about her life and her profession."

—*The Atlanta Journal-Constitution*

"In her revealing and sometimes shocking memoir, it's Bracco herself who's on the couch."

—NBC's Matt Lauer

On the Couch

Lorraine Bracco

Berkley Books

New York

THE BERKLEY PUBLISHING GROUP
Published by the Penguin Group
Penguin Group (USA) Inc.
375 Hudson Street, New York, New York 10014, USA
Penguin Group (Canada), 90 Eglinton Avenue East, Suite 700, Toronto, Ontario M4P 2Y3, Canada (a division of Pearson Penguin Canada Inc.)
Penguin Books Ltd., 80 Strand, London WC2R 0RL, England
Penguin Group Ireland, 25 St. Stephen's Green, Dublin 2, Ireland
(a division of Penguin Books Ltd.)
Penguin Group (Australia), 250 Camberwell Road, Camberwell, Victoria 3124, Australia
(a division of Pearson Australia Group Pty. Ltd.)
Penguin Books India Pvt. Ltd., 11 Community Centre, Panchsheel Park, New Delhi—110 017, India Penguin Group (NZ), 67 Apollo Drive, Mairangi Bay, Auckland 1311, New Zealand
(a division of Pearson New Zealand Ltd.)
Penguin Books (South Africa) (Pty.) Ltd., 24 Sturdee Avenue, Rosebank, Johannesburg 2196, South Africa

Penguin Books Ltd., Registered Offices: 80 Strand, London WC2R 0RL, England

Cover design by Andrea Ho; Cover photo by Sante D'Orazio
Book design by Claire Vaccaro

PRINTING HISTORY
G. P. Putnam's Sons hardcover edition / June 2006
Berkley trade paperback edition / May 2007

ISBN: 978-0-425-21510-4

The Library of Congress has catalogued the G. P. Putnam's Sons edition as follows:

Bracco, Lorraine, date.
On the Couch / by Lorraine Bracco
p. cm.
ISBN: 0-399-15356-X
1. Bracco, Lorraine. 2. Actors—United States—Biography. I. Title
PN2287.B675 A3 2006 2006044818
791.4302'8092—dc22
[B]

PRINTED IN THE UNITED STATES OF AMERICA

10 9 8 7 6 5 4 3 2 1

Contents

For Margaux and Stella

Introduction

Even before the hardcover edition of *On the Couch* was published, I was used to people approaching me to talk about their depression. I was sitting with my literary agent in a coffee shop before we went across the street to meet with the people from Putnam, my eventual publishers, when a woman came up to our table. She said she'd read an article I was quoted in and thanked me for speaking up about the kind of depression she'd been afflicted with for a long time. Encounters like this happened quite often. Once *The Sopranos* started, and before I'd mentioned my depression—before I'd come to terms with the fact I was depressed—people I didn't know would talk to me about Dr. Melfi, or talk to me as if I were Dr. Melfi, the psychiatrist I played on television. I don't know why people found Dr. Melfi easier to speak with. Maybe it was because they identified with her character. Certainly the sad and woeful stigma of depression played a part—Dr. Melfi might be easier to approach than a flesh-and-blood person. But after I sought treatment and went public, I'd get a mix of people, some for Jennifer Melfi, some for Lorraine Bracco.

Then the book came out, with its description of what I went through before I sought treatment and how much I was helped, and readers came forward. More people than ever were talking to me. When I was signing copies of the book, it was definitely Lorraine my confidants were relating to. I am immeasurably more comfortable discussing this issue than I used to be. Recently I gave a speech to a group of mental health professionals in Texas, which in itself is something that, ten years ago, I'd never have thought I'd be doing. For one thing, I would have been scared to death to talk about myself in public in this way. I also would not have thought that I had anything in common with people who might be suffering, or that I would have anything substantial to offer on the subject of mental health. Yet here I was, talking to a roomful of real-life Dr. Melfis. In my speech I said:

> The irony hasn't escaped any of us. I play a psychiatrist on *The Sopranos* who treats Tony Soprano for depression. Meanwhile, in real life I am actually someone who has suffered from depression and had to seek the help of a psychiatrist. And now here I am, hoping to encourage other depression sufferers to seek help.

It's important to me that the message I tried to get across in *On the Couch* continues to spread. We need to take care of our own mental health and that of our loved ones. I said it in the book, and I make no apologies for saying it again here: You must be aware of the danger of depression.

Every time someone stood up at a book signing and talked about his or her own experience with depression, I felt that writing the book had been worthwhile. Not everyone in my family was completely happy I was putting our story on paper, but when people would tell me that reading my book made them realize they were not alone, I was glad I did it. Sometimes even their best friends didn't know how they were feeling, and talking to me was the first time they had spoken about it at all. They felt comfortable enough to talk, even in front of a group of strangers, because I'd laid everything out between the covers of a book.

Not all of us, of course, are stricken with depression, but thirty-five million Americans will be, at some point in their lives, depressed badly enough to require treatment. So chances are that you or someone you know has been affected by depression. Your story will be different from mine. Each person who speaks with me has his or her own unique story to tell and every depressed person has gone down a different path. Depression comes in many forms and for many reasons. It might be the loss of a loved one or even the loss of a pet. I came home recently after being away and my dogs were still at the kennel and the house felt so empty without them. I missed them, no matter how much of a pain in the butt they can be when they're around. I understand how the loss of a beloved pet can hit you really hard.

Divorce rates are sky-high in this country, and getting divorced can have the psychological impact of a death. Even if it was an unhealthy relationship and you're glad to be out of it, it's still a major loss. A well-meaning girlfriend may try to get the newly single you out and about and tell you to "get over it already," but it's not always as simple as that. Any major life change, even if it is ultimately for the better, can leave you feeling depressed.

Depression has many faces. Not everyone goes through the kind of child custody battle I did. Fewer people still are successful and well-paid actors when they become ill. Even if you don't connect with the events I describe, my reaction to them may well be familiar.

It's good for you to give voice to your feelings and it's necessary for the rest of us to listen. I get letters from people who say that reading my book helped them better understand what people in their lives had been going through when they were depressed. If *you* are depressed, I hope that this book will enable you to talk about it with a friend or loved one, or to go out and find a doctor to help you. Every time we engage in this kind of dialogue, we're taking away a tiny piece of the stigma surrounding depression and mental illness. Until we're all as ready to talk about depression as we are about getting the flu, this work must go on.

The fact that people related to Dr. Melfi is a testament to the quality of the writing on *The Sopranos*. What I have tried to do is to use her to spread the word about depression. Look, she's a well-intentioned person; a terrifically well-realized character. I wish

I could have gone to her myself for treatment. We work really well together—I'm sure going to miss her when she's gone!

Two aspects of my work have moved me deeply. The first is that clips of Dr. Melfi's sessions with Tony Soprano are used in teaching therapy. They're not used in a "How to" way but as examples of a therapeutic relationship. I think that's incredible. This is a TV show that's made for entertainment but the writing and the acting are good enough for the scenes to be used as academic training sessions. That makes me very proud.

Of course, the fact that the Melfi/Soprano relationship has been at the heart of *The Sopranos* through its whole run, and the fact that it's one of the central characters in the whole drama, Tony Soprano, who's being treated has also done a lot to destigmatize therapy.

I am also proud of the book you're holding in your hands. I've already said that readers have told me how they've found it helpful. It goes deeper than that even. A friend of mine told me about a friend of his who had gone to see a psychiatrist. The psychiatrist had recommended that the person begin a course of medication but the friend was resistant. "I'm stronger than that," she said. "I'm bigger than that." "Do me a favor," the doctor said. "Would you read the first chapter of this book?" (Meaning *this* book.) More validation! First, they're using Melfi as a teaching tool in school, and now a psychiatrist is telling a patient to read the first chapter of my book in order to break through the reluctance to take much-needed medication. Unfortunately, for many people, taking antidepressants is viewed as a sign of weakness. If my book helps even one person realize that antidepressants can be just as necessary and acceptable as medication to control high blood pressure or cholesterol, it makes it all worthwhile.

If you choose to go down the therapeutic road, the kind of path I describe in *On the Couch*, be prepared for a bit of a bumpy ride. I'm not going to pretend it's easy. I write about looking forward each day to taking refuge under the covers and blocking out the world in sleep. In bed I felt safe. For a long time, that seemed like the best option for me. Most of us feel like that every now and then, but not three hundred days in a row! It was like having a fever every day. Eventually I confronted the situation and went for help, but it took some time.

Going through the process of writing and promoting this book helped distill my thinking about my experiences. Stepping back, I see two big scary words staring back at me: *honesty* and *responsibility*. Yikes!

You need to be honest to overcome the shame you may feel about depression. You have to be honest with yourself. This is where the hard part starts. First of all, it's embarrassing to admit to yourself and to everyone who loves you that you're not doing well. How often does someone say to you, "Hey, how are you doing?" It's a common courtesy. And we usually reply, "I'm really good, thank you very much." But you might be screaming inside, "My life is falling apart. I'm miserable. I'm lonely. I'm sad. I think feeling alone and being lonely is the worst."

The first step in the honesty process is to admit your plight to yourself, and then you can go on and say it out loud. Now, when somebody asks me, "How are you doing?" I can say, "Today, not so good." I'm willing to say that now. Here's another one. "Hey, how was Thanksgiving?" Here's another chance for you to be honest. I hope this will never apply but if it does, go ahead and say, "It was really bad." I've reached the point where I'm not going to keep chanting, "Oh, yeah, yeah, you know," which is what I would have done in the past. I'm going to tell the truth whether people like it or not.

This is honesty—emotional honesty. It's not everyone who is willing, or able, to go there. It might be that you need to go down the long and winding road to face your demons, understand them, so to speak, and then do something to fix them, i.e., therapy or medication. We only have one shot at our lives, and if this is a journey we have to take, then we have to take it. The honesty comes as one of the rewards. You are able to turn around and reply to someone who says, "How're you doing?" by telling them, "Not so good." Of course, you also have to be honest with someone sitting you down and really asking how you are doing. I found that being able to finally give a truthful answer was so empowering. I didn't have to put up a false front. I didn't have to reply with the cheery, "Okay, thanks" every single day.

Not everyone likes to hear the honest response. "Oh my God, I asked her how she was doing and she actually told me!" You can sometimes see it on their faces. An uncomfortable look comes over them, and they mumble something and quickly walk away. If someone reacts like that to me, it's okay because at least I was honest with myself. You can't control anyone else, but you owe it to yourself to be honest. If I ask a friend how they are and they tell me they're feeling down, I'm going to say, "Okay, what's going on?" I want my friends to feel they are able to talk to me, and if someone opens up to me, you can bet I'm going to do all I can to help.

Honesty is also absolutely necessary for the friends and loved ones of people suffering from depression. You shouldn't see someone you care about suffering and not say or do anything, although many of us do. It can be awkward or embarrassing to get involved with someone's life. It can be downright scary because you never know how someone will react. Perhaps some of the people you know may not be able to handle a more honest you. They may like you better the way you were. Because when you reach out and tell someone you love that you think they should go see a doctor, it may hurt them—even if your intention is to help. But please don't let that stop you from being compassionate.

The key is to be sensitive; you don't want to overwhelm or emotionally assault anyone. I don't charge around diagnosing everyone I meet, but I do try to stay aware and remain watchful and look for the signs that I know and recognize.

I try to tell it the way it is. I've always wanted to, even if I fell very short for a long time. But I know I'm more true to myself today than I've ever been. I'll never forget one day a director said to me, in that straightforward way they can have, "You know, I could never be in love with you, Lorraine, you're too brutally honest." From where I am now, I'll take that as a compliment.

I think young people of my daughters' generation are in a better position to be honest about depression because so many of my generation—their parents—have been in therapy. After all, we've had Woody Allen to grow up with. Maybe we can be more accepting and we can start to end the stigmatization of therapy. It's up to parents not to say things like, "Shoot me if I ever have to go to a psychiatrist." If you say it often enough, your kids are going to believe it. Stigma and shame can be taught in the home as much as racism and homophobia. Tolerance and understanding are learned in the home too, I'm sure of it. So, education, education, education. The more we all know about mental illness, the better position we're in to be open about it and to deal with it.

Honesty is also about being aware of our vulnerabilities. Sometimes we're just weak and there may be a relatively simple chemical reason for it. If it could be put right with diet or vitamins or exercise alone, we could very easily help the millions of people who fall prey to depression. But it often isn't that simple and sometimes medication is necessary. We're continually finding out more about how our bodies work. Postpartum depression is one significant issue that we're becoming much more aware of, and that we are talking about, that we are accepting as a real problem. A woman's body is very complicated.

I've got another *F*-word for you: Fifty. Menopause isn't much fun, I can tell you right now! It's another thing we as women have to keep an eye on, not just the physical aspects but the mental ones too. The hormonal changes we undergo can cause depression in some women.

Women place great value on being stoic. We're supposed to do it all and keep smiling, pretending we have it under control. It's not uncommon for women to work, take care of the kids, her husband, her aging parents, and manage the household. And God forbid we complain! Ah, nobody listens anyway! Women make it even harder for themselves by always thinking there's someone worse off. "Oh, I'm fine. Look at what so and so has to put up with." But every once in a while we need to stop worrying about everyone else and look after ourselves. And it only gets worse as we get older. We need to acknowledge all we do and how difficult it can be. We need to sometimes say, "Gee, this is hard. I'm having a tough time. I need a break." We need to take care of ourselves.

I heard a great quote recently: "Well-behaved women rarely make history." I love it! It's attributed to Laurel Thatcher Ulrich. She's a professor at Harvard, so she must be smart, right? What this quote means to me is not that you get places by being rude. It doesn't mean you have to be mean and horrible and despicable. Rather it's about taking control and not being pushed around. Here's where the other big word comes in. It's about taking responsibility for yourself. This is another thread that runs through *On the Couch*; how I had control over my life, then I lost it and had to go out and get it back.

Taking charge can be a very different proposition for a woman than for a man. It's hard to take responsibility for yourself if a man won't let you. We may have come a long way, but there are still great societal pressures on women. To a great extent, men are still in charge. Inequalities remain in the workplace: lower pay for women for the same work, for example, and glass ceilings that hinder our progress. Many men in power feel threatened by strong and independent women and prefer and promote dependency. There are so many cultural pressures—to be thin, to look young, to act in a "ladylike" way. (A successful woman in the workplace will often be written off as a "bitch.") We internalize these stresses and all the while are distracted from what are the genuinely important issues for women.

Many of the circles I move in are very male-oriented. Take the movies, for example. All the big male movie stars are making millions and millions of dollars while we're scurrying around for the scraps. Don't get me wrong, I love all these guys, but who made us not equal to them? This kind of disparity helps ensure that we are kept out of the real positions of control in all kinds of industries.

What threw everything into sharp focus for me was realizing that I was the breadwinner for my two girls. Once that thought snapped into my head, I had no choice but to take control of the situation. I couldn't stay in bed all day and be depressed. I needed to do something. I admitted something was wrong and I knew it wasn't physical. I wasn't bleeding, I wasn't broken, I didn't have a toothache. But something was badly awry and I wanted to get better. I had two children to bring up, and I had to figure out what was wrong, so I took a very aggressive position about my treatment and I saw it through. I went to a medical professional and began a program of therapy backed by medication.

This is taking responsibility for your own life. You've taken charge, beginning with the call to the doctor's office. Once you have started, it becomes your responsibility to follow through on what you've started. Like it says on the bottle of antibiotics: finish all of this medicine unless otherwise directed by your doctor. You have to complete the treatment. You can change course if you're not entirely happy with it. As you'll see when you read on, I adjusted my treatment at one point. But you have to complete the journey of treatment to make it to the other side.

More Americans are seeking medical attention and thank God for that. But many of them don't get adequate help because they aren't active participants in their treatment. They don't ask questions, they don't fully commit to the process, and they don't take responsibility for their own well-being. Hey, no one should be more concerned with your health than you are. And remember, you won't be any good to anyone if you don't take care of yourself.

As I've said, before I realized I needed to get help, I spent my days in bed under the covers. I hid because I didn't want to face my depression. I am very thankful that I don't have an addictive kind of personality. As a society we're addicted to so many things—drugs, booze, sex, food, gambling. It seems like we can get addicted to anything, and I think depression underlies a lot of our dependency culture. People run away from their emotions and turn to addictive substances so they don't have to feel. Even when I was at my lowest I knew I didn't want to be like that. I didn't want to be numb. I wanted to be alive. I felt a tremendous responsibility to my children and I didn't want them to see me curled up in bed avoiding life. I didn't want to set that kind of example for them. I want them to embrace life, live life to the fullest. So I would drag myself out of bed each day, plaster a smile on and pretend things were okay. I had to function for them. But that's all I was doing—running on automatic. I didn't get any satisfaction out of life. It was as if I were living in a murky fog. I spent a year like that, and I never want to miss out on my life like that again.

It makes me terribly sad to think there are a huge number of people who aren't living life to the maximum, who are not productive members of society making a full contribution. That really hurts me. When I was depressed I knew I wasn't living up to my potential. I'm a dynamic woman. I'm smart, I'm fun, and eventually I realized I didn't want to watch my life pass me by. And I don't want life to pass you by either. There's no reason why you shouldn't fulfill the potential you have and it's possible you're not because you're holding yourself back.

We have to admit to ourselves that sometimes it's convenient for us to hold ourselves back. It certainly feels easier and safer. When I was depressed I would say I was having a bad day. Enough bad days and it was a bad week then a bad month. I lost a whole year doing that. Friends were telling me, "Lorraine, go talk to someone," but I resisted for a long time. But as soon as I was honest with myself and took responsibility, I saw they were right. I could see it in my face and in my eyes when I looked in the mirror. I wasn't vibrant at all. It was like a dead person was looking back at me.

Getting treatment gave me my life back. Now, I like the woman I see in the mirror. I know I'm getting older but I look better now than I did when I was forty-four years old.

There's a second reason people—women mostly—come up to me to talk about the book. Having read about mine, people want to share their child custody stories with me. "I've been in court for three years," a woman will say. Or five years, or six. "Oh my God, I have the same story as you," she'll tell me, and I'll hear that she's had to sell everything to finance the court case.

I'm more convinced than ever that putting child custody cases into the adversarial court system is not the way we should be settling these disputes. You'll read about the terrible stress the court process puts on kids. It's not the best system for the children or the mothers and fathers. Whoever has the most money wins most of the time, which is not necessarily the best thing for the kids either. And after everything is said and done and all the money is spent, the chance that the parents will be able to maintain any kind of relationship is often gone. There's usually no way back. People are so consumed with beating their ex that the interests of the kids get overlooked. It's about power and control. Each side is so concerned with winning every battle that they both end up losing the war.

This is what I have been hearing: A lot of times the guy moves out, the woman stays in the house and they go through a horrible divorce. The woman now doesn't have the income to maintain her lifestyle so she has to sell her house. She moves into a rented apartment with her three kids who maybe used to be in private school. Of the money she made from the sale of the house, half of it goes to the husband, half goes to her. And the lawyers take whatever they can. Both parties start with lots of assets but once the lawyers get through with them, they end up haggling over dividing the debts. All the money's gone.

There's something badly wrong here. If you started from scratch and tried to come up with the worst possible system as far as the kids are concerned, it would look very much like the one we have now. What we should do is mediate these cases out of the courtroom. After my experience, when I see a couple that still gets along, a man who's made a friend of his ex-wife, and the children feel fine going back and forth, I say, "How did you do that?" I am so impressed. Statistics show there's a much greater chance of parents who mediated their custody dispute working together on the parenting of their children than people who went to court. The kids must come first.

As I write, we're shooting the second group of episodes in the final series of *The Sopranos* and in a few short months we'll be finished. I can't believe this incredible ride is coming to an end. I don't even want to think about it because it's been a dream and so satisfying for me. I got to sit across from Jimmy Gandolfini, a great actor. The writing has been extraordinary. I got to live in my own house and sleep in my own bed and go to work in my own city. These are no small things for an actor because we're usually nomads living all over the place.

I don't know if David Chase feels the same way I do about the end of the series. When he's done we'll have made more than eighty hours of television together and I think each episode is better than most movies Hollywood puts out. In years to come, the show will be considered an important piece of Americana.

Once I'm finished with Dr. Melfi I go back to being a bum actor. Where my next job is coming from, I don't know. I do have a producing/acting deal with the Lifetime network but the period right after a job is finishing has always been an insecure time for me. It's better now that the kids are older. I don't have to feel like the breadwinner twenty-four hours a day. Now it's more like twenty-two hours.

We'll see what parts come my way. I know there are no good parts like Dr. Melfi in the movies. And if there are, Meryl gets them, that's just the way it goes. When you look at my age group, women who are forty to sixty, say, there are plenty of extremely fine actresses looking at the same roles. Meryl Streep, Susan Sarandon, Annette Bening, and so on. Not a slacker among them! Whatever I take on, I know I'll be able to do a good job. If anyone cares to write a good part for a confident, fiftysomething actor who's got all her own wrinkles and curves, then I'm your girl!

One thing I know I'll be working on is a business venture I became involved with recently. I lived in France for ten years. In that time I learned to do a lot of things, and drinking wine was one of them. I'm very interested in wine and food, although the cooking gene has skipped me entirely. My daughter Margaux is a great cook—I can't believe what this kid can whip up! Bringing up the kids, I made sure they were well fed and I steered away from fast food, but I am no gourmet chef. On the other hand, thanks to France, I can order very well.

In Paris I really got to understand how to pair food and wine. This is something we're doing better in this country and we had a lot of ground to make up, because for decades we've been a Coca-Cola society. Now if I want to recommend a good Amarone to go with a particular cheese it's easy because I have my own, one of eight Bracco Wines I'm importing from Italy and selling in this country.

A lot of actors promote hair and beauty products, and I may too, but when this opportunity came along I thought, this I can do. I traveled to Italy and visited vineyards to taste the wine. I bought the wine I liked, we put my label on the bottles and shipped them over by the container and we launched Bracco Wines at a *Sopranos* cast and crew party at the Roseland Ballroom in New York City.

I like a challenge. It was a challenge to be a model, I'm always challenged as an actress, and I'm facing new challenges as a businesswoman. From my careers in modeling and acting to this wine venture, I never do something the conventional way. I like to be interested. I'm a very curious person. "What's this?" I'll say. "Who's that guy? How's that thing made? What's in that?" I'm a curious girl. If that's a fault, I'll live with it.

One of the things I'm most curious about is myself. A long time ago I learned I need nature in my life. Brooklyn born and bred I might be, but somewhere in here is a tree-hugger trying to get out. More recently I've come to learn I don't need a man to complete me. I found myself by myself—there was no man taking me by the hand and showing me the way. After my relationship with Eddie Olmos kind of fell apart, I spent a very long time alone. That was very good for me. It fostered my sense of independence. In time I came to understand I don't need anybody else to live this life. My life's not about being validated by another person. In the last ten years I've come to realize that. I don't have to be Daddy's little girl or somebody's trophy wife. I'm doing fine just being me. I've decided I want to buy my own underwear.

Here's something else I learned, one of the many life lessons I got from Martin Scorcese. One day he said, "Just tell me what you're thinking, just talk to me. Give me all your ideas, don't judge them." That was great lesson to learn as a woman. Here was a man encouraging me to express myself. He was interested in what I had to say rather than what I looked like or how I made him feel good about himself. Now I'm in a position to respond fully when someone asks for my ideas and opinions. I never would have been able to if I hadn't been through this process of fixing my depression. I was that curious, lively, funny girl who asked a lot of questions and who had a lot of ideas. I lost that girl, and in time I found her again. Now I can become the woman I was supposed to be, acting on all those ideas.

In time I discovered or rediscovered many other things about myself and how I needed to live my life. I learned how to be kind to myself, how to be easy on myself even when I was depressed and working so hard to get better. You have to accept the position you find yourself in. It's a time for introspection, an opportunity to find out what really matters to you. For the first time in ages, you might be able to plan ahead with a happy anticipation rather than a dull dread.

So, today, I'm looking forward. I'm happy. I'm healthy. I have a fantastic, renewed interest in life, and I'm going to embrace whatever happens. I jump up out of bed in the morning. I'm not saying I want to run a marathon anytime soon, but I might walk one. I'm gratified when people come up to me and say they read my story. It makes me feel I wrote it for something positive and if I help one person, it's worth it. Does it rock my boat to say I went through a really hard time? No. But you know what? I survived and came out better in the long run and there's something to be said for that. This story is about trying to be the best woman, the best mom, the most vibrant, aware person I can.

Here's the story.

One · Doctor, Heal Thyself

Hope comes in many forms.
·Dr. Jennifer Melfi

NOVEMBER 1996

The postman tried not to look at me as he handed me a large stack of envelopes. The letters were official-looking, and many were stamped with alarms that betrayed their contents: *"Extremely urgent"* . . . *"Second notice"* . . . *"Last chance."*

"My fan mail," I joked, but he didn't laugh. He looked embarrassed. Well, who wasn't?

"Some fans," I mumbled to myself as I added the letters to the growing mountain on my desk. I hadn't opened a single one. Even then, I knew it was nuts. Look at me, the famous actress in her gorgeous riverfront home, living her fabulous life. Was this someone's idea of a joke?

In their increasingly frequent correspondence, my current group of "fans" expressed hurt, disbelief, sadness, and regret. But it was still early in our relationship. They had yet to progress to anger, hostility, and retribution.

Dear Lorraine,

I'm sure it has slipped your attention that your account balance of $36,590 is six months past due. I know how busy you are, but . . .

Lorraine,

I hate to bring this up, but the law firm is after me about when they can expect another payment on your past due account, which now totals $1,422,872.23 . . .

Lorraine,

Your check for $940 for the hearing transcript bounced. Please send another check so I can process your request.

Lorraine,

Republic Bank will immediately commence foreclosure unless they receive a payment of $41,065 . . .

Lorraine,

I hate to be a pest, but . . .

The phone rang. I considered letting the machine pick up, but on the fourth ring, I grabbed the receiver.

"Lorraine?" It was my manager, Heather. Her voice sounded strained. "Have you read the script?"

"Huh? Umm, it's around here somewhere," I said vaguely.

"It's been two months," she pleaded. "They're waiting to hear."

"I know, I know." I looked around the room. Where had I put the damned script? "Heather, I don't think I can handle another script about the mob. I mean, how many Mafia roles can a girl play? If that's all they think I'm capable of, then shoot me now."

Heather was getting tired of me. "Lorraine, will you do me a fucking favor? Will you read the script? The guy's coming in Tuesday. He wants to meet you."

"Fine, I'll read it," I shouted back at her. "You're a pain in my ass, Heather."

"That's why they pay me the big bucks," she said, and hung up.

"Mafia television garbage," I muttered. Was my career in the toilet or what? I needed to make some real money here, and they were sending me television pilots about mobsters. Jeez. No wonder I was depressed.

I always figured there were two kinds of people in the world—the cheerleaders and the grumps. I was a cheerleader. The pep talker. Always ready with the pom-poms, always up for anything. I'm your girl. You need someone to take a carload of kids to a horse show? Call me. My energy knew no limits. I could sew a hundred sparkly beads on a costume for my daughter Margaux's school play, cohost a benefit with Bobby Kennedy for Riverkeeper, and still be on a set the next day, raring to go. But as 1996 drew to a close, my razzle-dazzle had definitely fizzled. The cheerleader had left the building, replaced by a listless, middle-aged woman who couldn't get out of her freaking pajamas until midafternoon.

I felt stagnant. Not calm and still like the Hudson River on a mild day, but stale, like a swamp, a place lacking a fresh infusion of life. When I first started feeling down, I'd told myself that I was worn out, and who could blame me? I'd just come through a six-year custody battle for my daughter Stella that was so horrible and so bruising I felt like I'd been beaten up. I'd won my daughter, which was a huge blessing, but lost everything else: my friends, my dignity, my reputation. Despite my work in movies like *Goodfellas,* I was a good two million bucks in debt, and on the verge of losing my house. I had my two beautiful daughters and a husband, yet I was as alone as I'd ever been in my life. My marriage to Eddie Olmos—only a couple of years old—was shaky at best, and it looked like I was going to be losing that, too. On my worst days, I imagined being penniless, having to pack up my daughters and move back in with my parents.

What the hell? I was an Academy Award–nominated actress. Famous, glamorous, living in the big house overlooking the Hudson River. I was the envy of the ladies in the local PTA. People stopped me in the produce aisle of the supermarket to ask for my autograph. If they could see me now. If only they knew.

When the court awarded me custody in September 1996, I didn't even have a chance to be elated. It should have been over, but of course it wasn't; there would be appeals and endless wrangling over child support, and the steady flow of bills, bills, bills. I just couldn't take it anymore. Eddie was working in Los Angeles, and our long-distance marriage wasn't working at all. I needed a shoulder to lean on, and it wasn't there. In the past, I might have felt sorry for myself and had a good cry. But at this point, I was too numb to cry.

At first I thought I just needed a few days to get my act together, a little time to recuperate. But a few days turned into a few weeks, then a few months. And I wasn't feeling better. I was feeling worse.

My days took on a blankness, one after the other, one day the same as the next. Thank God I wasn't a drinker, and I didn't do drugs; otherwise, I'd have been a goner for sure. Thinking back on how vulnerable I was, I really feel for people with substance-abuse problems. But my days were devoid of such drama. After Margaux and Stella left for school in the morning, I'd sit with my coffee, aimlessly paging through magazines or staring out at the river. Sometimes I'd get a surge of energy and put a load of laundry in, then forget it until Margaux discovered her favorite shirt mildewing in the machine and screamed, "Motherrrr!" I'd call my parents: "How ya doing? Good. Fine. Fine. Okay. Fine. Love ya." I was a bad actor. I plodded along, forcing myself to go through the motions, trying to be the same old me everyone knew. But I was counting the hours until I could get back into bed and pull the covers up over my head. Sleep was my only relief.

It wasn't until later that I'd be able to put a name on what I was experiencing: depression. It's a clinical condition that afflicts thirty-four million Americans at some time in their lives, which means that there were—and are—a hell of a lot of others out there feeling painfully empty and lifeless, just like me. But it took me more than a year to reach that realization. In the meantime, I didn't know what was wrong with me, and I definitely didn't know what to do about it.

Many people think depression is a big, dramatic black hole that swallows you up. But it doesn't have to be. It's not necessarily finding yourself thinking about suicide, which I never did, even on my worst days. It's something much worse, if you ask me. I'm an actress, so *drama* I can do. But this was the antithesis of drama. It was as though I were floating in a great thick bog of stillness, and it was that dullness I couldn't stand. The damping down of all my feelings. The absolute, complete joylessness.

Joyless or not, I knew it was extremely important to keep up appearances, so I wasted a lot of energy that I didn't really have pretending to have a sunny disposition, pasting a big, fat fake smile on my face. I had to show the world that I was okay and could be trusted. I had to prove that I could work, raise my kids, run my household, appear at charity benefits—do all the things I'd always done. At the time, I thought the worst thing in the world would be if anyone discovered how I was feeling. I mean *anyone*. No one could know—not my mother, not my sister, Lizzie, not my friends, or the people I worked with. So I hid in my house. I avoided talking to my friends. If anyone mentioned that I looked beat, I'd say,

"Yeah, I'm tired. It's been a rough year." Everyone pretty much took me at face value and let me off the hook. People don't want to know, they really don't. Not because they don't care, but because they don't know what to do. Basically, they're afraid.

Hiding my feelings was really just a symptom of my disease. The shame you feel when you're depressed is phenomenal. You think you're weak, and nobody wants to seem weak. Nobody wants to look *mental*, especially in show business. As it is, if you're a forty-two-year-old woman, you're hanging on by a thread most of the time anyway. If there's a *difficulty*, a *problem*, you can just forget it. God forbid a rumor should start. A few juicy tabloid mentions and you're toast. It's no wonder it takes so long for people to get help.

My daughter Stella was ten then, full of energy and spirit. She'd come bouncing in the door from school, calling to me, "Mommy, Mommy," talking a mile a minute about her day, sharing every exciting and mundane thing that had happened since that morning. I'd put a smile on my face while listening with only half an ear and thinking about sleep. That definitely wasn't me. I adored this little girl, and normally I hung on every word out of her mouth. It was all part of a vicious cycle. The worse I felt, the less I cared, and the less I cared, the worse I felt.

Stella mostly bought my act, but my sixteen-year-old daughter Margaux wasn't so easily fooled. She saw right through me, with that terrifying teenage acuity of hers. "What's the deal with you?" she'd ask, staring at me hard. I didn't know, so I just said, "Nothing.

Everything's fine." Margaux would roll her eyes, letting me know she didn't believe it for a minute. "Okay. Everything's fine," she'd say, parroting me sarcastically.

Even the animals had my number. The dogs would watch me morosely, their eyes seemingly reflecting my depression, their normally high spirits dampened by my mood. My plump, normally affectionate cat would push himself up and lumber out of the room when he saw me coming. "No way am I dealing with her crap," his disappearing tail seemed to signal.

My deepest fear was that I had permanently messed up my life. You see, although I can say I didn't exactly *know* what was wrong with me, I *suspected* plenty. Depression didn't just arrive out of the blue. It followed several years of a downhill slide, most of which was self-imposed.

In 1990, I'd been at the top of my game. I was nominated for an Academy Award for my performance in *Goodfellas,* and I felt as if nothing could touch me. In a business where your self-esteem is always on the line, it's impossible to describe the overwhelming relief of being successful, even if that success is fleeting. Being considered for an Academy Award is a powerful rush of affirmation in a very crazy, quixotic business.

But I had a secret that I kept well hidden behind my glittering smile. As my career became more satisfying, my personal life was failing. More than anything, I wanted a sense of loving calm at home, but this dream was shattered. It was such a wild juxtaposition: in the eyes of the world I was a movie star, and I'd have to stop a minute and think, *Holy shit. They're paying me to do something that I love*. But I'd get home and it was nothing but catastrophe. At this point, I'd been living with Harvey Keitel for eight years, and we were as good as married. We had the girls—my daughter Margaux, from my previous marriage, and our daughter Stella—and we'd just bought a beautiful house overlooking the Hudson River in Sneden's Landing, an exclusive enclave north of New York City.

But it wasn't all tea and roses. I wondered if Harvey had the capacity for contentment. He seemed to be filled with rage—at the world, at his parents, at the industry, and at me. Some people would say it was this rage that made him such a compelling presence on the screen. Well, fine. He's a brilliant, riveting, intense actor. But we were living with it every single day. When Harvey was home, the girls and I just wanted to stay out of the way. We tiptoed around, walking on eggshells. But a lot of the time he wasn't home. And there were times, sometimes days on end, when I didn't know where the hell he was.

For a long time, I covered it up. I was really good at acting like nothing was wrong. I'd answer the phone and say cheerfully, "Harvey's not here at the moment," as if he'd just stepped out for a breath of fresh air, when the truth was I hadn't seen him in four days. He had a drug problem; I knew that. But he'd promised me over and over that he was dealing with it. I'd finally stopped believing him, and I realized that the pretense couldn't go on forever. Instead, I started to hate him for what he was putting us through. I took it personally. I felt betrayed.

I was lonely and heartbroken, and I wasn't exactly thinking straight.

So I did something extremely stupid. In the summer of 1990, I had a fling with Edward James Olmos while we were on location in Idaho filming *A Talent for the Game*. I wasn't trying to destroy my relationship with Harvey, but I was hungry for another kind of love, something that was simpler and less intense. I think I just wanted to be coddled a little bit. It was a purely selfish act, for which I was deeply sorry. What I didn't count on was Harvey finding out. I believed he was incapable of seeing his own behavior with any kind of clarity, but he was like a laser beam when it came to my faults. I knew he would never forgive me, and his fury was absolutely terrifying. I finally asked him to leave. Harvey moved back to our loft in lower Manhattan, and I stayed in Sneden's Landing with the girls. But then I compounded the problem by marrying Eddie in 1994, thinking it would be best for everybody because he would bring stability to our lives.

All of my choices during that period were driven by a ferocious desire to stand up for myself and to fight for my dignity. I had a right not to be belittled and pushed around and controlled, and I was finally grabbing for it. I was scraping and clawing to get away from Harvey's hold, his ability to pull me up and make me feel like somebody one minute and like nothing the next. But Harvey seemed determined to punish me and to impose his will on me. There were ugly charges leveled against Eddie, which opened up a nightmare for all of us, as well as the endless custody battle over Stella that nearly bankrupted me. And in the midst of everything, Stella became desperately ill with systemic juvenile rheumatoid arthritis, an autoimmune disease that left her screaming in pain.

It was one thing after another, one terrible stress after another piling up and bringing me down. During those long, difficult years, I repeatedly made withdrawals from my emotional account, until I was finally cleaned out. We all came away damaged—my kids, Harvey, Eddie, his kids, me—and everyone suffered.

It's hard to describe the level of shame I felt, and I truly believed that I had caused this misery. That sense of shame is also a sign of the disease. You know you're suffering from depression when you define your life by your failures instead of your successes. I felt I was to blame for everything. Who was I? Well, I was a woman in my forties who had made a big mess of her life. I'd sit on the deck of my beautiful house in Sneden's Landing, which I was on the verge of losing, and look out on the expanse of the Hudson River, brooding over my shortcomings and mistakes.

How could I call myself a good parent to my daughters, who meant more to me than anyone in the world? Was I even worthy of being a mother? What if I lost the house? What if I couldn't take care of my family? There was no easy solution in sight. The bank wanted to foreclose, the lawyers wanted to be paid, and there was no real work coming in. It was, in a word, tough.

So, if I felt down, I figured I had good reason. But I'm not the kind of person who sits around going, "Oh, woe is me," so I figured I'd snap out of it. I started every day out determined to get my ass in gear, but I'd invariably stall by midmorning. Then the first call from my lawyer would send me straight back into my gloom. That's the thing about depression: It's internal. It's just there. It's not rational, it's not logical, and it doesn't go away when you tell it to.

The scary thing is, I was functioning well enough that I could have gone on for years, just getting by, just *existing,* with no joy or happiness in my life. And I was afraid that's exactly what would happen.

Finally, my old friend John Hoving, who happens to be a social worker, said to me, "You need to go to a doctor, and you need to get on an antidepressant." John had known me for twenty years, and he saw right through me.

"Oh, right," I said sarcastically. "That's all I need. Then I can add 'crazy' to my credits. It's hard enough for an actress my age to get work. Being a known mental case is not going to improve my chances." To my way of thinking, taking antidepressants was a big stigma that I would never be able to overcome. I was also worried that if I took medication, I'd stop being myself—not that "myself" was so terrific at that point. But I had terrifying ideas of what medication would do to me. I worried that I'd be a zombie, and I wouldn't be able to act. I'd never feel again.

John knew me well enough to back off a little. "Okay, but see a therapist. Really, it will help."

I scoffed at that, too. "What the hell is a shrink going to tell me that I don't already know?"

I kept plodding along. And nothing happened. I mean, *nothing.* No real work, no nothing. Fortunately, Heather was still bugging me about the Mafia show. So I finally sat down and read the damned script.

One night, when Stella was at Harvey's and Margaux was out with friends, I got a fire going in the fireplace, curled up on the couch under a blanket, and entered the world of the Soprano family. The script was David Chase's dark vision of the life of Tony Soprano, a second-generation mobster who lived with his wife and two children in an upscale North Jersey home, a tough guy on the verge of a nervous breakdown. The story opened with Tony suffering a panic attack so severe it sent him to a psychiatrist. The setup was immediately intriguing. On the one hand, Tony has life-or-death power over people. On the other, he's been abused by his mother, he can't satisfy his wife, and his children treat him with indifference or contempt. He's a wiseguy with a midlife crisis.

The script was funny and brutal and touching, all at once. It was an amazing work of emotional manipulation, the way it could make you feel sorry for Tony one minute and repulsed by him the next. All of the characters were very strongly defined and completely three-dimensional. It was a great piece of writing.

The part of Tony's wife, Carmela, was highlighted on my copy of the script. David had first seen me in *Goodfellas*, and he was taken with my portrayal of mobster Henry Hill's wife, Karen. He thought of me when he was casting for Carmela. This was a juicy role. Carmela Soprano was a complex character, a woman trying to balance the violence in her husband's world with her desire to be seen as a respectable upper-class lady and a typical suburban mom.

But she knew who she was, and she knew who Tony was, too. She was tough and real, and I totally got her. I'd done a lot of research in preparation for my role as Karen Hill, and I'd learned all about women who made this particular deal with the devil. I knew I could play Carmela, but I didn't really want to. Here's the thing. I'd already played the mob wife—in a big way. Been there, done that. And while I was reading David's script, I was completely taken with the character of Tony's psychiatrist, Dr. Jennifer Melfi.

Dr. Melfi was calling out to me. I identified with this woman. I could feel her. I *knew* her. Although the role was less substantial than that of Carmela, Melfi's place in the drama was absolutely central. I recognized Melfi as the moral through-line of *The Sopranos.* She was the voice of conscience and hope. I mean, what psychiatrist in her right mind would treat a gangster? She was going to help a killer feel better about himself? Melfi seemed to view the challenge as far greater than that. She wanted to believe that no matter how low a person sank, how devoid of common morality he seemed, she could help him change. I loved that about her.

I also found myself identifying with Dr. Melfi on a more personal basis. She was a flawed, lonely woman who questioned her own life. She battled private demons of her own. She drank too much. She was a failure at marriage. She and her son didn't get along. Privately, she suffered deep doubts, just like me. She was a woman who had sacrificed everything for her work and her desire to heal others' torments, and who ended up being tormented herself. She hadn't expected to be so sad at this point in her life, but she battled on. She tried to be straight with herself—to do the right thing. I saw Melfi holding out the hand of redemption to Tony Soprano, even as she searched for it in herself. A chill went up my spine. I was meant to play Dr. Melfi.

I called Heather first thing the next morning. "I read the script," I said.

"Thank God!"

"The thing is, I don't want to play the part of Carmela. I want to play Dr. Melfi."

There was silence on the other end of the line. Then, Heather slowly said, "Don't do this to me again, Lorraine."

I knew what she was talking about. In 1992, I had a chance to star in a big-budget movie called *Fearless.* It was an incredible opportunity to work with the great director Peter Weir, who'd done *The Year of Living Dangerously*, *Witness*, and *Dead Poets Society*. I had always wanted to work with him. Plus, the movie starred Jeff Bridges. What could be bad? The plot involved a guy whose personality is changed after he survives an airplane crash. They wanted me to play his wife. But I didn't like that role. I wanted to play the female survivor whose baby died in the crash. I stuck to my guns and ended up with nothing. The part of the wife went to Isabella Rossellini, and the part of the survivor went to Rosie Perez. I was right about it being a great role, though. Rosie Perez got nominated for an Oscar.

Poor Heather. I felt for her, I really did. She knew me better than anyone in the world, had been representing me and advising me since the beginning of my career. She'd talked me off ledges, fought for me, and put up with my crap. And now I imagined her sitting at her desk, running a replay of the *Fearless* debacle in her mind. "They're not looking at you for Dr. Melfi," she repeated. "For Carmela. Not Melfi."

"Yeah, well, that's the part I like."

She sighed. "Do me a favor. Go in and talk to David Chase. *You* tell him."

A few days later, I traded in my bathrobe for a decent-looking suit, Hush Puppies, and makeup. I even got my hair done. One thing they always say about me: I clean up good. By the time I arrived for my appointment, I looked like a professional actress.

David Chase was casting in a crummy little rent-a-room on Manhattan's Upper West Side. I climbed five steep flights of stairs—the first exercise I'd had in months—and limped into the room.

David was sitting at a cluttered table, and he looked at me with dark, heavy-lidded eyes as I entered the room. My first impression of David was that he was a complicated man—soft-spoken but intense. As he held out a hand to greet me, our eyes locked in a moment of mutual understanding. We clicked on a deep level. I felt it right away.

I told him how much I loved his script, and then I dropped the bomb about wanting to play Dr. Melfi. He gave me a look I have since come to know so well, the one that says, *Huh. What have we here?* I explained that I felt I'd already played Carmela. But Melfi was different. "I love this woman," I said. "Love her."

"Huh." It wasn't really a response. It was more like an exhalation of air.

"I guess what I'm saying is, well, Dr. Melfi is what I want."

He looked at me, and I looked back at him, and it was just like the point in the cartoon where the Roadrunner gets right up to the edge of the cliff and puts on the brakes—*eeeeeeeeeeck*. He's engulfed in huge clouds of dust. Waiting, waiting, waiting, the dust slowly clears . . .

"Okay," David said.

I was elated. I could hear my heart pounding in my ears.

Some creative artists won't stand for people interfering with their vision, but I was fortunate. David was interested in what I had to say. And as we talked, something clicked for both of us.

For David, the core of *The Sopranos* was Tony's relationship with his mother, which led to his panic attacks and ultimately to Dr. Melfi's office. It was personal with David. For years he'd been telling people stories about his own mother that would have them laughing hysterically at first, but ultimately leave them crying. They kept telling him, "You have to write about this." And in a way, with *The Sopranos*, he finally did. David said that, as a child, he had repeatedly suffered injury at the hands of his mother. She never missed an opportunity to harp on him, calling him stupid and complaining about his bad behavior. She never failed to remind him that he was completely unlovable. He recalled that she once threatened to put his eye out with a fork because he was being too rambunctious. He was seven years old! As an adult, David sought the help of a therapist to explore some of the scars his mother had left on his psyche. His interest in the therapeutic process only deepened. So, in *The Sopranos*, he chose to model Tony's cruel mother, Livia, somewhat after his own. He also wanted to explore a question that had occupied much of his time in therapy: Can your actions in life be understood—and even excused—if your psyche was warped by the sick behavior of a negative, guilt-inducing mother? What if you're a cold-blooded murderer? A mobster? A psychopathic maniac?

David felt he'd been helped by analytic therapy, but the process had also raised many questions for him, and in a sense *The Sopranos* was his attempt to work through and eventually answer them. David put Tony Soprano in a room with Dr. Melfi, hoping to discover whether even a guy like Tony could be saved. I wanted to embody the woman who tried to guide Tony toward redemption, and once David agreed to cast me, I became consumed with turning the character into flesh and blood.

We started filming the pilot in the spring of 1997. I was relieved to have a part that kept me close to home. When you're an actor with kids, you rejoice to have a local job that allows you to maintain a family life. All of the exterior scenes were shot in North Jersey, an easy commute away. That's another thing I admired about David. Despite the expense of shooting films in the New York area—the union take alone could kill you—he wasn't willing to film in Canada, which was what so many others were doing at that point. A big believer in total authenticity, he knew a street in Toronto wasn't going to look or *feel* like a street in Newark. And of course, the entire cast and crew loved him for it.

I made Dr. Melfi a Jungian therapist. Carl Jung believed that if people could get access to their unconscious minds, they'd find a treasure trove of important information that would help them solve their problems and live more satisfying lives. Most of the time people just skim the surface and take life at face value; they don't stop to analyze why they repeat their mistakes, or why they behave in self-destructive ways. Didn't I know it! In Tony Soprano's case, it was a big stretch to think that analyzing his dreams or becoming aware of his childhood wounds would make him wake up and say, "Oh, my God, what was I thinking, whacking that guy?" Even so, the pilot episode was suspenseful—Tony had opened a door by entering therapy. Would he walk through it?

For me, getting inside Dr. Melfi meant becoming very still. Tony was the storyteller; his therapist was the listener and interpreter. David wanted the therapy sessions to be shot starkly, with no moving camera angles. It was just Tony and Melfi, sitting across from each other in a room. Not only were the therapy scenes a dramatic contrast to the emotional and violent tone of other scenes, they were also different from what television viewers were used to seeing. I told David that I wasn't sure how people would react to the therapy sessions. "Either they'll be the weak link or people will be fascinated," I said. I had no idea which way it would go.

It was the first day of filming. Sitting very straight and composed in Dr. Melfi's chair, I looked across at Jimmy Gandolfini, who perfectly embodied Tony Soprano's tough but fragile pose. He was slumped in his chair, the big made man, embarrassed that he'd had a panic attack and fainted. I worked Melfi's face into a blank, open pose—polite but with a touch of intimacy. I relished that scene, where Tony tells Melfi about the depression he's been feeling ever since a family of ducks living in his swimming pool flew away. He loved those ducks. "I was sad to see them go," he says, and to his great shame starts to cry. "That's what I'm so full of dread about, that I'm going to lose my family, just like I lost the ducks. It's always with me."

What a riveting beginning! What a home run! We did great work on that pilot, and nobody doubted that HBO would pick it up. But then there was silence, not a single word from HBO for months. David sent me a copy of the pilot, and I couldn't stop watching it. It was so amazing. But as time went by, I began to get that feeling of dread in the pit of my stomach. *Oh, no. Don't tell me they're not going to pick up this show*. It was a different feeling for me. I'd always done movies, where the deal was sealed before we started shooting. In television, you get paid for the pilot episode, and then you wait for it to be picked up. If it's shelved, the payday is over. Even if it's a go, they'll maybe give you a dozen episodes. I hated the sense of always being on the chopping block.

As December approached, I was starting to get nervous. Our contracts were up on December 13. Finally, I called David. "What's going on?" I bleated into the phone. "I have never seen anything so fuckin' brilliant. I'm starving for more. Give me more!"

He was laughing. "Believe me, I'd like to give you more," he said.

"So, what's up?"

He sighed. "Chris Albrecht at HBO hasn't okayed it yet. He thinks it's too expensive."

"What can I do?" I had visions of holding fund-raisers, bake sales, penny drives.

"Why don't you call Chris Albrecht?" David said, half joking.

"I will." My next call was to HBO—as if Chris Albrecht would have an idea in hell who I was. But he came to the phone. I did a song and dance for him, and I think he was amused. Did it help? Who knew?

"You *called* Chris Albrecht?" Heather asked in amazement when I told her.

"I did. Somebody had to talk sense into the guy." My false bravado was obvious. I didn't feel very confident.

"I just got a call," Heather said. "HBO ordered twelve more episodes. We're in."

I screamed and raised my arms to the heavens, Rocky-style. Finally, something good was coming my way.

I suppose it would make a perfect story if I told you I completely transformed myself, became Dr. Melfi, rose out of my slump, and rode off into the sunset with the wind whipping my hair and the radio blasting "I am woman, hear me roar . . ."

Didn't happen. All during 1998, as we shot the first season of *The Sopranos*—the best job I'd ever had—I struggled through that pea-soup gloom. Even as I was immersed in the role of Dr. Melfi—a therapist, for God's sake—my depression was there in the background like a constant throbbing ache. It refused me the full measure of joy I deserved from this wonderful turn of events. My life was on the upswing, but my mood stayed on the downswing. That's the bitch of depression. It gets a hold on you, and the longer you wait to confront it, the harder it is to climb out of it. That internal vise just clamps down tighter.

But, in addition to being frustrated, I was also curious. My low mood had been easy enough to explain when my life was a mess. Now that things were looking up, why couldn't I respond? Why wasn't I elated? Why wasn't I out dancing in the streets? Why?

"Because you're depressed," John Hoving reminded me. "Doctor Melfi, heal thyself! Get thee to a therapist."

I continued to resist. Then one day, while flipping through a magazine, I stopped at an ad. It read: "You have only one chance to be a mother. Why do it depressed?"

Those words hit me like a ton of bricks. "All right already," I said out loud. "I'm going." I got a recommendation, and went to see Dr. Stein* the following week.

He was a lovely man. I felt it from the first moment: he wanted to help me. After he listened to me stumbling through an attempt at describing what I was experiencing, he said, "I'm going to put you on an antidepressant."

Uh, oh, I thought, and then I giggled. I was reacting exactly like

*Not his real name.

Tony Soprano when Melfi mentioned medication. "Here we go," Tony had groused. "Here comes the Prozac."

Actually, for me it was Zoloft. Dr. Stein explained that the medication wasn't a happy pill. "It's a tool," he said. "It will lighten your load, and make it possible for us to do the work we need to do."

I was reluctant. It was hard for me to accept the idea of taking a mind-altering medication. What if I couldn't act anymore? What if I wasn't *me* anymore? What if it changed my personality? I didn't think I could stand that. I thought even depression would be better than waking up feeling like a different person. I was scared.

So I told Dr. Stein all my fears, and he was extremely understanding. He didn't brush me off, and I appreciated that. He answered every concern, and then he said if Zoloft didn't work, we'd try another way. I relaxed once I saw that therapy wasn't going to be a rigid routine. I left his office and went directly to the pharmacy. I realized it could be the beginning of the end of my problems.

So I began to take Zoloft, and it was weird. I didn't feel anything. It wasn't like a druggy drug. I wasn't high, or groggy, or stoned. I was just myself. And within a couple of weeks, things just started to open up and get clearer. I felt lighter. The fog lifted. As I started to feel better, the first thing I wanted to do was clean the house. I had let so many things go. The chaos in my house represented the mess in my life. I was done with it.

I went through everything. Every drawer, every closet, every box. I had music playing loud, and I was singing along, cleaning out my soul. At one point, after I'd been at it for a few hours, I looked up to find a crowd in the doorway. Two kids, two Labs, a wirehaired terrier, and a large furry cat. Gaping (as much as dogs and a cat can gape). And I smiled my first truly genuine smile in a long time, and yelled out, "Everybody in the car. We're going to the Greek Village for dinner."

I was back on track. The medication hadn't "cured" me. But it gave me the jump start I needed. I was so grateful that I hadn't let the fear of being thought crazy or weak, insufficient in some essential way, make me wait for help a single day longer. Life was always good—but *enjoying* life fully was even better.

When the cast and crew gathered for the premiere of *The Sopranos* on a cold January night in 1999, it wasn't exactly a star-studded event. Although in later years the premieres would be held at the legendary Ziegfeld Theater, with eleven hundred seats jammed to the rafters, that first time we stuffed ourselves into a medium-size theater in the basement of the Virgin Megastore in Times Square, and there wasn't a flashing bulb in sight. It was a family event in every way. The post-premiere reception was held at John's Pizzeria.

I sat with Margaux and Stella on either side of me, and we all cheered wildly as the opening notes of "Woke Up This Morning" thrummed through the theater and Tony Soprano appeared on the screen, driving up to the tollbooth of the New Jersey Turnpike. As we watched, I kept reaching over to cover Stella's eyes so she wouldn't see the violence or the nude dancers at the strip club, Bada Bing. She had just turned thirteen, and I wasn't about to expose her to that. Naturally, she was insulted at being treated like a child.

The Sopranos was a hit, and I was glowing with pride. I tell you, after the gloom and doom of the past few years, I was filled with awe that life—my life—had been so graciously restored to me. So I decided to do something daring. I changed therapists.

I honestly don't know if it was Dr. Melfi's influence or what. I just knew I wanted a woman's voice, a woman's perspective. Don't get me wrong, Dr. Stein was a wonderful, compassionate man who got me through the crisis. But I also saw that the biggest issues in my life had to do with the way I'd let men get a hold on me. I'd never been in a completely healthy relationship. I'd never demanded equality. I wanted to make sure I changed that—better late than never. But in order to change it, I had to understand the part of me that made it happen. I thought I would feel safer exploring those areas with a woman therapist.

Dr. Stein was very understanding, going so far as to recommend someone. I'd been nervous about making a change, because I didn't want to have to start over. But, looking back, I'd tell anyone who asked for my advice to go for it and not be afraid. In therapy, you grow, and what you need at one period of your life may not be what you need later.

When Dr. Melfi tells Tony Soprano, "Sad is good. Unconscious isn't," I really got it. People tamp themselves down and tune out their reality. They take the pain that they're feeling out on themselves and others in a thousand different ways, wallowing in guilt and blame. It's such a waste. I'd never thought of myself as being unconscious, but in therapy, I was forced to admit that I wasn't always so willing to turn on the floodlights of my consciousness and really take a look deep inside, poke around and peer into all of the corners, every nook and cranny. I thought I was depressed because I'd had some hard knocks, but my new therapist, Dr. Sullivan*, kept pushing me to search more deeply. I felt comfortable with her. She was middle-aged, like me, and the woman-to-woman thing worked for me. She got me.

I'll admit I had a little fun with her. *The Sopranos* was a big hit by then. I knew she knew who I was. There's no way she didn't realize she was treating Dr. Melfi. But I never brought it up, not once, the whole time. To tell you the truth, she was probably relieved. What therapist wants to compete with Dr. Melfi in her own office?

Depression is a process, and treatment for depression is a process. It doesn't happen overnight, and it doesn't take a straight and certain path. There are weeks when you meet with your therapist and report that you're starting to feel better, and other times when you don't feel so great—maybe even worse than when you started. It takes time, and a degree of patience with yourself. In some ways, it's like being overweight. You might start a diet, but that doesn't mean that suddenly you won't want to eat things that you shouldn't. It doesn't mean you're going to lose the weight overnight. It took a long time to gain the weight, and takes a long time to lose it. Depression is the same thing—it takes time to start to feel better. It's a long path.

*Not her real name.

"I don't get it," I said in one of my therapy sessions. "How can an optimist like me be depressed?"

"Maybe you're not an optimist," Dr. Sullivan said.

I didn't like that. "Usually, I am," I told her. "I've always been."

"You've been unhappy for a long time," she observed.

That stopped me. I *had* been unhappy for a long time. Damn. I realized it was true. My therapist was right.

I think we all have areas of our lives we'd just as soon leave unexamined. Those "God knows what I was thinking" moments. Those "Let's just pretend this never happened" moments. I was especially good at that. When I was growing up, my mother's attitude was, if you didn't talk about it, it never happened. There was no point in dwelling on past mistakes. I'd taken that lesson to heart. To me, being a survivor meant moving on. Dr. Sullivan taught me that you don't have to live in the past to understand how it shapes you.

I came to see that my failed relationships were part of a larger puzzle. It wasn't accidental that I was drawn to exciting, intense men who turned out to be emotionally troubled and unavailable. What I saw as their power was really weakness, and I allowed the weakness to control me. I realized that, too often in my life, I had made decisions because one man or another, who seemed to know better than I did, told me it was what I should do. It was time for me to start setting my own course. First, I had to own up to the ways I'd damaged myself and those I loved. It was grueling work.

One day I said to Dr. Sullivan, joking, but not really, "I thought I was depressed before . . ."

She smiled. "This is what consciousness feels like. It's painful at first, but this isn't a wasted period. Use the time in which you finally understand you're depressed as an inward voyage. Don't grab for all the exterior fixes that won't feed your soul." That concept resonated with me. I found the idea of an inward voyage, a chance at true discovery, exciting. I began to think about what kind of person I wanted to be. What kind of mother. What kind of woman. What kind of human being.

I started hanging out at the local Barnes & Noble, setting up in the self-help section. I'd sit on the floor and immerse myself in books about self-empowerment, the spiritual journey, being a woman, finding your strength. I was such a regular that the staff began to notice me. They probably thought I was doing research for my role as Dr. Melfi. One day a young man brought a chair over. "Ms. Bracco, maybe you'd be more comfortable sitting," he said. I gave him a bright smile, said thank you, and sat down. I didn't budge for two hours.

I put myself on the couch. I know people think that there are some things that are just too painful to talk about. I know I thought that. But once you begin traveling down the road of self-examination, you have to go all the way and ultimately take responsibility for everything, good and bad. It's like waking up just before dawn and watching the day begin. Sunrise is a glorious time, the world coming awake again after a long dark night, the sun breaking over the horizon and coloring the sky red and purple and blue and taupe.

Sunrise was exactly what I was seeing, exactly what I was feeling. I'd been telling myself, *You made your bed, now lie in it,* and I was finally recognizing myself again, seeing my old feistiness kicking back in. Now I heard myself saying, *Hell, no. I'm not lying in this bed. I'm getting up. I'm walking out the door. I'm outta here!*

One day, about a year and a half after I started therapy, I said to Dr. Sullivan, "I don't think I need the medication anymore. I'm really doing well. I lost myself for a little while, you know? I did; I lost myself. But I'm finding myself, and I want to stop taking the Zoloft."

"Good," she said. "We'll gradually wean you off the medication. But keep talking. Keep asking. Keep seeing."

Today, when I walk down the street, fans will call out, "Hey, Dr. Melfi." At parties people want to get me in a corner and tell me all their problems. That makes me laugh. I'll kid them, saying, "My practice is very busy right now. Why don't you call Doctor Phil." But seriously, folks . . . I have to remind them, "You know, I'm not really a psychiatrist. I just play one on TV."

What I am is a woman who is not that different from most women. Our culture glorifies people who are on television or in movies, but being a celebrity doesn't insulate you from the struggles of life. I'm here to tell you that no one gets an exemption. In fact, sometimes it's harder, especially if you've bought into your own P.R. I'll tell you, when you take the makeup off and look in the mirror, you don't see some airbrushed image looking back at you. My mirror these days shows a fifty-one-year-old face that's seen better days. But I like to think that what's inside has never been better. I am more alive today than I was at twenty-one. That's a fact.

I always say that Dr. Melfi is my payback for depression. But maybe the best thing she's done for me is to provide a way to reach out to other people. And so, I'm inviting you onto my couch, to a safe place where the truth will be told. I'll show you how I got lost, and maybe you'll see something of yourself in me. I'll show you how I got found, and my story might give you the courage to search for your own joy.

As I said, I'm no Dr. Melfi, but I do believe her with all my heart when she says, "Hope comes in many forms."

Two · Princesses Aren't Born in Brooklyn

Own your feelings.
· Dr. Jennifer Melfi

JANUARY 1979

Warning bells should have been going off in my head when I leapt into marriage with a man I knew didn't love me. In 1979, I was a twenty-four-year-old model living in Paris. Ah, Paris, the city of romance. I was ready for love. When I met Daniel Guerard, a French salon owner, I was smitten. I ignored all the signs that told me to run the other way. I excused his wandering eye and wandering hands as being just so French. Frenchmen were like that—all of them just oozing sensuality. It didn't mean Daniel wasn't devoted to me in every way that mattered.

At the time, I still truly believed that Prince Charming existed, and that strangers from opposite sides of the ocean and very different backgrounds could meet and fall in love. Look at my parents.

They met in England after World War II. My mother was a nineteen-year-old British girl from a working-class family, a secretary at the military base where my father was stationed. Ironically, she worked in the department that was in charge of processing war brides. Sheila Molyneux was a proper, well-bred English girl who also happened to be gorgeous. She had soft brown hair, deep blue eyes, and a drop-dead figure. Dad used to say she was the image of Irene Dunne. And Sal Bracco was pretty sharp, too, a spunky Italian-American soldier, with wavy, dark hair and a handsome, sweet face. Dad wasn't a big guy, at least not physically, but he had a big personality, and though he was only eighteen, he had confidence to spare. The first time he came into the office at the base and saw my mother, sitting all prim and pretty at her desk, he went head over heels. He knew he had found "the one." He set out to win her over—and trust me when I say that when my father sets out to do something, he succeeds. Mom, of course, had been warned about the American soldiers, and wanted nothing to do with him. But you have to know my dad. He started talking, she started laughing, and that was that. She finally agreed to go out with him.

Dad's flair was inherited. His grandparents had been very influential in their Detroit community, where his father had owned Club Morocco, which had featured big-name headliners like Bob Hope and Danny Thomas at the height of their fame. He was larger than life. Dad used to say, "My old man was the king."

Unfortunately, my paternal grandfather ruled his roost from the wrong side of the law. When Dad was twelve, they arrested his father in a sweep involving arms trafficking, and he died in jail of a cerebral hemorrhage. The family pulled up roots and moved to

Brooklyn to live with relatives. They wanted to put that chapter behind them, and I was an adult before I knew anything about Grandpa's shadowy life. Even today, Dad doesn't like to talk about it.

On their first date, my father took my mother to a dance at the USO, where the famous bandleader Glenn Miller and his orchestra were playing. My mom got up the nerve to approach Glenn Miller, asking for his autograph and requesting that he play her favorite song. He opened the next set with her request. My mother remembers to this day dancing with my father in that dark, crowded USO hall, and falling in love with him to the tune of "Stardust Memories."

A few years ago I was honored to be asked by the USO to be entertainer of the year for a fund-raising event. I brought my mother and father with me that afternoon, and I told the assembled crowd how my parents had fallen in love at a USO dance. At that, my mother reached into her purse, pulled out an ancient piece of paper, and held it up. It was Glenn Miller's autograph. The room went wild. She never told me that she'd kept his autograph in her purse for fifty-some years.

Have you ever heard the expression "Opposites attract, but they don't attach?" My parents proved the old adage wrong. They were different, but they stuck for life. Where my dad is forceful and dramatic, my mother is quiet, though she's got a strong side, too. My parents were raised in different worlds, on opposite sides of the ocean, but they saw eye to eye on all of the important things. And their attraction today, sixty years later, is as great as ever. My dad still looks at my mom and says, meaning every word, "You're the most beautiful woman in the world." He's right, too. I might also mention that he still cuts a pretty dashing figure himself.

How did my mother's parents feel about this sweet-talking American soldier who had swept their daughter off her feet? Not only did they like Dad, they thought the idea of Mom living in America was the best thing in the world. In the years following World War II, the British economy was in lousy shape, and many families felt their war bride daughters had grabbed the golden ring. So Sal and Sheila married in England on October 26, 1946. Dad got a pass and borrowed a cottage for the night. He still talks about their extremely frigid wedding night. "How cold was it?" he asks dramatically. "It was so cold I couldn't find my equipment. It had run for cover." But somehow, they managed to make do, frozen or not. Love comes with its own fireplace.

Dad had a couple of months left to serve, so Mom joined the stream of war brides signing up for passage to America. Maybe because she'd worked in the office that processed foreign brides, she got a prime spot on the grand transatlantic ocean liner the *Queen Elizabeth*. She was delighted, although she wasn't prepared for the stormy sea or the rough voyage. "I wore an emerald green suit," she recalled. "It matched my face."

Mom had been eager to come to America. She saw it as a grand romantic adventure. But by the time the ship entered New York Harbor, her enthusiasm was waning. It was a freezing December day, and the icy river air hit her face like a thousand pinpricks. When she finally disembarked, exhausted and shivering, she was met by her new *famiglia*—an imposing welcoming committee of the Bracco clan that wasn't so welcoming. These were big, loud, domineering people—and I'm talking about the women here. They didn't expect their precious Sal, their little prince, to marry an outsider. Forget that she was British. Worse, she wasn't *Italian*. What kind of home was she going to make for Sal? You can imagine the conversations before my mother even showed up. You can imagine the conversations *after* she showed up.

They took her home to Brooklyn and started showing her the ways of Italian-American life. She was horrified. She thought, *Oh, my God, my new husband is thousands of miles away across the Atlantic, I'm an Englishwoman, I've never cooked spaghetti, and I've never even heard of lasagna*. What a culture shock!

It's telling that Mom's memories of the adjustment mostly had to do with food. She was shocked to find food being the primary topic of conversation in her new family. "We never talked about food in England," she said. "I realize we weren't exactly known for our food, but in England people talked about their gardens. Here I was, in a family that discussed the many ways of meatballs, at length and in depth."

Mom didn't do much talking at first. She was too busy trying to work up the courage to eat calamari and octopus, not part of regular English fare, you know. She was relieved when somebody whispered to her that she didn't have to eat it if she didn't want to.

My dad arrived home a month later, and he made her feel a lot more comfortable. "I knew she'd come around when I caught her raiding the refrigerator in the middle of the night, eating leftover octopus salad," he chortled. Well, maybe it wasn't the love of octopus; maybe she was just pregnant.

They moved to an apartment in the Bay Ridge section of Brooklyn and got ready to make their personal contribution to the baby boom. Their first child, a son, was born in October 1947. They named him Salvatore after his father, but his nickname was Sally Boy. To his humiliation and chagrin, it stuck. God, he hated that nickname. Sally was a *girl's* name, even if you tacked "Boy" on the end. Needless to say, there are still a few holdouts who call him Sally Boy to this day, and Sal's fifty-nine.

After he got out of the service, Dad went to work at the Fulton Fish Market and eventually built his own business there, ABC Fillets, where he filleted flounder for the wholesale market. For the next twenty years, his workdays began at two in the morning and ended just as we were getting up.

My mother loved Dad, and she doted on little Sal, but she was desperately unhappy during those first years in Brooklyn. "I wanted to keep my own individuality," she told me many years later, "and it didn't work. I tried to be my English self, but it wasn't possible with fifty Italians crawling up your neck, carrying on and yelling. At first I thought, when in Rome do as the Romans do. But it didn't happen. I never belonged. I didn't understand their lifestyle, or their food, or anything."

With Dad working nights at the Fulton Fish Market, Mom was all by herself in the apartment with just a baby for company. She cried with loneliness. To her, it felt as if everybody had family except her; her family might as well have been on another planet. You have to remember that in those days, international phone calls were a rarity, and visits were pretty much out of the question. Mom felt herself growing more and more distanced from her family in England, literally and figuratively. She had no contact with her siblings: her two older brothers were married and off living their own lives, and her little sister, who was almost ten years younger, led a life completely foreign to my mom, given the distance and the age difference. It was a bleak time for her.

The nights were especially tough. When it was late, while my dad was at work at the fish market, Mom had a lot of time to think, and she'd despair of her lost youth—what she'd left behind, and what she'd hoped for her future. She had expected a brighter, fuller life, and instead she felt trapped, a stranger in a strange land.

In September 1951, when my brother Sal was nearly four, she announced to Dad, "I want to go home. I've had it here." And with that she packed a bag, took Sal, and headed back to England on the next boat.

I'm sure Dad was stunned, but I have to admire Mom's guts. Hearing this story opened my eyes to a side of her I didn't fully know or appreciate. She was tough in her own way, and her flight back to England was her signal to Dad that conditions at home had to change. I have to tell you, it was a brilliant strategy, because Dad spent the next three months courting her all over again, sending her wonderful gifts every week. This approach definitely impressed Mom's parents. "He seems like a nice guy," her father said as Christmas neared. "Look at what he sends you—all the packages and the letters. I think it's time for you to go back." What my dad and her dad didn't know was that Mom had planned to go back all along, but before she did, she wanted to make sure that things were going to be different. Well, no surprise there—she got her way. Shortly after her return, my parents and little Sal moved to the ground floor of a two-family house on 85th Street, in the Bay Ridge section of Brooklyn, an acceptable distance from my father's hard-core Italian clan.

Mom was happy. She loved the new neighborhood, and started making friends. She was active in St. John's Lutheran Church, and she joined the choir. Around the time when Sal was in the first grade, she decided she was ready to have another child. She hoped for a little girl, and she got her wish when I was born on October 2, 1954. She dressed me like a doll, but even as a baby I wasn't exactly doll-like. I was messy and high-spirited, a tomboy in the making. My frilly dresses always had a muddy fringe. I looked up to my brother Sal, and I figured out pretty early that if I wanted to play with the big boys, I had to be tough. It's a good thing my sister Elizabeth arrived, when I was three. Now, *she* was a beautiful doll. Such a little lady. I *ate* dirt. Lizzie *repelled* it.

Thanks to Mom's influence, our household wasn't typical of the Italian-American families in Bay Ridge. But I'll say one thing. Mom knew how to put on a big Italian spread. When she married Dad, she figured out pretty quickly that she had to master Italian cooking if she was going to survive in the Bracco clan. In a world where you were judged by the quality of your meatballs and the thickness of your sauce, Mom more than held her own. I still remember the Sunday feasts at my grandmother's apartment in Brooklyn, with platters of ravioli and lasagna and, of course, meatballs. Mom, trim and pretty with a flowery apron covering her dress, looked triumphant as the *real* Italians nodded their approval. She was one of them. Apart from those dinners, we were mostly busy with our own lives as a relatively normal family of the 1950s. My dad was definitely the head of the household. He ruled our roost. Mom was strong in her own way, but her primary goal was to keep the peace, and she deferred to my father on all other matters. Like all families, we had our ups and downs, but after what I've seen in my adult life, I appreciate even more how lucky Sal and Lizzie and I were to have parents who loved us and always put us first.

In the summertime, Dad rented a cabin at a family camp in upstate Brewster, New York, back when it was still considered the country. We loved it there, and made many friends with families who, like us, returned year after year. Dad would work all week and then come up on the weekends, when he was a big hit, organizing sports activities and playing cards with the blind owner of the camp, Henry. I remember that Henry had a set of Braille playing cards, something that was totally new to us. We all thought that was pretty amazing.

Our friends always said how lucky we were to have such cool parents. Of course, you never think your own parents are cool, but looking back, I see what they meant. Dad and Mom were fun to be around, and Dad was popular with Sal's friends, volunteering as a Boy Scout leader and sports coach for Sal and his classmates. I tagged along sometimes, but I was a girl, and in those days there was a very clear dividing line between what girls did and what boys did. Mostly, I think, Sal just thought of me as his annoying little sister.

By the time I was eight, things were starting to change in Bay Ridge, and my parents began to talk about moving east to the Long Island suburbs. The change that affected us the most was the construction of the Verrazano-Narrows Bridge, which would open in 1964, connecting Brooklyn to Staten Island. Many people lost their homes as construction cut a path through our neighborhood. Bridge work at the end of our street made it a messy and more dangerous place to live.

Our move to Long Island was expedited by a scary incident that occurred one summer afternoon in 1963. I was playing near the construction site with my two girlfriends, Mary* and Joyce*, when a man approached us and showed us an official-looking badge. "I'm a detective," he said with a friendly smile. He said he was doing some police work in the area, and then asked us if we'd like to see the inside of a detective's car. Joyce said she had to go home, but Mary and I were interested.

We got inside the car with the man, with Mary sitting next to him and me by the door. Mary was a beautiful girl, with long blond ringlets and blue eyes. She was very ladylike—the complete opposite of me with my cropped dark hair and smudged pedal pushers.

The detective smiled at us and asked if we'd like a soda. We nodded yes. He handed me a ten-dollar bill—a huge amount of

*Not their real names.

money at the time—and told me to go down the block to Weber's deli and buy us sodas. I ran off happily. The deli owner looked at me strangely when I handed him the money, saying, "Goodness, that's a big bill. Doesn't your mother have an account?" He was right; we never paid cash at the deli. Although he was suspicious, he let me go, with the sodas and the change clutched tightly in my fist.

I started running down the street, then stopped dead. The car was gone. Then I panicked and started crying. I raced home and sobbed out the story to my mother; within minutes, the street was filled with *real* cops as well as many of the neighbors. This was just around the time Dad was arriving home from work, and when he saw us talking to the police, he leapt out of his car and ran over to us. I didn't fully understand what was happening, or why everyone was yelling and crying, but I do know I felt as if I'd done something bad. In my child's mind, I thought if I'd stayed in the car, the man wouldn't have taken Mary away.

Miles away, a plainclothes policeman was walking down the street when he noticed a man in a car with a little blond girl. He stopped to investigate, only to discover that it was the phony detective with Mary. It turned out that the man had been convicted before of sexually molesting little girls.

When Dad found out they'd arrested the guy, no one could hold him back. "I'm gonna tear his eyeballs out," he told my mother before heading down to the police station. They had the perpetrator in a cell, and when Dad got close to him, he started shouting, "Put me in the cell with him. Let me get at him." The cops told him he'd better calm down or he'd be under arrest, too. That was the whole idea. "Good," he yelled. "Then I'll be in the cell with him." They finally hustled Dad out of the station and sent him home.

We moved soon after that incident. I'm sure it made my dad do what he could to speed up the purchase of a house in Westbury in central Nassau County. We later learned that nothing ever happened to the sexual molester. When it was time to testify in court, Mary's family never showed up. They simply disappeared. As a result, the child molester—a repeat offender—walked.

When Dad announced that we were moving to Westbury, Lizzie and I couldn't have been more excited. But Sal—Sal was very upset. He was fifteen, in love with his first girlfriend, and in his mind, moving to Long Island was like being exiled to Siberia. He begged my parents to let him stay, promising that he'd live with a friend, that he'd find a place. Naturally, they wouldn't hear of it. I mean, really! He was a fifteen-year-old kid! Finally, in desperation, Sal made a rather theatrical last-ditch attempt to change their minds. He grabbed a wad of cash my dad kept hidden, and held it up, while in his other hand he held a cigarette lighter. "Let me stay or I'm burning this money," he threatened. He meant it, too. He was love-crazed. Somehow my dad talked him down and saved the money. I think it involved the promise of a car.

Westbury, Long Island, was considered a safe place, like many bedroom communities in the sixties, and a welcome environment to raise children. During the height of the baby-boom years, many families left their crowded urban apartment buildings and tiny row houses in Brooklyn and Queens to raise their kids in neighborhoods with cleaner air and open spaces. We lived in a pretty little enclave of about one hundred families, mostly Jewish, between Cantiague Park and the Westbury Music Fair (now known as the North Fork Theatre at Westbury). Every family on our street had two or three kids, and backyards with swing sets, lush green grass, and flower gardens. People didn't lock their doors, and kids rode their bicycles for miles without encountering serious traffic. In the summertime, we hung out at Jones Beach, ate snow cones, watched ball games, and had picnics in the park. It was wonderful to have the ocean practically in our backyard. Dad's commute to lower Manhattan was longer than it had been from Brooklyn, but he didn't encounter much traffic at one in the morning, and his drive home was free and clear, since all of the traffic was heading toward the city, not away from it.

I'd have to say that we all thrived in Westbury, but the person who really spread his wings was Sal. He blossomed at Hicksville High School. Sal was smart and popular—a real star. He was president of his class, and he was the stage manager for the annual Battle of the Bands. One band was led by Billy Joel, who was in Sal's class and was already playing professionally.

It seemed like our phone never stopped ringing with all the girls calling for Sal. I always raced to answer it, and when a girl asked for Sal, I'd say, "I'll put you on the list. You're number seventeen today."

There was a definite pecking order in our house: I annoyed Sal, and Lizzie annoyed me. Anyone with a younger sister knows exactly what I'm talking about. We shared a room, and she drove me crazy with her Pretty Miss Perfect routine. It would take her an hour every morning just to select her outfit for the day. She'd stand in front of the closet staring in as if she were trying to channel the gods of style.

Lizzie could get away with anything in our house, because she was the baby. Even when she got older, Mom would say, "Don't yell at the *baby* . . . don't hurt the *baby*." She was a little sweetheart. Not like her big sister.

It's funny, looking back, that we ended up in a Jewish neighborhood, but my mother loved it. She and I both made a lot of friends there and most of them were Jewish. I was the only Catholic—and I was only minimally Catholic. After my First Communion at age seven, the only time I saw the inside of a church was on Christmas and Easter. Clearly, my parents weren't very religious at all. Of course, I was *very* curious about what it meant to be Jewish. Sometimes I'd have dinner at my friend Linda's house on the Sabbath, and I marveled at the rituals—how beautiful it was when her mother lit the candles and said the prayers in Hebrew. For me, it was like entering a magical world.

When all of my friends joined B'nai B'rith, I begged my mother to let me join, too. She rolled her eyes and got that look on her face like, *What am I gonna do with this kid?* But no one had explained to me why I couldn't join, or what was different about being Jewish or Catholic or any other religion. I was completely in the dark.

My friend Hedy's grandmother lived with her family. She

seemed really old to me, but she was probably only in her fifties or maybe sixty at the most. She didn't speak any English, only Yiddish. One day I went over to Hedy's house after school and her grandmother fixed us a snack. As we sat at the kitchen table, I noticed that Hedy's grandmother had numbers tattooed on her arm. I didn't have many social graces, so I pointed at the tattoo and asked, "What's that?"

The old woman's face turned white, and Hedy nudged me. I knew I had said something very rude. I felt terrible. I started to apologize, but Hedy's grandmother ignored me, chattering in Yiddish to Hedy. "She wants to know if you've heard of Auschwitz," Hedy said. I confessed that I had not. Schools didn't teach about the Holocaust in those days, and my parents had never talked about it. So that day I got my first lesson on the evils of Hitler's Germany. As Hedy explained it to me, her grandmother sat silently, with a haunted look in her eyes. I could feel her agony, and I thought my ignorance had caused her more grief. Impulsively, I got up and put my arms around her. "I'm so sorry this happened to you," I said. I was a silly girl, but that day made a lasting impact on me.

I often wondered, who am I? I wasn't like my friends. I didn't have any distinguishing characteristics that I could point to. As for looks, I was certainly no beauty. I was gawky and uncertain, too tall, too funny-looking.

I longed to be like my gorgeous mother. Even as a little girl, I knew she was a head-turner. We'd be walking down the street in

Brooklyn and truck drivers would honk their horns in appreciation. Men would call out, "Hey, beautiful." I'd hang on to my mother's hand, demanding to know, "Mommy, why are those men talking to you?" She'd just smile to herself in a secret way.

Beauty was a mystery to me, and I wasn't exactly growing into my looks. When I was twelve years old, the kids on the bus voted me the ugliest girl in the sixth grade. Kids can be so mean, but at the time it felt right, even to me. I had buck teeth and braces. I still sucked my thumb. I had a really awful perm, given to me by my mother. I was a good head taller than all of the other girls, and literally towered over the shrimpy little prepubescent boys.

But although I envied my mother's beauty, I sensed from a fairly early age that I wanted a different life than the one she had chosen. I was restless and full of unfocused dreams. I didn't want to grow up to be a doting wife and mother. I had no patience for domesticity, no interest in cooking or keeping my room neat. I'd rather do manual labor than iron a shirt. It seemed that my mother spent all of her time keeping our house spotless, and that was not going to be my life. I had a lot of ideas percolating inside of me, but they didn't seem possible. I would look at myself in the mirror, and I just didn't see in my reflection any of the movie stars I idolized. I didn't look like Doris Day or Kim Novak. I certainly was no Sandra Dee or Debbie Reynolds, either. I was not an all-American girl, the way my favorite magazines defined her. For a while I went through a stage where I wanted to be Barbra Streisand, because she was so unusual. If only I could carry a tune!

Unfortunately, what I lacked in looks I was unable to make up for in smarts. I was a terrible student. No matter how I tried, I couldn't buckle down. I just didn't get it. Today, I would have been diagnosed as having some kind of learning disability, but no one knew about that in the late sixties and early seventies. You were either a good student or you were a screwup. By the seventh grade, I was sliding along, headed nowhere in particular, coasting into what was sure to be a completely unremarkable future. Then a teacher named Artie Horowitz took an interest in me, and it changed my life.

Mr. Horowitz was the seventh-grade English teacher at my middle school, and he also directed the school plays. You know how every school's got a cool teacher? That was Mr. Horowitz. He was cute, young, still single, with a mod hairstyle and a mustache. He wore bell-bottoms, which was very radical for a teacher. He could pull off that look, and kids just thought he was awesome. I loved Mr. Horowitz—all the kids did. A bunch of us stayed after school and painted scenery for shows and auditioned for plays. It was a lot of fun, and one of the best things about getting involved in the drama club was feeling like part of a group—with a caring adult in charge. He was an authority figure, but he reached out to us on our level. Mr. Horowitz was the first adult who talked to us like we were real people.

Mr. Horowitz always took a special interest in me. I wasn't a good student, but he pushed me and encouraged me to read books and apply myself. My lack of ambition and acceptance of mediocrity in myself really bothered him, and he refused to let me off the hook. Somehow, he saw something in me that I had yet to see in myself.

In high school, I fell in with the creative crowd. We weren't the jocks or the eggheads or the beauty queens. We girls wore our hair long and straight, ironing out the waves. We dressed in bell-bottoms and miniskirts, platform shoes, banana jeans, and big hoop earrings. We thought pastel separates were the kiss of death. We weren't exactly edgy, but in small ways we tried to assert our individuality.

When my braces came off at age fifteen, I blossomed. I started to feel pretty. The "ugliest girl" days were far behind me. I became a little more interested in style and fashion. My two best friends in high school were gay boys—not that I knew it then. One aspired to be a photographer and the other a fashion designer, and I was their model. We spent long hours in my backyard doing what we considered to be high-concept shoots. I'd be draped in gowns with spangles and faux furs, striking what passed for dramatic poses against snowy suburban backgrounds. We had no idea what we were doing, but it was more fun than hanging out at the bowling alley. I vividly remember standing in the snow up to my knees, peeking out from under a big furry hat, smiling for the camera, and thinking, "I'm not going to be like anybody I know."

I was also good friends with a boy named Jeff Kurland, who would later become a major costume designer. Among his many projects, Jeff has done the costumes for most of Woody Allen's movies. In high school, Jeff used to tell me, "Get your book together, girl." By book, Jeff meant a model's portfolio of fashion shots. He was the first person who seriously thought I could be a model.

Talk is cheap, though, and daydreams are just that, unless you do something to make them happen. And I was not distinguishing myself in high school—just drifting along, barely making the grade. It was obvious that I wasn't college material, and it's not something my parents pushed for. In Dad's view, boys went to college. Girls? It didn't matter so much. Sal was the first person in our family to ever go to college. He attended SUNY in Old Westbury and lived at home. My parents practically burst with pride the day he graduated.

Sometimes a couple of us girls would go over to the middle school to visit Mr. Horowitz at the end of our school day. We'd find him in the auditorium, where he'd be working on the latest play. He was always happy to see us, and he never missed a chance to talk about the future. Most of my girlfriends were college bound, but when he'd ask me about my plans, I just shrugged. Mr. Horowitz kept asking, though. "What do you want to do with your life, Lorraine? What's your passion, Lorraine? What's the one thing you want to do?"

Looking back today, it seems amazing that he bothered. What was it about me that made Mr. Horowitz try so hard? I've often wondered about that, and I've come to the conclusion that Mr. Horowitz was one of those rare people who decides to give a damn, for no other reason than that he's in a position to make a difference. It's why he became a teacher in the first place. It was more than just a job to him. He lifted me out of my doldrums because he cared. He hated to see people float on their inertia. If it weren't for Artie Horowitz, I wouldn't be where I am today. It's a simple fact.

One day when Mr. Horowitz was pestering me about my goals in life and what I wanted to do with myself, I answered, practically in a whisper: "I think I want to be a model." I was voicing the most distant dream of the ugliest girl on the school bus. It sounded ridiculous, even laughable, as the words came out of my mouth. But to his everlasting credit, Mr. Horowitz didn't bat an eye. "Okay," he said, "why don't you find out if you can do it?"

"How?" I gaped at him. What, was he kidding?

"Call the agencies. Make an appointment."

"How do you know what to do?"

"I don't." He grinned. "But if it's what you want, you have to take action. You can't just say maybe." He did some research and found the telephone numbers, and told me to talk to my parents. "If it's okay with them, I'll drive you into the city and bring you back," he said.

Amazingly, my parents said yes, and one day after school I hopped into Mr. Horowitz's red Camaro, and off we went. It's kind of hard to imagine this happening today.

Our first stop was the Ford Modeling Agency on East 60th, where we met Eileen Ford herself. She was intimidating—not one for chitchat. She took one look at me and shook her head. "Too heavy," she said in her clipped manner. "Needs a nose job." I was glad my dad wasn't in the room. He'd have plenty to say about that!

Dad couldn't stand pretentious people or fakery. Funny that I was about to enter a world that was mostly composed of just that.

As we left the agency, I felt a little stung by Eileen Ford's harsh scrutiny. "Maybe we should go home now," I said. But good old Mr. Horowitz just smiled at me, and drove me to my next appointment at Wilhelmina. He parked the car right in front of the building at 37th and Madison, and we went in.

Willie was an absolutely stunning woman, tall and glamorous. Before she started the agency she'd been one of the most famous models in the world. I was awestruck in her presence. I don't think I'd ever seen anyone quite like her. She paced around chain-smoking (I think there were two or three cigarettes going simultaneously), and best of all, she actually treated me like a human being. Willie studied me for a long time, and then she said, "I don't know what it is about you, but I like it."

"Really?" I couldn't help myself. I must have looked shocked. I'd been ready for failure, especially after meeting Eileen Ford, and I definitely wasn't prepared for acceptance. I thought my "different" look would doom me, but Willie liked to take chances on girls who didn't fit the all-American, blond, blue-eyed mold. She told me to come back the following week to do the paperwork, and just like that, I was in. I was going to be a model represented by Wilhelmina!

I was floating as Mr. Horowitz and I came out to the street. As we headed for the car, we noticed a parking ticket flapping on the Camaro's windshield, which made him groan. He was working on a teacher's salary, so there wasn't a lot of wiggle room for extra expenses like parking tickets. He went to take the ticket, and stepped off the curb into a pile of dog shit. I was horrified. I hoped it wasn't an omen. But then again, no good deed goes unpunished.

The next week I took the train to the city one day after school and after meeting with Wilhelmina once again, she gave me a contract. When I walked into the house with a contract for fifty dollars an hour, my Dad twirled me around the living room. It was the first time I had ever done anything that really made my parents proud, and I liked that feeling. Fifty dollars an hour was a lot of money at a time when the minimum wage was only $2.25.

During the summer of my sophomore year of high school, and for the following two years of high school, I continued to work as a model. Modeling become such a significant part of my life that by the time I was a senior I was given permission to take half days at school. I did numerous catalogue shoots, and occasionally appeared in *Mademoiselle* and *Seventeen*. One of my biggest jobs was for Butterick Patterns, which really impressed my mom. I was not a natural, believe me; I've never been a natural at anything. But I worked hard, and I had the advantage of naïveté. Sometimes, if you don't know you can't do something, you end up doing it in spite of yourself. Willie was incredibly supportive, a combination big sister and adviser. She really took me under her wing. "Kid," she'd say (she always called me Kid), "you've got it." Boy. Whatever "it" was, I was sure glad she thought I had it.

I didn't talk about my modeling jobs much around school. It embarrassed me a little. I'd never been the prom-queen type, and maybe I thought the kids would laugh at me. I could see that the girls were phony-happy for me, and some who'd never spoken to me before would sidle up and coo, "Oh, Lorraine, how's it going?" I didn't like that feeling of fakery, so I clammed up and didn't talk about it much.

As the year ended, my friends were all getting ready for college. I was planning to move into the city and be a full-time model. I was going with the flow, not really thinking too hard about the long term. At seventeen, I was younger than most of the other models, and I had my whole life ahead of me.

I shared a tiny apartment in Peter Cooper Village with another model named Nancy Carpenter, and started pounding the pavement. Literally. My days were filled with "go-sees." Go see this photographer. Go see that art director. I was getting enough work to make ends meet, but I wasn't into the cutthroat side of the business. My attitude was always "What will be mine will be mine." I wasn't going to stab someone with a stiletto heel to get there.

One day in Wilhelmina's famous waiting room, I met a girl who was drop-dead gorgeous, but obviously troubled. She was pacing the floor, upset and mumbling. I did what I always do: I walked up to her and asked, "Is something wrong?"

It was the right question. She took off and let go with a torrent of information—how her father didn't want her modeling, and threw her out of the house, and now she didn't even have a place to sleep.

"Wow." That's all I could manage. I was amazed. My parents had always been so supportive, and I couldn't imagine parents being any other way. "Well, you can't sleep on the street."

"Right." She was miserable. So I said, "Look, I have a queen-size bed. If you want, you can come home with me."

And that's how I became lifelong buddies with Shaun Casey, who went on to make millions as the face of Estee Lauder. Shaun was friendly with another hot model of the day, Patti Hansen, future wife of Keith Richards. At some point she ended up staying with us in the apartment.

Patti was the original wild child. She and Shaun were great blond Amazons, and they had the world on a string. Men with flowers, candy, and champagne were lining up outside the door in limousines. I felt like a gray wren next to them. They'd blow into the apartment around 10:30 at night, and pull me away from the television. "Come on, Bracco, we're going out," they'd say.

"I'm in my pajamas." I felt like I was twelve years old.

"Get dressed. And Bracco, could you put on some makeup? And comb your hair." Laughing, they'd drag me out into the night. It was a dizzying few months—after all, Shaun and Patti were the "it" girls of the time—but their club scene never became my scene. I was still a kid who went home to Westbury on the weekends.

In the spring of 1973, after I'd been working full-time in the city for a few months, I met Christa, who ran Willie's sister agency in Paris. She told me that with my look and personality, I'd do very well in Europe. A lot of American models did stints in Europe to build their portfolios.

"Come to Paris," Christa said. "You will be our girl next door."

At first I refused her offer. I didn't want to leave my family, and, I never thought my dad would permit it. He was very strict with his girls—the typical Italian father. He always kept Lizzie and me on a short leash. But when I told my parents about Christa's offer, they shocked the hell out of me by telling me to go.

I stared at them in disbelief. "You've got to be kidding. You *want* me to go?" I have to say, I felt a little hurt. In some weird way, I guess I was offended. Maybe they didn't love me. Maybe they just couldn't wait to get rid of me. It may seem strange now, but I took their support as a rejection, which just goes to show how insecure I was. The reality was, they were letting their little bird fly away, because they loved and trusted me.

Dad handed me a thousand dollars and said, "Don't worry. If you don't like it, you just give me a call and you can come home right away. Anytime you want."

As it turned out, I *did* like it. In fact, I loved it from the moment my plane landed at Orly airport. Paris was electric—a combination of both Old World charm and New World glamour. Christa's agency was housed in a six-story building in the heart of the city, and it was a bustling enterprise. There were four floors of offices, a full-service kitchen, and on the top floor a warren of rooms where new models stayed until they could afford to get apartments of their own. There were four rooms, two girls to a room. Need I say that it was bedlam?

Christa's partners, Jacques and Dominick Silberstein, introduced me around and wined and dined me like I was a star. It was unbelievably thrilling. I was enthralled with every detail of my new life, and couldn't wait to get up in the morning. I was very serious about learning French. For the first time in my life I was motivated to study. I was a talker, a communicator. If I couldn't talk, I'd wither and die. It amazed me that I had an ability with languages. It had certainly never been apparent in school. But within a year of my arrival, I was able to speak and understand enough to get by.

My roommate at Christa's was Susan Wyatt, a beautiful, elegant southern girl—a real lady. She seemed to epitomize the phrase "fashion model" far more than I did. I was used to a more casual existence, just throwing on jeans and a sweater, running a comb through my hair, and being ready to fly out the door. Not Susan. Her daily beauty regimen was lengthy and elaborate. I'd lie on my bed in our little room and watch her as she slowly and artistically applied makeup, curled her lashes, and combed out her hair. It was a real education.

"Stop watching me," she'd say, annoyed.

I'd laugh. "No, I can't help it. This is fascinating. I'm learning."

She'd give me a look, as if to say, *Not you. You'll never learn.*

And we'd both laugh. We were enjoying ourselves. Everything was an adventure—learning the language, figuring out the metro system, sitting in cafés and people-watching. We were having too much fun to realize what a cutthroat business we were in, and Jacques and Dominick never made it feel that way. They were adorable men—charming, handsome, and oozing with French charm. I started dating Jacques during the first year. It wasn't that serious—like most Frenchmen I knew, he had a girlfriend—but it helped me improve my French.

A lot of people warned me that the French were very cold and dismissive, and that they didn't like Americans. But soon after I arrived, I had an experience that endeared me to the French people forever. I was on assignment for a magazine in Normandy, in the picture-perfect coastal town of Deauville. While we were setting up for the shoot, an old man wearing a black beret and walking with a cane approached us. He began speaking rapidly in French to the editor and pointing at me. I hadn't learned enough French yet to understand, so I stood dumbly by, wondering what on earth his interest in me could be. The editor was frowning, and she looked very annoyed, but he was persistent. Finally, she turned to me and said, "He wanted to know if you were American, and he said to tell you that you should know about the heroic deeds the Americans performed during World War II. He wants you to pass his thanks on to your father, grandfather, uncle—anyone in your family who served."

I thought that was incredibly sweet. I turned to the old man and smiled brilliantly. "Yes, yes," I said, nodding my head.

He was mesmerized—that much I could tell. He spoke to the editor again, and she threw up her hands in disgust. "He wants to know if you will sing 'The Star-Spangled Banner,' " she said.

"Really?" I stared at the man, and I could see that he really wanted me to do it. Believe me, my singing voice wasn't much, and I didn't know all the words, but I was so touched by his request that

I couldn't refuse. Standing as tall as I could, and placing a hand over my heart, I sang:

Oh, say can you see
By the dawn's early light
What so proudly we hail'd . . .

Tears streamed from the old man's eyes as I sang, and I felt kind of choked up, too. For the first time since I had arrived in France, I felt the strong connection between our two countries. In a strange way, I felt at home.

Let's face it, overall, the business of modeling is a shallow one, but the experience made a woman out of me. My ten years in Paris exposed me to a world far beyond my neighborhood. Americans can be parochial, and when you never look outside your own culture you don't have a chance to stretch your mind. Living in Europe, and traveling for my work to Berlin and Kenya and Brazil and Morocco and Rome and Düsseldorf and Milan, I truly found myself.

I worked all the time, shooting for print ads, catalogues, and features in *Elle*, *Marie-Claire*, and *Cosmopolitan*. I worked with some of the top fashion designers of the day—Jean-Paul Gaultier, Azzedine Alaia, and Kenzo. I wasn't in the supermodel class, like Patti Hansen and Shaun Casey, but I didn't care. Remember, I wasn't Miss Ambition. For me, the experience alone was thrilling—and if I could support myself, too, I was happy.

On one occasion, Jacques took me to Barcelona, where he introduced me to Salvador Dalí, the brilliant Spanish surrealist painter.

We visited Dalí at his apartment at the Ritz. Dalí was wild. And he loved women, which was very funny, because his wife was extremely jealous and she didn't try to hide it. Dalí's new project was the jewelry of Spain, and he asked me if I would pose for a picture in his bathtub wearing gobs of jewelry. I assumed he meant nude, so I got on my high horse a little, but he waved his hand impatiently. "No, no, in a gown. In a gown." Well, how could I refuse? Later, another model and I stood there in evening dresses while he draped us in fifty million dollars' worth of gold and jewels. Then we lay down at opposite ends of the Ritz Hotel's huge sunken bathtub. Dalí had neglected to mention one detail—the five hundred live escargots that he dumped into the tub around us. (Dalí always did everything in fives. It was his magic number.) Jewels and snails. He was a madman. My dad still has that photo, signed by Dalí himself, hanging on the wall of his basement workshop.

Dalí's wife was extremely jealous of the young girls Dalí had in the suite. Not that he ever did anything, but she'd sweep into the room and literally hiss at us with the force of a steam radiator. Her husband was a lover of women, and that was her cross to bear.

Later, Dalí did ask to paint me in the nude, and I had to decline. I wasn't up for it. You can take the girl out of Brooklyn, but you can't take Brooklyn out of the girl! That's a regret I have now. I could have been part of a Dalí painting forever. But not then. At that time, it was just too much for me. So he gave me a pencil drawing of an erect penis as a consolation gift. I was mortified. I didn't realize at the time what a big compliment it was. I'll say this for Dalí. He may have been a surrealist, but he was a *realist* with me.

The man who helped transform me from a girl to a woman was a Polish prince named Jean Poniatowski. It was 1975, and I had already ended it with Jacques. I had just turned twenty-one. I had a friend, Patrick, who was always talking about his sister Sabine. Sabine was married to a prince. "Prince of what?" I asked. European royalty was very confusing to me.

Patrick explained that Sabine's husband, Jean Poniatowski, was a direct descendent of Stanislaw Poniatowski, the last king of the Polish-Lithuanian Commonwealth. So Jean had a title, but no kingdom. However, the Poniatowski family was extremely prominent. In addition, Jean was director of the French *TV Guide*, which made him even more well connected.

Patrick told me that his sister was divorcing Jean to be with another man, and the children were going with her.

"How terrible," I said.

"Oh, not so terrible." Patrick shrugged. "They are very friendly, very close. In fact, since Sabine moved out, Jean goes there every Wednesday for lunch with his children. He doesn't ever miss it. Everyone gets along."

I was impressed. It sounded very sophisticated to me. Very live-and-let-live.

One night, Patrick and I were at a nightclub, and I met Jean for the first time. He was an adorable man—with piercing blue eyes and blond hair, and a cute little space between his front teeth. He was charming and sophisticated. He spoke perfect English, and his personality was very genuine—funny and witty and warm. I asked him if I should call him Prince, and he laughed and said, "No, Jean is fine." I liked him immediately, and I was very drawn to him, even though he was forty-five and I was only twenty-one. He liked me, too, and when he asked me out to dinner, I eagerly accepted.

Walking into a restaurant with Jean was an event—every maître d' in Paris knew him. "They treat you like royalty," I marveled. For some reason, he thought that remark was hilarious.

When Jean and I started dating, I was aware of entering a world that was completely foreign to me. He was an amazing man. He was also a grown-up, with a house in Neuilly, a wealthy suburb of Paris. He had a close-knit group of friends—wealthy and prominent couples, all in their forties. I was the odd woman out in every way. I was young. I was American. And on my earnings, I certainly didn't have the wardrobe for the constant travel and glamorous parties. Let me tell you, their social whirl was dizzying. It was nothing for Jean to take me to dinner with captains of industry, Arab royalty, and French politicians. But I absolutely refused to let Jean buy clothes for me or give me jewelry, although I did let him talk me into wearing some spectacular jewels on special occasions.

And when I say special occasions, I mean magical nights to remember. The one I will never forget was a grand formal dinner at the Versailles Hall of Mirrors. Before we left Jean's house, he pulled out a $300,000 diamond necklace. "You should wear this tonight," he said, gently placing it around my neck and clasping it. I felt like a princess that night, and I got a chill every time I caught sight of my sparkling neckline in a mirror. I have to say it made me nervous, though. I kept catching myself holding on to the necklace with one hand, as if I were afraid it would fall off and be lost. I guess that's how you spot someone who isn't used to wearing expensive jewelry. They hang on to it for dear life.

I had a lot of learning to do if I was going to feel comfortable in Jean's world. We'd attend state dinners at which I counted twenty-seven pieces of silverware at my place setting, and had to wait for Jean to pick up a fork before I made a move. One evening I was invited to a dinner party at Jean's for the prime minister. I dressed carefully, and left our apartment early to go across the street to Lenôtre, a fancy pastry shop. I picked out a few treats, and as I came back out to the street carrying my little box, I found myself in the middle of a police sweep of prostitutes. The oldest profession was practiced everywhere in Paris, and prostitutes were a big part of the lively street life near the Champs-Élysées. They came in every variety—tall, short, fat, thin, old, young, elegant, scruffy—walking alone or in groups, boldly calling out to the drivers of passing cars.

As I tried to walk around the action, a policeman grabbed my arm and started to lead me to the area where the prostitutes were being corralled. "Oh, my God," I cried. "No—I live right there." I pointed wildly to my building.

"So, where are you going now?" he asked suspiciously, looking at my evening attire.

"To dinner," I gasped. "In Neuilly. Jean Poniatowski. Call him. He'll tell you."

The police officer's demeanor instantly changed. Jean's name was like magic. He practically escorted me to Jean's door.

Jean and his friends often arranged trips together to exotic places like Morocco and Rio. We were once invited to go quail shooting in Scotland, on the Queen's property, and we stayed in a castle. Jean took me to Poland and showed me Kraków, Warsaw, and the gorgeous countryside. He opened my eyes to the splendors of the world. Everyone adored Jean, and any of his friends would have said that he fully deserved the title of prince because he was a prince of a man.

With Jean I felt like a great sophisticate, but I was more like a little girl playing dress-up. We never lived together; I always kept my own apartment on avenue Victor Hugo and hung on to my independence. I had a career. I wasn't a party girl, and I let Jean know it. Sometimes we'd be out in the evening and I'd announce, "I've got to go. I'm up at five tomorrow for a shoot." And I'd take a cab back to my apartment.

My current roommate, Julianne Wasiak, mostly had the Victor Hugo apartment to herself, and that was fine with me. She was dating Bill Wyman of the Rolling Stones, and walking into that apartment really drove home our different lifestyles. I was her age, but I was living the life of a forty-year-old society woman. I was a twenty-one-year-old girl who said things like, "Could you turn the music down?" To a Rolling Stone! More than once I'd come into the apartment late to find members of the group crashed on the floor. I'd carefully step over dozing forms and tiptoe to my bed.

Looking back, I think I was lucky to be outside of that culture. I was protected from the ugly part of it. In the 1970s, many of my counterparts got involved with hard drugs. They lived dangerous lives—too much booze, too much sex, too many drugs. They grew old before their time. They lived on the edge. I never wanted that, but if you're immersed in such an intense environment, it's hard to escape it. Did I do a couple lines of coke in my day? Yes. Did I smoke some pot? Of course. But it was never my thing. I was safe with Jean, and I spent very little time at my apartment.

Our relationship was strong. After the first year, it was obvious that it wasn't a fling. We loved each other. And I loved Jean's daughters, who spent every other weekend with us. They were adorable. Marie was six and Sarah was four, and we had such fun together. They used to sit with me and lay their heads on my lap. I saw that nothing was more important to Jean than his girls, which made me love him more.

As our relationship progressed through a second year, I began to wonder if this was the man I was going to be with for life. We never discussed it, but I knew he cared about me. He even came with me to the States and met my parents. They liked him—it was impossible not to.

Jean and I had been seeing each other for almost three years before I finally got up the nerve to ask him about our future. Did he love me? Were we meant to be together always? It was the fall of 1977, and I was twenty-three years old. Jean was forty-eight, and he was officially divorced from Sabine.

"What are your intentions with me?" I asked Jean one evening over dinner.

He looked surprised by my question, and then he laughed. "Intentions?"

"I was just curious," I went on. "I mean, you know, where are we going with this relationship?"

He laughed again, and I got the message.

I was so hurt. I was fighting not to cry. I said, "Yeah, well, I guess princesses aren't born in Brooklyn."

Somehow I managed to get up from the table. "I'm going back to my apartment," I said. "I'm working tomorrow." And I got out of there before the tears started.

I was devastated. Our romance was over for me. I would have been okay with it if he'd said, "I love you, but I can't deal with this right now. I just got divorced. Talk to me in a year." But he just laughed. What was I? A fling to him? Arm candy?

Jean pursued me. He told me he loved me. I didn't believe him. I believed the laugh. Many years later, when Marie wanted to know why I didn't marry her daddy, I told her, "Because when I asked what his intentions were, he laughed."

Eventually, Jean and I would become friends again. I was always made to feel like a member of his family, and he helped me out when I needed it. A few years ago I flew to Morocco for Marie's wedding. "You have to be here," she told me. "You're my second mommy." You can't imagine what that meant to me.

After Jean and I parted, I realized that I had been living his life instead of my own. As much as I loved the world that he showed me and everything that he made me aware of, it wasn't me. I didn't have to go far to reclaim my life. It was right there at 25 Victor Hugo. To my relief, my wild roommate Julianne had left for the States, and my model friend Lisa Crosby moved in. Even better, my old friend Shaun Casey was working in Paris. Shaun and Lisa took me in hand. They threw away my matronly skirts and blue patent-leather Celine loafers, decked me out in minis and high heels, and off we went to see Grace Jones at La Palace. I was back.

By 1978 I could afford to rent my own place—a one-bedroom apartment on rue St. Simon. I also inherited a cat from an Australian woman who was going home. The cat's name was Simon. I loved being independent. I felt confident and happy. I bought my first couch for that apartment. I gave my first dinner party. I was dating a little. It felt great to be living my own life.

That year, I met Daniel Guerard, a hairdresser with his own salon, on a fashion shoot. Unlike Jean, Daniel was very intense. He had dark hair and dark eyes, and he had a way of drawing you in with those eyes. He was interesting to me. Even his moodiness was interesting to me. What did I know? We flirted for a few months, and I could feel myself becoming smitten. Daniel could make you feel as if you were the only girl in the room. Unfortunately, with Daniel, you were *never* the only girl in the room. Still, I fell hard for him, and simply ignored the signs that I wasn't the only one in his life. I wasn't even number one in his life, but the fantasy was just too intoxicating.

Then I got pregnant. At the time I was doing a two-day advertising shoot with the great Italian photographer Oliviero Toscani. Toscani was using trampolines to create that free "I'm flying" look. The first day, I was good on the trampoline and having a great time. But on the second day after five hours of leaping into the air, I started to feel a little green around the gills. I got down and ran into the bathroom and threw up. I finished the shoot, but when I was still feeling nauseated two weeks later, I went to the doctor and found out I was pregnant.

When I told Daniel, he asked, "What do you want to do?"

I loved him, and I thought he loved me. I told him, "Where I come from, if you're pregnant, you get married."

He kissed me very sweetly and said, "Then that's what we'll do."

It wasn't exactly the most romantic proposal, but I pretended it was a great fairy-tale moment. I'd already decided that Daniel was my very own Prince Charming. That was my story, and I was sticking to it. I simply ignored my inner voice, the one screaming at me again and again: *Hey, Lorraine. This guy just wants to sleep with you. He doesn't love you. He's no Prince Charming. Lorraine? Lorraine? Ah, never mind.* I was sure that I could make Daniel into the man of my dreams.

Living in fantasyland is like having an incurable disease. It does not respond well to treatment—no matter how many jolts of reality there are, or how often those jolts are administered, none of them penetrate and change the course of the disease. I suppose, deep down inside I knew that Daniel didn't love me in the way I wanted to be loved, but I really thought that marriage would change that. Although I had no reason to believe that he was husband material or father material, I decided that marriage would make this man *my* man.

We flew to New York and were married in January 1979 in a small ceremony by a justice of the peace in Glen Cove, Long Island. I wore a beige Donna Karan tunic and pants—a loosely fitted outfit designed to hide my already bulging belly. My parents hosted a party at Regine's, but they weren't so thrilled. Dad didn't like Daniel one bit. That was obvious. I could see him eyeing Daniel with a look that said *I've got your number, pal.* Nothing was said overtly—that wasn't my parents' way. They hoped for the best, but they didn't expect the best.

I, on the other hand, thought marriage and a new baby would make everything right. When we returned from the United States, I was five months pregnant, and eager to start preparing for the baby. Daniel was less than enthusiastic, but he put up a half-hearted front.

Then, when I was six months pregnant, I started having contractions. My doctor told me that if I didn't want to lose the baby, I'd have to lie flat on my back for the rest of my pregnancy. He recommended a clinic, and I spent two months there. Bored silly and worried about losing my baby, I learned to do needlepoint. I actually got pretty good at it.

I'm sure Daniel was glad to have his freedom. He didn't even manage a daily visit. His wife was a beached whale, and he wanted no part of the situation.

I was happy when my mother agreed to fly over and spend the

last month with me. She was due to arrive April 26. On April 25, I started to have strong contractions, and Margaux was born just as my mother was landing at Orly. Mom was so excited when she called and found out I'd delivered that she left her mink coat on the luggage cart in the airport. It was returned to her the following day. You've gotta love the French!

Margaux was a gorgeous baby, my little spring flower. I thought her arrival would make everything perfect between Daniel and me. I loved watching him with our baby girl. I imagined the years of joy to come as he played the role of the doting father with his little princess of a daughter and his loving wife by his side.

My dreams for the future lasted about five minutes. Daniel wasn't Daddy material any more than he had ever been husband material. I was spending more and more time alone in the apartment with Margaux. Daniel was incredibly restless, like a caged animal, when he was with us at home. He let me know that he felt trapped. What I didn't feel coming from him was any love. He was remote and indifferent. I would have preferred it if he'd yelled, screamed, stomped his foot. But he simply withdrew.

I was so lonely. One day, when I was talking to my sister Lizzie on the phone, I asked her if she wanted to come and stay with me for a while. She'd just turned twenty-one, and she was still living with our parents. She wanted to be an actress. "Please come to Paris," I begged, and she happily obliged. With Lizzie there, I felt a little bit like I had a family again. It didn't matter as much that Daniel wasn't around.

Lizzie and I took Margaux all over Paris. We played games in the apartment. I started to laugh again. When we were kids, we'd never been close. Three years was an insurmountable distance. But as adults, we had so much to talk about. When I returned to work, Lizzie took care of Margaux, and they bonded for life during those months.

Lizzie wasn't blind: she could see what was happening with my marriage. As she prepared to go back to the States, she asked me if I was going to stay with Daniel. I told her yes. We were married. We had a child. It was our responsibility.

Who was I kidding? Maybe I was the one who was blind. Daniel did feel trapped, but it had nothing to do with me or Margaux. I finally figured it out. How dense was I? Daniel was seeing another woman—in fact, he'd been seeing her since before we were married. She was the love of his life. At first, I had been the exciting prize. Now it had all been turned upside down, and I had been transformed into a boring chore—his demanding shrew of an American wife, complete with a crying kid.

The knowledge was devastating. I was too overwhelmed to summon up my old fighting spirit, and too ashamed to ask my family or friends for help. I couldn't get my mind around this betrayal. I felt emotionally starved, and therefore I starved myself. I stopped eating, and began wasting away. I looked in the mirror and didn't even recognize myself. Who was this girl with the dead eyes and thin, pale face? Where was that person I had once been, the one with such a powerful life force? What had Daniel done to me?

A better question was, what had I done to myself? It was easy to blame Daniel for being a lousy husband, but the truth was, he'd never pretended to be anything but who he was. I'd tried to make a fantasy come true, and now I was lost. I was twenty-six years old, married to a man who didn't love me—who, in fact, was in love with another woman. I was emotionally abandoned in that relationship. For all intents and purposes, we lived together, but he wasn't there. Maybe he'd never really been there, but I had refused to see it.

Margaux was my saving grace. She was perfect, a dream come true. She made me steady, and kept me on the straight and narrow. But it was beginning to dawn on me how much power I'd allowed Daniel to have. I'd given him control over whether my soul was alive or dead. It took me a while to recognize that he wasn't doing it to me; I was letting it happen. I was thin and depressed, having panic attacks. I was a mess. Throughout 1981, I battled with myself, trying to decide whether to stay or leave.

On New Year's Eve, I was once again alone with Margaux. I crawled into bed with her long before midnight. I had already made my resolution. I looked at my daughter's sweet face and I promised her a better life. I was going to take her out of this.

I called Jean, who was always so kind to me, even after we had stopped seeing each other. I tried to keep my voice steady and not burst into tears. "I need to borrow five thousand dollars," I said.

"Of course," he replied gently. He didn't ask questions, but I could hear the concern in his voice. I nearly wept to think that someone could be so kind to me.

I used the money to rent a small apartment. I packed Margaux's and my things and left. Daniel got what he wanted. He was free.

Leaving Daniel was the most liberating thing in the world. Women should know that they are so much better being off on their own than being with someone who is emotionally absent. It wouldn't be the last time I found the courage to walk away from a bad relationship with nothing but my dignity. No matter what, I was going to survive—for my baby Margaux and for me.

Daniel made a pretense of appearing deeply hurt. He liked the masquerade of being the poor, abandoned husband and father. I felt he was good with words, but weak when it came to action. After we split up, he'd come by every month or so to spend a couple of hours with Margaux, in his lackluster way trying to look the part of the devoted dad. He was a lousy actor. It made me sad, but I let him visit Margaux without complaint. I was through trying to make Daniel someone he wasn't.

Here's the lesson I learned: You can't change other people. You can only change yourself. After I left and got away from him, the dead look in my eyes slowly began to disappear. I started feeling good and looking good again. I was regaining control of myself, and I realized that I had no one but myself to blame for the catastrophe of my marriage. It was time to face myself, take a good long look in the mirror, and start living again.

For all practical purposes, I'd been a single mother for the first two years of Margaux's life. But now it was serious business. Daniel was paying my rent in lieu of child support, but I needed to make money to support us.

I was still modeling, but other opportunities were starting to come my way. While I was still with Daniel, I'd been approached about playing the female lead in a French romantic comedy called *Duos sur Canapé* (*Duets on a Loveseat*). I thought they were kidding. "Sorry, I don't know how to do that," I said. To me, the idea that being a model prepared you to act in a movie was ridiculous. I knew how to pose, how to capture a look or an aura, but open my mouth and speak? Me, with the Brooklyn-accented French? No, thank you.

The director, Marc Camoletti, was so intrigued by my refusal that he intensified his pursuit. It was hilarious. I finally agreed to do the movie when he promised to get me a coach. I thought he meant an acting coach, but all I got was a girl from Berlitz who drilled me on correct French pronunciation. Now I could speak my lines correctly, but I still couldn't act. Also, it was a very physical movie—a classic romantic romp—and I had no idea what to do. I was terrible in that movie. I hated every minute of the experience, and I vowed never to do it again. "Boring!" I declared.

I wound up having very small parts in a couple of other movies. I did them for the money, but a friend suggested I might actually enjoy acting if I had some training. I took a few seminars with John Strasberg, the son of the famous Method acting teacher Lee Strasberg of the Actors Studio in New York. John encouraged us to make acting organic—to live in the role. I threw myself into the lessons, and I loved them. But at the time I couldn't imagine myself really making it as an actress.

I'd done a brief stint as a deejay for Radio Luxembourg as a vacation fill-in, and I found I liked it. When the offer came to help produce an MTV-style show on French TV, I accepted. At the time, French TV was a dreary, government-owned mishmash that in no way reflected popular culture. This was a very exciting venture, initiated by Pierre Lescure, who would later become a major French television mogul. Years later, Pierre would go on to create an independent channel patterned after America's HBO. Canal Plus was France's first paid cable channel.

By now I was twenty-seven years old, and I'd been living in Paris for nearly a decade. My parents never pressured me to come home, but I knew it was what they wanted. My mother was eager for the chance to dote on her granddaughter Margaux, who was growing into such a darling little girl. They didn't see a compelling reason for me to stay. At the time, I remember feeling that it was important for Margaux to be near her father, but he hadn't exactly been Mister Dad. Maybe it really was time to think about moving on.

Then I met Harvey Keitel, and my life changed in a big way.

Three · Harvey's Seduction

Can we say that there are certain kinds of people that are drawn to fire, looking for an inevitable result, like a moth to a flame?

· Dr. Jennifer Melfi

SEPTEMBER 1983

The phone rang insistently, and I was annoyed. I had been having a really bad day. I had a hungry kid running amok around the place, dirty laundry piled on my only good chair, and I looked like a used rag.

"All right, all right," I yelled, grabbing the phone. "Hello?"

"I turned this city upside down looking for you," a voice growled.

I sank into a chair, my heart pounding. "Well, Harvey," I said. "I guess you found me."

"Let me take you out for dinner," he said.

"I can't. I'm here with my daughter," I told him, and then, before I had time to think, I invited him to join us. He said he was on his way.

I rushed around like a maniac, picking up toys and clothes and stuffing everything into a closet. I had just applied lipstick and brushed my hair when the bell rang. Slightly breathless, I flung open the door, and there he was.

Harvey Keitel was an imposing guy. He wasn't a big man, but he had a presence that filled my doorway. He drilled into me with his eyes. Those eyes were wild and powerful. I felt a rush of heat pulse through me from my head to my toes.

Finally, I said, "Well, all right. You want dinner? I've got some chicken cooking." I stood back and motioned for him to come inside. While Margaux and I picked at our food, we watched Harvey tear into that chicken like a starving man. It was something I would come to learn about him. He always did everything at full throttle. He didn't hold back.

I'd met Harvey at a party the week before. Some friends were in town from New York, and they had invited me along. I'll admit I hadn't really wanted to go. By this time, I'd been separated from Daniel for a year and a half, and although I'd finally started dating a little, an evening out meant paying for a babysitter, and I was just barely making ends meet. My friends insisted that I join them, and promised to take care of the sitter.

Soon after walking into the party, I was introduced to Harvey, and bam! It was one of those electric moments. I thought, *My God, what is* this *about?* He took my hand and said one word: "Hello." In that word I heard the familiar accent from home.

"Brooklyn," I said with a grin.

He nodded. "Brighton Beach."

"Bay Ridge," I announced.

We smiled at each other, delighted in the discovery of our common roots.

I was blushing furiously. "Um, you can let go of my hand now," I said, laughing. I felt very silly. I knew immediately that he wanted me and I wanted him. My instinct was to run in the other direction, but I didn't. Within an hour, we were walking out of the party together. We stood in the street kissing in the rain.

That night, I did something unusual for me. I slept with him, and then sneaked out before morning without leaving my number. I was tired of being disappointed, and my attraction to Harvey was so immediate and so strong that it had "heartbreaker" written all over it in black Magic Marker.

But when Harvey wanted something, he didn't let go so easily. I have to say that I was flattered when he tracked me down. It was very romantic.

Harvey is a very intense man, and I was drawn to his intensity. He seemed so powerful to me. He was as fierce in life as he was in his films.

Dr. Melfi would have had plenty to say about Harvey's veneer of toughness being a survival skill he learned as a child. Harvey was born in 1939 in the Brighton Beach section of Brooklyn, the youngest of three children, to parents who had emigrated from Eastern Europe to escape the growing anti-Semitic fever of the times. Even as a little boy he felt like an outsider—at home, where his parents were by turns remote and chiding, and on the streets, where his small stature and bad attitude forced him to learn how to fight and get tough very fast.

Harvey didn't like to talk much about his parents, except to say that he'd felt emotionally and physically abandoned by them. His most vivid memories were of being a small child crying because his mother wasn't there, or begging for her to stay with him, only to have her rage at him for his neediness. Eventually, he learned not to cry for his mother or expect his father to be a protective presence in his life. He realized that he would have to fend for himself.

Harvey eventually mastered the façade of fearlessness, even though he was painfully shy and had a slight stutter. Fearlessness was his most compelling—and daring—role. He continued to play that role as a young adult, joining the marines right out of high school. The marines provided a sense of belonging and achievement that he'd never felt before. He often spoke of how he lived the credo "Semper fidelis"—"always faithful." Loyalty was essential to him, and he maintained that personal code, even in the faithless world of acting.

Harvey was twenty-two before the acting bug bit him. Before that, everything had been about survival. Acting was his first true passion.

As gruff as he seemed to be, Harvey could also be incredibly loving. After the years of Daniel's indifference and questionable fidelity, Harvey's attention was like a healing salve to my wounded soul. There was no question that Harvey was focused on me and me alone. He wasn't a player or a lothario. He didn't have other women waiting in the wings. When he held me in his arms and told me that he'd been looking for me all of his life, I was completely convinced. I knew that he was serious and that he meant it. At forty-four Harvey didn't have a string of ex-wives and a bunch of abandoned kids the way some actors did. He wanted quality, not quantity.

After Harvey tracked me down, we saw each other constantly. He even extended his stay in Paris for a couple of weeks. It was a sweet, low-budget courtship. We took Margaux to the circus, walked along the Seine, and ate at out-of-the-way Vietnamese restaurants. I was both thrilled and scared by the intensity of our connection. I wanted Harvey, but I had to protect myself and Margaux. I had to play things smarter this time.

Harvey took me out to dinner on my twenty-ninth birthday. He was leaving for New York in a few days. I was going to Africa to work as a producer on a documentary film. We agreed that we were going to pursue our relationship, and we both meant it.

Once he was back in New York, he called me almost daily, wondering when I was going to visit. I was surprised at how much I already missed him, but I wasn't planning on a trip home any time soon. Then fate intervened.

On November 9, I received a hysterical call from Lizzie. She was crying, and I could hear my mother making soothing noises in the background. When she calmed down enough to talk, she told me that her boyfriend, an actor named Jimmy Hayden, had died of a drug overdose. I'd never met Jimmy, but I'd known Lizzie was serious about this guy. His sudden death was a terrible tragedy. Jimmy, who was separated from his wife at the time, had been starring in the play *American Buffalo* on Broadway and was beginning to garner great reviews. He'd had a good role in the film *Once Upon a Time in America*, which was scheduled for release in 1984. The famous illustrator Al Hirschfeld had even drawn his portrait. He was young, promising, and had everything to live for, including his relationship with my lovely sister. And just like that, he was gone. "You have to come home," Lizzie sobbed. "I need you." Lizzie had never said that to me before. I knew I had to go.

I promised her I would, and immediately called Harvey. I asked him if he knew Jimmy Hayden, and he said he'd met him once through Robert De Niro. "He was Lizzie's boyfriend," I said, "and he died of a drug overdose yesterday. Listen, Harvey, I'm coming home for the funeral. Could you pick Margaux and me up at the airport?"

Margaux and I flew to New York the next day. I never went back.

My memories of those first days back in New York are vivid. The joy on Harvey's face as we walked out of customs at the airport. The way my father, mother, Sal, and me surrounded Lizzie at the cemetery, keeping her together with our support. Margaux nestled in Lizzie's lap, offering comfort the way only a child can. My intention was to be there for Lizzie, but I saw that I was there for myself, too. I needed a family, and so did Margaux. What was I doing, spinning my wheels in Paris? I'd been telling myself that I stayed so Margaux would know her father. But the truth was, Daniel wasn't very interested in his daughter.

After Jimmy's funeral, Margaux stayed with my parents on Long Island. They were ecstatic to have Margaux with them. She was their first grandchild and they could never get enough of her. I stayed with Harvey in his TriBeCa loft, so I could be closer to Lizzie. I was busy helping Lizzie, getting to know Harvey better, and rediscovering the city. Two weeks became a month, and there just didn't seem to be a reason to return to France.

I called Daniel to tell him we were staying in New York, and he put up a little fuss, just for show. But why should things change? It had been this way for years now. *Basta. Finis.* Enough. His words of mild protest fell on deaf ears. How long do you let people feed you their line of bull? Forget the words. What have their actions been? And believe me, his years of sullen, half-assed actions assured me that I was doing the right thing. His words were empty, his emotions meaningless.

Margaux and I moved into Harvey's loft in TriBeCa, an area of downtown Manhattan that was just starting to emerge as something of a nouveau artist's colony. It was still pretty grungy, still frontier territory, and it didn't feel like much of a real neighborhood—just long, dark streets of old converted warehouses and closed-up shops with heavy metal accordion gates. TriBeCa felt abandoned, and vibrated with none of the chic or charm of SoHo or Greenwich Village. Far from being the gentrified yet bohemian neighborhood people know today, filled with art galleries and shops, it was pretty desolate, and eerily deserted at night. We had to walk many, many blocks to find the most basic services, like a laundromat or a grocery store. But the high prices that had pushed the art scene south of SoHo had created a little community there, and it was growing. Twenty years later, it's amazing to see TriBeCa lofts now priced into the stratosphere, easily competing with apartments in SoHo and on the Upper East Side. Even after the devastation caused by the terrorist attacks of 9/11, the neighborhood has continued to thrive. From an artist's perspective, a lot of the credit has to go to Robert De Niro. In the late 80s, he made a real statement by establishing his production offices, living space, and the Tribeca Film Center in the area, as well as the Tribeca Grill in 1990. But that was all a distant and unrealized dream when I arrived there with Harvey in 1983.

Harvey was intrigued by the fact that I really didn't know his work as an actor. In a way, it was good for him, because he could see that I honestly wanted him for himself, not because of some image I'd picked up on the screen. And it was good for me, too, because I might have been influenced by what I later learned. But of course he wanted me to know him as an actor, so he suggested several films he liked, and I started my own personal Harvey Keitel film festival in the loft. I watched his films by myself and then we would talk about them at night. He got me a copy of director Martin Scorsese's first big film, *Mean Streets.* It was a violent story about a couple of small-timers, young hoods who'd grown up in New York City's Little Italy. It starred Harvey and Robert De Niro.

The movie is an amazing piece of work, and Harvey explodes off the screen. His performance hit me right in the gut. That night, I said, "Wow. You're a real lighthearted guy, Harvey."

He stared at me for a second, wondering whether I was serious. And then he laughed. "You're something different," he said. I smiled back at him.

Harvey's films did seem to veer toward the dark side. He'd also been cast in Scorsese's *Taxi Driver,* playing the young Jodie Foster's pimp, and portrayed a schizophrenic in James Toback's *Fingers*. His lightest role might have been the hotheaded French soldier intent on gutting a rival in Ridley Scott's *The Duellists*. Obviously, when directors were casting comedy, they weren't thinking of Harvey Keitel.

Within a few months we were committed to each other. Harvey would have married me in a heartbeat, but I told him I didn't ever want to get married again. It wasn't rational. Harvey and I were as good as married. But my experience with Daniel had been so traumatic, and had so damaged my self-esteem, that I equated marriage with a death of the self. I needed to hold back, hold on to that corner of my independence that still remained. A piece of paper doesn't say *Respect me until death*. It's just a piece of paper. I wanted to be loved. No paper guaranteed that. Nothing could.

The adjustment to being in New York was tougher than I'd expected. I had left behind a huge, exciting life in Paris, and I didn't know where I would fit in. Harvey was incredibly supportive. "Take your time. Don't be so hard on yourself," he'd tell me. But I felt homesick and lonely in TriBeCa. Everything was foreign to me. The culture shock was enormous. I'd buy yogurt at the market and nearly gag. It didn't taste like real yogurt. I'd forget myself and speak to the guy at the newspaper kiosk in French. Half the time I didn't know whether I was coming or going. How would I ever adjust? When my parents came to visit the loft, they looked uncomfortable and a bit shocked. They didn't understand the concept of an urban loft. I heard my father mumbling, "I worked hard all my life so my daughter could live in an empty warehouse?" I knew he thought my New York life was a comedown.

I worried constantly about what I was going to do with myself. Since I had some experience in production from French television, I thought maybe I could do that. Harvey's friend Robert De Niro very kindly got me a job as a production assistant on a film he was shooting with Meryl Streep called *Falling in Love*. I lasted about a month, during which time I was paying more money for babysitters than I was making. The sixteen-hour workdays left me no time or energy for Margaux, who at four was full of life. And Margaux needed me then. New York was a very tough adjustment for her, especially when you consider that she was really like a little immigrant child. She understood English, but she could barely speak it—though she was perfectly fluent in French. When I registered her for Washington Market School, a Montessori preschool on Duane Street, they expected a child who spoke fractured Brooklynese, like her mother. Ronnie Moskowitz, the director, was pretty surprised when this gorgeous little Parisian girl showed up on the first day.

"She doesn't speak English!" Ronnie exclaimed.

"Aw—she'll catch on," I said. "She understands it." I was very blasé about it. I shouldn't have been, but I was. She was a very smart girl.

She did learn English, of course. In fact, Margaux loved everything about New York. And me? I was still at loose ends, banging around with no apparent rhyme or reason. It was driving me crazy.

"Just relax," Harvey told me. "I'll take care of you."

That was a lovely thing to hear, but I wasn't sure if that's what I wanted. Still, Harvey was a very convincing guy. He liked the power of being in charge of our lives, and in many ways it was a relief to no longer have to concern myself with the burden of supporting myself and Margaux. I believed that with Harvey beside me, I could find my way.

One day Harvey said to me, "Why don't you come with me to the Actors Studio? Just sit in on a class and see what you think." I jumped at the chance. To tell you the truth, I was so lonely that if my boyfriend had been the mailman, I would have hung out at the post office with him. But Harvey's invitation was more serious than just a way to fill my time. He saw a potential in me that I didn't know existed. I'd loved the acting seminars I'd taken with John Strasberg in Paris, but I still didn't think I'd ever be an actress.

The Actors Studio was a New York institution, and it took the art of acting very seriously. This was the reputed home of "The Method," an approach codified by the great Russian acting teacher Stanislavsky. Method acting emphasized finding the "truth" of each moment in a performance. For nearly thirty years, until his death in 1982, the legendary acting teacher Lee Strasberg was the director.

Strasberg personally cultivated some of the great actors of our time. I felt honored just to be an observer. I'd *never* have been invited to participate.

Every Tuesday and Friday for the next year, I went with Harvey and sat in the back of the room. I never said a word. Just watched. I was awestruck by the level of talent in the room each week—Paul Newman, Estelle Parsons, Ellen Burstyn, Robert De Niro, and many others, including the great teachers Marilyn Fried and Penny Allen. And, of course, Harvey. I was paying attention. I was learning. Finally, one day, after a year of watching, I said to Harvey, "I think I could do this."

Harvey was pleased to hear me say it. You see, Harvey really believed in my talent—believed that I was special. Through Harvey, I came to believe in myself. He taught me that being an actor is not a question of whether you're a "natural" or not. Although he was certainly brilliant, Harvey didn't think he was a natural actor. He attributed everything to passion and hard work.

Harvey's generosity was limitless, which is really something when you consider that he had to fight for every role he got. He arranged for me to study with Stella Adler and Ernie Martin, two of the greatest acting teachers in the city. I think he liked playing Pygmalion.

Harvey is one of the greatest film actors of his generation. He's just phenomenal. He understands the work of an actor, and he lives by it. You can see his intensity onscreen, his intelligence and ferocity. It makes him an exciting actor and a very difficult man. And as an actor, I have the greatest respect for him, because when you work with someone like Harvey, he's going to raise your game. He's going to make you better, which is what you want. Harvey is challenging, not just as an actor, but as a person. He has a ferocity, but also a certain vulnerability. He's got a lot going on inside. He can be very dark. He knows the belly of the beast.

Harvey was as uncompromising in art as he was in life, and sometimes that made it difficult for him. But I saw that I could use a little of that uncompromising spirit in my own life.

I threw myself into my studies, and found that I loved it. And Harvey, though he was still intense and tortured, was easing up. For Harvey, he was almost lighthearted! We traveled together. He would go on location to shoot movies and I would go with him. That was a good period for us, and in 1985, when I got pregnant, we were both overjoyed.

Our daughter was born in New York City on December 10, 1985, at Lenox Hill Hospital. We named her Stella. Everyone assumed that she was named either for the character in Tennessee Williams's *A Streetcar Named Desire*, or for the legendary acting teacher Stella Adler. The name was chosen for neither of those reasons. During my pregnancy we had been in Naples, where Harvey was starring in *Camorra*, Lina Wertmüller's film about an Italian mobster, in which I also had a small part. We used to take Margaux with us while shooting the movie in the Quartiere Stella, and we were touched by the children who played there—so full of life, and yet so utterly poor. We chose the name Stella for our daughter as a way of bringing the memories of those beautiful little children home with us.

Harvey was mesmerized by Stella. He couldn't believe that this beautiful child, with her delicate little fingers and toes, her perfect little mouth, her fine fuzz of blond hair, was his baby. When you grow up like Harvey did, essentially left to your own devices, it can seem like a miracle to have a vulnerable child of your own, a child that you can pour all the love in the world into. And Stella soaked up that love like rays of sunshine.

I breast-fed Stella for a couple of months before starting her on the bottle. Harvey was glad because now he could get involved. It worked perfectly—the insomniac Harvey did all of the night feedings. When Stella would start wailing in her crib, he'd be there in a flash. "Why are you crying?" he'd ask in a sweet voice. "You know the milk is coming. There's no reason to cry." I can still picture him sitting in the dark in front of the loft's big window, with Stella nestled in his arms, talking to her softly as she sucked at the bottle.

Since Harvey was an all-or-nothing kind of guy, his passionate attachment to Stella could be overwhelming. When she was a year old, we felt a lump in her groin, and Harvey nearly had a nervous breakdown before we could get to the phone to call the doctor. He was convinced it was cancer, and he was about to lose his little girl.

On the phone, the doctor said calmly, "It's probably a hernia."

"A hernia?" Harvey screamed. "The kid's not even walking. What, you think she's been lifting furniture?"

But it did turn out to be a hernia—something that afflicts about 1 to 5 percent of young children, but is especially rare in girls. We took her to the hospital to get it repaired, and Harvey was a complete wreck—a big puddle on the floor. "She's going to die, she's going to die," he mumbled over and over.

"Harvey, it's a hernia. She's going to be fine," I said. "You're not helping here."

"Oh, God," Harvey groaned. I wasn't sure he would survive the day.

These were happy days for us. I felt incredibly blessed. I had two beautiful daughters, a devoted, supportive partner, a life full of friends, and the beginnings of work I loved. Our loft was an easy place to be. Harvey's close friend, the actor Vic Argo, whom he'd met doing *Mean Streets,* was a frequent visitor. Vic was a great guy, and he treated us like a second family. Sometimes when Harvey was working, Vic would hang out with the girls and me. We'd have Play-Doh contests in the apartment or walk to the park.

Vic introduced me to his agent, Heather Reynolds, and we clicked immediately. Heather was a real beauty—a tall, blond, slender woman around my age, with big blue eyes. I liked her fresh, forthright manner, and felt that I could trust her. She agreed to be my agent on a handshake and later, when she became my manager, that deal was made on a handshake, too.

Harvey's friends told me at the time that being with me and the girls was mellowing him, making him more balanced. Now, you could never accuse Harvey of being mellow, but it seemed to me that he was getting what he needed most from us—the loving family embrace he had craved since childhood. In my simplistic view, if your life was good and you were with people who loved you, you should be happy. I didn't understand the way old wounds from childhood could fester even when there was joy in the present moment. I had no idea that low self-esteem, ground into you from childhood, didn't lift automatically when you achieved success.

So I was thrown for a loop when, out of the blue one day, Harvey didn't come home. You have to understand, Harvey was a guy who called to check in four or five times a day. He was always in touch. So when he didn't show up for dinner and didn't call, I was alarmed. I waited up for him until late in the evening, then fell asleep expecting him to walk in any minute.

When I woke up in the morning and Harvey was still not home, I got a horrible feeling of dread in the pit of my stomach. After I took Margaux to school, I picked up the phone and called Vic Argo.

"Vic, Harvey is missing," I said, my voice shaking. "He never came home last night. I'm scared."

There was a pause on the other end of the line, and then Vic said, "Stay calm, Lorraine. I'll be right over."

Now I was really freaked. I'd heard something in Vic's voice that gave me a chill. Did he know something? Was Harvey okay? I waited anxiously, feeding Stella and putting her down for a nap. When the bell rang, I ran for the door. Vic entered the apartment, and his face was grim. He took my hand and led me to a couch where we sat. "Lorraine," he said, "I swear, I thought those days were over."

"What days?" I didn't know what he was talking about. So he told me. Before he met me, Harvey had occasionally dropped out of sight for days at a time. He was wrestling with his soul. He was doing cocaine.

"Cocaine?" I stared at Vic, mystified. "Harvey doesn't do drugs." But as soon as I said it, I knew, and my heart sank to the ground.

Vic tried to be reassuring. He told me that it had just been an occasional thing with Harvey, and if he was using again, we could help him get over it. His words didn't register. I could feel my anger building. How could Harvey do this? We had two children. We had a life. How *dare* he!

Vic promised me that he would try to find Harvey, but as I kissed him good-bye, my head was spinning.

Harvey didn't come home that day, and after the second morning with no word, I was spent. I shuffled aimlessly around the apartment, unable to believe that my wonderful life had been shattered. I kept Margaux out of school because I was afraid to leave the phone. I called my sister.

"Lizzie," I said, and burst into tears.

"Lorraine, what's wrong?"

"Can you come over?"

Lizzie came and sat with me all morning. We played with the kids, fixed lunch, and distracted ourselves from the phone that didn't ring. In the early afternoon, she bundled up the kids and took them to the park. I was in the kitchen cleaning up from lunch when Harvey walked in.

"Where have you been?" I screeched. "I thought you were dead."

He looked at me though bloodshot eyes, and raised his hands in a conciliatory gesture. "Please," he said. "I'm sorry. I'm really sorry. It has nothing to do with you."

"Nothing to do with me!" I hollered, grabbing a plate and throwing it past him. It spun like a Frisbee and stuck into the freshly spackled wall. Harvey didn't react. So I threw another plate, and another, screaming at him, shrieking like a wounded animal, "Where have you been? What kind of drugs are you doing?" It was not my proudest moment. I was out of control.

Harvey was still maddeningly wordless, but he got the point. He looked at me with a flash of anger that scared me, marched into the kitchen, picked up the remaining plates, and smashed them onto the floor.

I was shaking with fury. I wanted answers. Harvey wouldn't give them to me, except to say that he had needed to get away and work through some things on his own. He was suffering from old demons. "It has nothing to do with you," he assured me, and he promised that it would never happen again.

"How can I believe you?" I cried.

He was ashamed and embarrassed, but he had little more to say. Then he went to bed and slept for two days. I prayed he meant it when he said it would never happen again.

Harvey truly believed in me, but I had some big barriers to overcome as an actor. Maybe the biggest was my lack of confidence in myself. Could I really get inside a role? Could I be convincing? Plus, there were, shall we say, *technical* difficulties. I had always been a slow reader in school. Reading out loud petrified me.

This gave me big problems in the script department. I couldn't just take a script and read it cold. I had to spend hours memorizing lines so I could pretend to read them later.

I know now that dyslexia is nothing to be ashamed of. We should be enlightened enough in this day and age to recognize that. In fact, every actor who overcomes dyslexia should be applauded. Unfortunately, everyone in the film business has this paralyzing fear of admitting *any* weakness that might be the deciding factor in not getting a role. I'm happy to say that I'm over that now. But in 1985, I was still pretending. I didn't want to disappoint Harvey.

Harvey was working with his friend David Rabe, a Tony Award–winning writer who was married to the actress Jill Clayburgh. David had written several major Broadway plays, and Harvey thought he was brilliant. David had an old play, *Goose and Tomtom,* but he didn't like the way it had been produced. He set out to cast and direct a new production, and he'd invited Harvey and a bunch of other actors over to his apartment to read. The group included producer Fred Zollo, Danny Aiello, Christopher Walken, Ellen Barkin, and Sigourney Weaver.

Just as Harvey was preparing to leave the apartment, David called. Sigourney Weaver couldn't make it, and he was thinking about canceling the reading.

"Don't cancel," Harvey said. "Lorraine will read."

I was dancing around Harvey, mouthing *No, no, no,* but he ignored me.

"I can't," I said when Harvey hung up the phone.

"Don't be ridiculous," he said. "You'll be great."

So I allowed myself to be dragged to the reading. *Goose and Tomtom* was the story of two bungling, low-level wiseguys infatuated with the same woman. When she told them that her jewelry had been stolen by yet another wiseguy, they kidnapped his girlfriend and held her for ransom. I was to read for the part of the girlfriend, Lulu.

I humiliated myself at that reading. I couldn't read one line straight through without stumbling. Everyone was looking at me, shaking their heads. Harvey was totally confused. "Do you need your glasses, Lorraine?" he whispered. I said no. I was so nervous that I was shaking.

As soon as the reading was over, I got up and ran for the door. Tears were spilling out of my eyes, and I didn't want anyone to see me crying. But David Rabe followed me out. He grabbed my arm as I was going through the door. "Lorraine, wait," he said. I turned around, my eyes wet, my face blotchy with shame.

"Lorraine," David said calmly, "that was a fantastic reading."

"Oh yeah, right," I sobbed.

"I'm serious," he said. "If I ever do this play, I'd like you in the role of Lulu."

I stared into his kind eyes, grateful that he was helping me save face. But I didn't believe him. I hung my head low and then fled, waiting outside for Harvey to join me.

But David actually meant it. In July 1986, I played Lulu in a series of workshop performances of the play at Lincoln Center. It was the first time I had performed before a live audience. Madonna played the love interest, and Harvey and Sean Penn played the bungling wiseguys.

I only fell off the stage once.

Harvey gave me confidence I didn't yet have. I'm not too proud to say that he made my career happen. One day in 1985, Harvey was walking down the street and he bumped into the film director Ridley Scott. Harvey had starred with Keith Carradine in Ridley's critically acclaimed first film, *The Duellists*, which had been shot in France in the 1970s. They stopped to chat, and Ridley told Harvey that he was looking for an actress for his next film—a kind of tough girl from Queens.

Harvey said, "You should meet my girlfriend."

Ridley laughed. He thought Harvey was kidding. But Harvey persisted. "No, really. You should meet my girlfriend. She's your girl." Could you ever hope for more support than that?

The part that Ridley wanted to cast was Ellie Keegan in *Someone to Watch Over Me*. In the story, she was the blue-collar wife of a Queens cop, to be played by Tom Berenger. In the course of protecting a beautiful murder witness—Mimi Rogers—the cop has an affair and puts his marriage and the safety of his family at risk.

Harvey worked with me on the audition, and so did Victor. I arranged to get my hands on the scenes I was going to read for Ridley and his casting people. Harvey, Vic, and Heather tried to do everything they could to protect me from reading at auditions cold, especially after my humiliating experience with *Goose and Tomtom*. Even now, when I have to do a read-through for *The Sopranos*, I break into a sweat. They weren't exactly thrilled, but I got the scenes ahead of time. This became my pattern for all of my future auditions. I had the agent get the sides of the script beforehand. I would either memorize the lines or at least get the gist of it, so if I screwed up, I could still get through the audition.

Vic Argo came over to our apartment and read with me for the Ridley Scott audition. We went over the scenes again and again and again. Vic would read with me and read with me and read with me. And Harvey would work with me on making it real, making me understand the circumstances of the character, so I wouldn't just say the words. I'd understand what the subtext was, the action taking place; what was really going on. And I'd discover the truth of each moment that way. It helped more than I can say.

I'd be going over my lines with Vic, and Harvey would be in the other room, and in the middle of my reading, he'd yell out, "Helloooo! What are you talking about?"

And I'd say, "I'm telling my husband that . . ."

He'd storm into the room. "No, no, no. I don't mean what are you saying. I mean, what's going on? Your husband just walked out on you. He left you for this rich babe. You are alone. You have a kid. You have no job. You're trying to keep your family and your home together. That's what you're fighting for. Not those words. The words are the last thing that should make any difference. You have to decide how important that family and that home is for you, Ellie Keegan. And then you'll be able to say those lines for real."

Harvey opened my eyes. And I fought through the layers of emotion to *feel* Ellie Keegan. I began to feel the humiliation of her husband cheating on her in front of everybody. I came to know what it was like to fight for my life and the life of my child.

It wasn't easy, but when the day of the audition arrived I was prepared. The casting people weren't that glad to see me. I could feel their annoyance and hear them mumbling about Ridley picking up people on the street to come in for readings. I couldn't blame them, but I gave them a reading they wouldn't forget. I didn't really know how it all worked, but when I walked out of there, I was sure that I had nailed that part. I was certain that I had gotten the job.

What I got was a screen test and a preliminary deal. I flew to California for the screen test, and I was ecstatic when I got the role. Ridley Scott is one of the greatest film directors, and he was wonderful to me. He made it one of the best experiences of my young life as a working professional actor. Even though I knew next to nothing, he worked with me so beautifully, so sensitively, that I will always be grateful to him for the experience.

I still had a lot to learn. There are a lot of different ways you can screw up. I made sure I always arrived on the film set or the location, wherever it was, early. This way, I'd have plenty of time to prepare, to get into my character.

We filmed the interior shots on a set in L.A. One morning I arrived at the set of Ellie Keegan's kitchen early, as usual. The kitchen table was covered with dirty coffee mugs and ashtrays full of cigarette butts. Disgusting. There was also a sign on the table that said "Hot Set." Now, I didn't know what that meant. And the character I was playing, Ellie Keegan, this was her house, her kitchen. I thought, "If this were my house, I wouldn't leave the kitchen table filthy like this. Ellie Keegan wouldn't." So I cleaned it up. I made that table shine.

Eventually, Ridley and the crew arrived at the location to begin the day's filming. And all hell broke loose! Screaming, shouting, carrying on. It was horrible.

At first, I didn't understand why everyone was so upset. Then I found out why they were going crazy. Oh. Oh my God. It was the table. It had to appear exactly the way it was when filming stopped the previous day, and I mean *exactly*. Down to the last cigarette butt. And now little Miss Busybody had swept it away. The art director, the property department guys, they were screaming at each other, the accusations and blame flying. There were tears, protestations of innocence, threats of murder, promises of dismemberment.

I watched for a while, and then I took a deep breath and went to face the music. I figured I'd be lucky to get out of there with all my limbs intact. I sidled up beside Ridley, who was looking on the scene with horror, and I quietly told him what I'd done.

The look on that man's face! The look of absolute wonder and awe. Disbelief. Then he started laughing. And I fled. I mean, I *ran* out of there. I was humiliated. And then I started hearing everyone laughing. Laughter pouring out. As I left, I saw people turning beet red, with tears streaming down their faces. Laughing. Someone eventually explained to me what a "hot set" was (it means you leave it exactly the way it is!). The prop guys had Polaroids they'd taken, which enabled them to reconstruct it exactly as it had been before I cleaned everything up. Why was it so important? It's about continuity, so the scene looks just as it did when they shot it the day before, so they can match up bits and pieces of different scenes in an editing room. They lost a few hours of shooting time that day, but I learned a lesson. And Ridley? Ridley was just lovely to me. It was my first important film role and he made it happen. He could have, maybe should have, fired me right then and there, but he didn't. And when the shoot was over, and he was in the editing room putting the film together, he sent me a gift. An elegant little Tiffany alarm clock, inscribed *For all of the early morning calls you'll be answering. Love, Ridley.* He thought I was going to be working as a film actress for a long time. What a darling man. He really did treat me with kid gloves.

He knew this was my first role in a major film. I was so fired up, so psyched to have this role. The first day of shooting—and the first scene I shot—was with Tom Berenger. We were on location, shooting in Brooklyn, at this restaurant right under the Brooklyn Bridge. It was a big scene, and I was raring to go. I was so prepared.

Unfortunately, I was ignorant of some of the fundamentals of filmmaking. It was a complicated process. Harvey once told me, "If acting was just about memorizing lines, anybody could do it." He was so right. When you make a movie, each scene is shot from a variety of angles—first wide, then tighter, then close-ups. For each of the subsequent shots, it is essential that the actors duplicate exactly what they were doing, right down to scratching their noses and crossing their legs, also a matter of continuity.

I had no idea. After we shot the scene the first time to Ridley's satisfaction, I thought we were done. I didn't realize we had to duplicate it several more times as the camera shot from different angles.

The continuity girl came over to me and said, "Okay, Lorraine, when you said this line, you touched your hair over there. When you said your next line, you put your left index finger on the right corner of your lower lip. Then . . ." Huh? I was stunned. I said, "Wait. You want me to repeat everything I did?" And I burst into tears. I couldn't help it. I wasn't ready for that. They didn't teach you that at the Actors Studio.

Ridley spotted me and came flying over. "What's the matter, darling?" he said. And I told him. Huge tears were pouring down my cheeks. I panicked. I sobbed, "You can have me try to remember the lines, and try to stay in character, or you can have this continuity stuff. But I don't think I can handle all three at once. Pick two great or three terrible. Your choice."

The continuity question was huge. Because eventually, Ridley and the film's editor, and a whole bunch of other people, were going to be going over this film frame by frame, take after take, scene after scene. And if elements in a scene didn't match up, then they couldn't use bits and pieces from here and bits and pieces from there to put together the scenes the way they wanted them. Continuity is crucial to the editing process, and therefore crucial to the entire film.

What did Ridley Scott do? He said, "I'll worry about it in the editing room." That's very unusual, that a major director like Ridley would just put aside his concern about such a key element to make it easier on me, the new kid on the block. He was so amazing. So I dried my tears, composed myself, and went on.

But I was such a rookie. If it weren't for Ridley Scott, my film career would have been over, maybe on the very first day of shooting. I learned so much, it was ridiculous. I didn't know so much, it was ridiculous. But he was my champion. Maybe I brought something out in him, but he was a true gentleman in every sense of the word. He not only gave me this opportunity, he was gracious and patient and gallant throughout. He is a great man, a great film director, and a true friend. It was a great introduction to the business at the hands of a master. Whenever I see Ridley now, I just throw my arms around him and give him a big hug, and his return hug is heartfelt. He's such a good guy.

Lizzie was trying to break in as an actress, and while I was doing *Someone to Watch Over Me*, she was excited to land a small part as a waitress on an episode of the TV drama *Crime Story*. We commiserated about the business, talking like old pros, which we definitely weren't.

I was more interested in talking about Lizzie's love life. After Jimmy died, she avoided getting involved in a serious relationship. It took her a long time to get over that. But now, she'd met a guy, a young actor named Aidan Quinn, and she was crazy about him. Aidan was a talented actor and a beautiful man, inside and out. He came from a strong Irish family in Illinois, and had spent several years in the Chicago theater before breaking into film. My parents thought the sun rose and set on Aidan. They wanted to see their baby happy. We all did.

In practically a whisper, Lizzie told me she thought Aidan was going to propose. "I'm so happy for you," I told her. "Aidan will be a great addition to our little melting pot of a family."

Meanwhile, reception for *Someone to Watch Over Me* was lukewarm, but I got some good reviews. I was getting noticed, and it felt great. Harvey was very proud of me, but he was frustrated and angry about the direction of his own career. He was working a lot, but the roles were not career-making breakthroughs. He was as good as or better than most of the actors he was losing roles to, but Harvey just didn't know how to play the game. He was a terrible schmoozer. He often said that talent should speak for itself, and maybe he was right, but it didn't work that way. He had a reputation for being too intense, and that was like a red flag to studios. Intensity may have been genius on the screen, but in real life it scared people away. Harvey made the studios nervous.

Harvey was particularly aware that Robert De Niro, whose career had started at around the same time, had far surpassed him in both juicy roles and public acclaim. Robert was like the favored sibling who gets all the love. Harvey liked to tell the story of being in a restaurant with Robert after *Mean Streets* came out. A woman at another table started choking, and Harvey rushed over, stuck his hand in her mouth, and caused her to vomit up the piece of meat that had been lodged in her throat. According to Harvey, the newspaper headline the next day read "Robert De Niro Saves Woman's Life." As for Harvey, "I was standing there with a handful of vomit."

The girls and I would have been happy with less intensity at home. Harvey worked relentlessly on his roles. Depending on how it was going, he could be up or he could be down, and we were never sure which guy would come through the door each night. He was like a walking time bomb of stress. "Relax, Harvey," I said, like a mantra. Our life was good, and I wanted him to be able to enjoy it.

When Martin Scorsese picked him for the role of Judas in his film of Nikos Kazantzakis's book *The Last Temptation of Christ*, Harvey was thrilled. It was a big opportunity for him, and I was happy, too, but I was also preparing to see the emotional spigots turned on full blast. I knew Harvey. He would *become* Judas. He'd try to touch heaven, and he'd descend into hell. But at least he wouldn't be doing it in our kitchen: the movie was filming in Morocco.

As Harvey headed for Morocco to film *The Last Temptation of Christ*, I was hired by executive producer Dick Wolf to play Sonny Crockett's wife on the hit TV series *Miami Vice*. I'd never acted in a TV drama, so I was nervous, but everyone encouraged me to do it. Well, why not? I left the kids with my mother and flew to Miami Beach.

From the get-go, it was obvious that this was going to be tough. *Miami Vice* was a huge series, and the paparazzi were hanging from the trees. Everyone was hyped about Sonny's new love interest. But Don Johnson and I had no chemistry whatsoever. He was the star of the series, and he just looked at me like I was an alien being. It didn't help that I had absolutely no experience in acting for television. Television is very fast-paced, compared to moviemaking. I felt as if I had been thrown into a maelstrom. I couldn't keep up. I was lost half the time, and after two days of filming, everyone was getting pretty frustrated and hot under the collar. There was no chemistry, too many flubs, and too many takes.

Dick Wolf called me in and fired me. He was kind but brutally honest. He didn't see any point in dragging it out. Boom—I was gone, just like that. I'm sure everyone breathed a sigh of relief, although Edward James Olmos, one of the stars of the series, was incredibly sweet to me.

Mostly, I felt humiliated. I'd never been fired from anything before. Being fired is a gut-wrenching experience. It makes you want to never show your face in public again. And, as an actor, it throws you into a cauldron of self-loathing. I called Harvey in Morocco, crying. "I got fired, Harvey. I feel terrible."

Harvey replied, "Good. You're not TV material." He meant it as a compliment, which I'm not so sure I deserved. "Why don't you and the girls come to Morocco for a few weeks?"

And that's what we did. It was some of the best time we ever spent together. We had the most wonderful experience, and in the end, I was glad I wasn't working on a tense TV production down in Miami. This location shoot for *The Last Temptation*, with all of us together as a family, was so much more meaningful. By the time I returned to New York, I felt healed from my first firing and ready to get back in the game.

Four · Nobody's Sweetheart

Amour fou. *That's what the French call it.*
Crazy love. All-consuming.
· DR. JENNIFER MELFI

JANUARY 1988

My agents suggested that maybe I should take speech lessons to get rid of my Brooklyn accent. They thought it limited me in the kind of roles I could get. Actually, my accent wasn't pure Brooklynese, but more of a hodgepodge of Brooklyn, Long Island, and Europe. It was very hard for the speech coaches to pinpoint it. I told them, "If you can't identify it, how are you going to fix it?" I disliked the speech classes, with the endless, boring repetitions. It wasn't exactly my cup of tea. For example, we'd have to stand there and go through a list of nonsense syllables:

Mah . . . maw . . . moh . . . moo
Nah . . . naw . . . noh . . . noo.

And then there were the limericks.

There was a young lady named Bright,
Who could travel much faster than light.
She started one day, in a relative way,
And came back the previous night.

You get the idea. I was no Eliza Doolittle, that was for sure. I finally gave up on the idea of trying to lose my accent. Hey, it's who I was. Besides, I didn't really think it would matter all that much. After I did *Someone to Watch Over Me*, I began to understand that people noticed me *because* I was different. I stood out. It seemed to be the main thing I had going for me, and it seemed crazy to go all vanilla and give up the thing that gave me my edge.

One day in late 1988, I got a call to read for director Mike Nichols, who was casting the movie *Working Girl*. I read the script and immediately got very excited. "This is for me!" I told Harvey. I knew this character, Tess McGill, in my guts. She was the secretary who did her job day after day, got walked all over, and never said a word in protest. She was the one nobody thought was too bright. Her potential went unnoticed. She lived on Staten Island, rode the ferry to Manhattan every day, and had big dreams, but it seemed like they'd never get her anywhere. She acted sort of tough to hide her vulnerability. Best of all, when her big chance came, she grabbed it and showed what she could really do. I loved her spirit.

I prepared for the audition with Mike Nichols like it was going to be the first day of the film shoot. I knew Tess inside and out. Call me melodramatic, but I thought I was born to play that role.

I showed up to read for Mike at his beautiful town house on the Upper East Side. I'd never met him before, but I certainly knew of him—the man's a legend. He'd risen to fame as a performer, first as a partner in a comedy team with Elaine May. Both he and Elaine had gone on to separate, successful careers as both writers and directors. Mike loved the women in his films, and *Working Girl* was no exception. It was a romantic rags-to-riches story, but not an outright fantasy. Tess was as close to real as you could get.

I gave a great reading, and Mike was just lovely to me. I liked him a lot, and I felt we'd connected. I was the working girl, no doubt about it.

I floated out of Mike Nichols' town house. The part was mine. I loved the feeling I was experiencing, a mixture of confidence and joy. I was elated. I walked until I found a pay phone, then called my manager. "Heather," I boomed out when she answered her phone, "I definitely got this part. I nailed it!"

There was dead silence on the other end of the line. "Heather? Are you there?"

"Yes," she said, subdued. "Oh, Lorraine, I'm so sorry. They already called. You didn't get the part."

I couldn't speak. My mouth was hanging open. In the time it took me to leave the town house and find a pay phone, they'd already rejected me. I was devastated. I hung up and started walking home. It was several miles from the Upper East Side downtown to TriBeCa, but I kept tottering along in my heels, crying. By the time I got back to our loft, I was a complete wreck. And my feet were killing me.

Harvey took one look at my face and said, "What happened to you?"

"I didn't get the part," I sobbed out, tears pouring down my cheeks.

"Whew!" He blew out a breath. "The way you look, I thought you were hit by a bus."

I spilled out my tale of woe, and Harvey tried to give me a pep talk. "You win some and you lose some," said the man who would know. But I didn't want to hear it. I was inconsolable.

In one of those cases of cosmic irony, we had tickets for the hit Broadway musical *Les Misérables* that night. I sat in the theater and sobbed during the entire first act—and they hadn't even gotten to the really sad parts yet. I was completely obsessed with myself and my misery. Forget the misery of the starving French during their revolution! It was all about *me*.

Harvey turned to me at the intermission, and I could see he was getting fed up. "If you can't stand the heat, get out of the kitchen," he said sharply.

"I know, I know," I said, trying to wipe my eyes. The tears kept coming, though. I was heartbroken.

Harvey softened and took my hand. "Okay," he said, "this is the deal. You're allowed twenty-four hours to cry and feel sorry for yourself, and that's it. Then you move on."

And so that's what I did. I tried to put it behind me. I said to hell with it and made an effort to bury my disappointment, or whatever it is actors do when they feel so rejected. Being an actor is like riding a seesaw. So many rejections, so little time. You're up, you're down. Sometimes you stay down a long time, but if you do get back up, it's the only thing that matters. I'd watched Harvey ride that seesaw. He had a level of passion and discipline I admired. My little collapse over losing the *Working Girl* part was, to Harvey, just another part of the business. Actors are rejected a thousand times for every job they score. It's a very demeaning, frustrating path they travel. I often wonder if most actors would choose it if they knew what it was going to be like—a lifetime of rejection with an occasional *huzzah* of approval. It's a crapshoot, and a hell of a way to try to earn a living.

I moved on, but that doesn't mean I wasn't aware of what was happening with *Working Girl*. Who did Mike Nichols cast in the role I was born to play? Melanie Griffith. He chose Melanie Griffith! She was the complete opposite of me. How could I have had the vision of the movie so wrong? Mike wanted to make a Cinderella story. He wanted a sweetheart, a gorgeous piece of blond fluff, and I'm nobody's sweetheart.

I took some comfort in recalling what Stella Adler taught me. She hated what she called cutesy-pootsy acting, and she always encouraged me to be true and tough. Stella said, "It doesn't matter if it feels good or bad. It only matters if it's right." But what was right for me?

I was flailing a bit, and in need of a course correction. That year I did two quick movies that got ho-hum reception at theaters. In *The Dream Team*, the story of four mental patients who escape during an outing, I play the former girlfriend of a mental patient. It was fun and silly, and I loved working with Michael Keaton and Peter Boyle, whom I adored. But it wasn't a career maker.

In *Sing*, a *Fame*-style heart-tugger about a teacher who convinces the school punk to star in the high school musical, I played said teacher, Miss Lombardo. The movie reviews were damning, although Roger Ebert actually liked me.

But I was biding my time, still waiting for that special role, the one that was right for me.

Then, in one of those moments of serendipity that can only come from the heavens above, I got the call to read for Martin Scorsese. It was late 1988, and he was casting for his new mob drama, *Goodfellas*. I thought Marty was a genius, but I didn't want to get my hopes up. You see, I already had auditioned for Marty once before. Way back when, when I was just starting out, Harvey and Robert De Niro had pushed me to read for a part in Marty's film *After Hours*. My audition was good, and I've always been impressed that Marty called me a couple of days later. "Listen, Lorraine," he said in his energetic, rat-a-tat style, "I'm not going to give you the part, and I'll tell you why. It's not that you aren't talented. You are, and you should continue to study. It's *my* problem."

"Oh." I didn't know what to say. How do you respond to that?

"I've got to bring this movie in on budget. I can't fool around, and you're not ready. Don't worry about it. We'll work together again. I promise."

I thanked him, hung up the phone, and sighed. *Yeah, yeah, yeah.* But there I was, all these years later, getting the call from Marty's office. And this time I got the part. It was a once-in-a-lifetime opportunity.

Goodfellas was based on Nick Pileggi's best-selling book, *Wiseguy: Life in a Mafia Family*, the story of Henry Hill, a lifelong punk associated with the Lucchese crime family. It spanned his life from street kid to low-level hood to drug dealer to FBI informant. The film ends when he is forced to turn on his mob pals and enter the federal government's Witness Protection Program.

Goodfellas was really the story of two families. There was the gang of guys who grew up together as hoods, and were closer than blood brothers, and the mob boss, played by Paul Sorvino, who was always like a father to Henry. And there was Henry's life with his other family—his wife, Karen, and his two kids—and the way a wiseguy's immorality broke every rule of living a decent, ordinary life. These guys cheated on their wives, their mistresses, and each other. They had no moral compass. Their motto was "Screw unto others before they screw unto you."

Marty had wanted to do this movie as soon as he read Nick's book. He was attracted to the gritty reality of the underbelly of mob life—not the grandiose glamour of the classic Coppola film *The Godfather*, but the dark, petty smallness of the underlings, the low-level guys. The street soldiers in *Goodfellas* never got rich.

They never retired to country estates. Their lives were brutal and messy. Marty was attracted to this side of mob life, because it reflected what he'd seen growing up on the Lower East Side of Manhattan, in Little Italy. "These are the worker bees, the drones," he told us. "We're capturing the everyday banality of it."

At the same time, Marty wanted to show the seductive side of being an outlaw, and he did that by establishing a fast-paced beat—as he said, like a crazed roller-coaster ride through the underworld. His use of voice-over was a great device to keep the film moving along at a bruising pace.

I never actually auditioned for the part of Karen Hill. It happened like this. Marty called me and asked if I'd come over to his apartment and talk to him about the new movie he was casting. Of course I would! At Harvey's urging, I read Nick Pileggi's book before the meeting.

Marty lived in a high-rise in the West Fifties. As I rode the elevator up to his floor, my heart was thumping. I didn't know what to expect.

Marty's apartment was very dark. As he ushered me in, I saw that there was another person in the room. He stood up, and I found myself looking into the bluest eyes I'd ever seen. And that's how I met Ray Liotta.

For the next couple of hours, the three of us sat and talked about Henry and Karen Hill. I didn't fully realize it at the time, but in Marty's dark apartment, Ray and I were learning how to inhabit our characters. The chemistry between us worked, and it turned out to be a big deal that I'd grown up in a Jewish neighborhood, because Karen Hill was Jewish.

Marty offered me the role of Karen Hill, and I was elated, but there was a dispute about money. I was seriously doubtful that I should accept for the amount offered, but Harvey told me, "You should never miss an opportunity to play a great role and work with a great director over money." The purity of Harvey's devotion to the art was an inspiration to me. And he was right. The role was mine to play.

Harvey would be in Los Angeles filming *The Two Jakes* while I made *Goodfellas*. I'd be in the city, but I realized that the demands of the shooting schedule would be intense. I rented a loft downstairs from us and installed a full-time babysitter to take care of the girls.

Doing *Goodfellas* was like joining a family, and I don't just mean *The* Family. It was a once-in-a-lifetime experience, that chance to work with Marty and all of these unbelievable people. Not just the actors—Robert De Niro, Joe Pesci, Ray Liotta—who were, of course, phenomenal, but the crew and the production team were absolutely top notch as well. Marty's parents were there during the filming, too, and they were great. Catherine Scorsese was especially memorable in a scene as Joe Pesci's character's mother, which she completely ad-libbed.

Martin Scorsese is an incredible filmmaker and an extremely intense man. He is complicated, smart, intriguing, candid, and very funny. On his films, everything is important, down to the underwear, the socks, the shoes. Everything has to be just right. The crew loves and respects him. Most of them have worked with him over the course of many films. He knows what he wants to see and hear in each and every frame. He knew what music he wanted to use in each scene before the film was even shot.

Marty trusted me, and because of that trust, I was free to create Karen Hill. I had to create my character from the inside, psychologically, because I was unable to meet the real Karen Hill, and there weren't any live role models around. People weren't coming up to me and saying, "Meet my mob wife." So, while I was basically in the dark, I was lucky to have Marty and Nick Pileggi as my ever-present guides on this journey.

Marty showed his casting genius when he chose Ray Liotta to play Henry Hill. I knew there were several leading actors who wanted that part, but Marty saw exactly what he was looking for in Ray. Ray *was* Henry Hill, in all of his complexity. He could switch gears in an instant, from being the white knight that swept Karen off her feet to being the cold thug. Ray and I clicked—we understood who we were as a couple in that movie. Marty called us "the kids," which was funny. By the end of the film, we weren't "kids" anymore. We literally lived through the sad decline of the Hills—Henry's descent into drugs, and Karen's descent into being a partner in her husband's crimes. We felt their desperation and their despair. Sometimes I'd look at Ray-as-Henry through Karen's eyes and think, *How did I end up like this?* The work of making that movie was life changing for me. It was the first time I understood what being a real actress was.

One of the things that makes Martin Scorsese such a great artist is his clarity about who his characters are. For *Goodfellas*, he could detail every moment of every character's life—who their friends were, what they wore, what they ate, how they felt. Marty encouraged me to develop my vision of Karen, and he spent time rehearsing scenes with me and the rest of the cast. As I got deeper into the role, I was surprised to find that I really *got* this girl. She came from a very strict Jewish home, and her mother was the family's dominating force. Karen's father was reduced to a little nothing, to ashes, by this woman's vitriol. He was also dull—passed out and snoring on the couch every night by nine p.m. And Karen didn't want a man like that. She was looking for a *man*, and when Henry Hill showed up, she knew he was her knight in shining armor. She wanted to be swept away by him, without actually being implicated in his dark world. She thought she could live a life of pretense and deny responsibility for his behavior. She thought she could have Henry, enjoy the spoils of his criminal life, and still keep her hands clean.

There is a powerful scene near the beginning of the movie that brings this idea home. It was one of my favorite scenes to perform because there are nuances to it that show Karen's heart. At this point in the film, Karen doesn't know Henry very well, but she realizes he's an old-world guy with a hair-trigger temper and a macho protectiveness toward his girl. One day she calls Henry, crying, from a pay phone where she's stranded. He rushes to her rescue, and she sobs out the story of what happened. She was driving with Bruce, her neighbor from across the street, whom she's known all of her life. He started grabbing her, she slugged him, and he pushed her out of the car. Henry drives Karen home, and as they pull up, they can see Bruce and his brothers hanging out around Bruce's cherry-red Corvette. Henry tells Karen to go into the house. Then he reaches under the driver's seat and pulls out a snub-nosed .38. He walks across the street, marches right up to Bruce, and smashes him in the face with the butt of the gun. And keeps on smashing him, until Bruce is lying on the ground, his face reduced to bloody pulp.

The camera moves to Karen, standing perfectly still in the doorway of her home, watching. To me, this was a beautiful moment because the viewer is expecting her face to show a normal reaction to witnessing such violence and brutality. I worked hard on that scene so that I didn't portray the least hint of shock, revulsion, or horror. I'm watching . . . watching . . . and then I bring just the tiniest sparkle into my eyes, the slightest curve to my mouth. That was the thing you had to know about Karen. She's excited by Henry's power. In a voice-over, Karen says, "I've got to admit the truth. It turned me on."

The young Karen was easy to read. She was the bored good girl, hungry for a life of excitement. She was rebellious. She had low self-esteem, but when she walked into the Copacabana nightclub on Henry's arm, she became "somebody." She wanted more of everything, and at first it was easy to justify Henry's lifestyle. She chose to see Henry as enterprising, rather than criminal, saying, "He and the guys were making a few bucks hustling, while other men were sitting on their asses waiting for handouts."

It was harder to get Karen as she aged, because her motivations were increasingly complex. Who was this woman who tolerated such danger and uncertainty in her life? He brought her into his world, and she learned from him. She learned so well that she eventually became his accomplice, his partner in crime. Any moral judgments she may have once held were swept away by the life she led with Henry. Where did she think all of the money and clothes and furs and jewels and fancy cars were coming from? And even though he cheated on her, even set up a nice apartment for his "goomah," his mistress, Karen stayed with him. Oh sure, there's a scene in their bedroom where she puts a gun in his face and threatens to kill him, but he ends up on top of her on the floor with the gun in *her* face, and she's crying hysterically, "I'm sorry. I'm sorry." Henry Hill must have felt he could con anyone. All women were just whores to him, people to use and manipulate—even the mother of his own kids. And Karen came to see them as united, "you and me against the world." It was a bizarre universe, where good and evil were reversed. Karen stayed with Henry when he went away to prison, even brought him the drugs he sold to the other cons. She made a scene when she found out his latest mistress was visiting him, too, but she didn't leave him. Karen followed Henry into the Federal Witness Protection Program when he ratted out his friends in the mob. By then she had no choice. She was implicated in everything Henry did.

The scene in the movie where Karen puts a gun in Henry's face had a lot of emotional drama, because it was the only time she manifested the same level of madness that Henry did. Was she going to pull the trigger? You really didn't know for sure. Shooting that scene also provided a dramatic moment for the crew—especially the cinematographer, Michael Ballhaus. The scene called for Henry to pin Karen to the floor and roughly knock the gun out of her hand. During one of the takes, Ray Liotta pitched the gun wildly, and it hit Michael squarely in the forehead. Blood began pouring down his face.

"Not again!" Marty screamed, running over. Again? It turned out that the previous year, while shooting *The Last Temptation of Christ*, Willem Dafoe, playing Jesus driving the moneylenders out of the temple, had flung a bowl of coins, accidentally striking Michael in the same spot! Marty was distraught. Michael Ballhaus was one of the best cinematographers in the business. He got in close and really worked the scenes. But all of this friendly fire was going to kill him. Michael got patched up, and we all vowed to be more careful. Someone get that man a pith helmet!

I wasn't interested in playing Karen as a victim, or as a sympathetic character. I didn't want to pass judgment on her life. Rather, I was searching for the truth of who Karen Hill really was in my portrayal. I was intrigued by the way the wives of mob guys were able to put blinders on. They were so indignant, so outraged that the government had the nerve to harass their husbands. Just like the other wives, Karen justified Henry's criminality. But at the same time I felt that she considered herself very different from those women: smarter, classier, prettier—above them. But the sad truth, which she'd learn when she was in too deep, was that she was subject to the same fate—a husband who didn't value her. She was essentially expendable.

I never met Karen Hill, but I felt for her and her two children.

I think she saw the Witness Protection Program as their second chance. After portraying her, I felt I knew that she still believed that they could have a normal family life of backyard barbecues and dinners with friends after going undercover. It was unimaginable to me that she would have allowed herself to be ripped away from her parents—and allowed her children to be so abruptly separated from their lives—to inhabit a new identity somewhere else, if she had known that Henry couldn't adapt. But I am not sure she ever really had a choice. I have always felt that this second part of their lives would have made a fantastic film.

A lot of women are screwed up about love. When *Goodfellas* came out, so many women came up to me and said, "Oh, my God, what an incredible love story." Well, let me tell you, that wasn't a love story. It was more like a descent into addiction. Karen Hill was hooked on Henry. He lived in her veins. And Henry turned Karen into more than just his wife—she became his accomplice in crime. It was a relationship based on her initial rebellion against her family, and her addiction to the outlaw excitement Henry Hill brought into her life.

Karen Hill experienced that crazy, intense, passionate kind of love, which can be so potent and all-consuming. Many of us can relate to that—how exhilarating it is to be involved in a love affair that seems larger than life!

At first, my relationship with Harvey had some elements of that wild kind of love. Harvey swept into my life with such confidence and pursued me with such determination that he was impossible to resist. I was vulnerable, a single mother struggling to get my life together, and Harvey appeared to be so strong and fearless.

In reality, Harvey had vulnerabilities, too, of course. His stemmed from an insecure and difficult childhood. What I originally saw as strength ultimately turned out to be something else, especially when it came to the day-to-day practicalities of life and raising children. Harvey was tough and sure and implacable, but it made for a difficult domestic partnership. As with everyone and all relationships, it takes a lot of time before such things become truly clear. I thought I was being rescued, but instead I became an enabler, working overtime to keep all of the disparate elements of our life together.

I was crazy about Harvey, and I know he was crazy about me, too. Maybe that was part of the problem, "crazy" being the operative word, perhaps a central part of our unique puzzle. Harvey and I shared a crazy love, crazy passion, crazy fights, and crazy jealousies. It got more and more crazy all the time, until it seemed it was all crazy all the time. Not good for a stable, long-lasting relationship. Not a great environment in which to raise children.

I can see it all now. Unfortunately, I couldn't see it when I was *in* it. As I wrapped the filming of *Goodfellas*, I didn't have a premonition that Harvey and I were headed for a showdown.

Five · Ms. Enabler

There's no such thing as total control.
·Dr. Jennifer Melfi

MARCH 1989

TriBeCa was a desolate place to raise kids. They couldn't run free. They couldn't even walk free. At age eleven, Margaux was never allowed out of my sight. I couldn't let her ride a bike down streets where massive delivery trucks rattled over the cobblestones, or go out and roam around with her friends on deserted sidewalks intersected by dark alleyways. To reach the deli or the video store, you had to cross busy streets that had no traffic lights. At age four, Stella was a bundle of energy, always trying to wriggle her hand out of my tight grip no matter where we went. Like all city parents at the time, I raised my kids with the ever-present memory of Etan Patz, the beautiful little boy who had been snatched from a street by a sick predator and disappeared a few blocks north of where we lived. His faded picture still clung to telephone poles and was taped on windows, although he'd been gone for ten years. Neighborhood parents, myself included, were haunted by this child, frozen in time at six years old.

With the money I'd earned from *Someone to Watch Over Me*, Harvey and I had bought a small weekend place in upstate New York, in an area called Kripplebush, near Mohonk Mountain. We'd escape there when our schedules permitted, which wasn't nearly often enough. Aidan and Lizzie had a place in the area, too, which was fun. We really loved it up there. Eventually, though, the weekend commute to the country could be more of an ordeal than a soothing getaway. We'd join the gridlock of escaping New Yorkers, and arrive exhausted and crabby after two or three hours on the road, only to turn around and return a day and a half later.

I couldn't help comparing Margaux's and Stella's childhoods to my own, remembering how free I'd felt in Westbury, Long Island, playing for hours in the backyard, roller-skating down the sidewalk, or listening for the music of the Mr. Softee truck. On summer days, we'd disappear for hours, visiting each other's houses or swimming at the pool at Cantiague Park. Our mothers weren't watching our every move, sick with worry if they lost sight of us for an instant. Some of my best childhood memories involved holiday fun that my children could only imagine. They spent Halloween nights safely locked behind the deadbolts of our TriBeCa loft. Trick-or-treating was virtually nonexistent for city kids. Nor could they enjoy the pure fun of decorating a house and yard with Christmas tree lights and statuary—my father's specialty—or build a snowman.

Harvey liked to wear his badge of honor for having survived the urban jungle as a kid, but that hadn't been my reality. My parents moved to the suburbs because they wanted their kids to have freedom and opportunity and safety. They did it for us. The more I thought about it, the more I regretted that our kids were losing out on that precious taste of childhood freedom and whimsy. And while one could argue that there were many advantages for children living in the city, there were only so many times you could trek to the Bronx Zoo, and the Rockefeller Center Christmas tree lighting and the Big Apple Circus only came around once a year.

When the weather was nice, I'd take the kids to Washington Market Park, a small, crowded cement playground located at Greenwich and Chambers streets, in the shadow of the World Trade Center. (After 9/11, it was used as a staging area for rescue workers.) There was a giant red metal jungle gym, a gazebo, and a sprinkler that spit sprays of water on hot days. The parents and nannies would sit on benches and watch the kids romp, and I always thought there was something depressing about it—like we were trying to pretend that we were experiencing the great outdoors, even though we were constantly assaulted by the sounds of heavy traffic and blaring horns on the West Side Highway a block away. I remember the haze of soot filtering through the uncertain sunshine, and the noxious aroma of diesel fuel and car exhaust fumes that filled the air. My kids needed the healthy scent of fresh clean air and the rich loamy aroma of turned soil, even if it was from a tiny flower bed, not this congested clot of downtown Manhattan.

As for me, I needed a place where I could find peace. Not that changing locations was the answer to the problems in our relationship, but I hoped a change of scenery would shake loose some of Harvey's demons.

The first time Harvey disappeared for four days without notice—provoking the famous plate-throwing incident in 1986—I was so caught off guard that I was willing to believe his promises that it would never happen again. But it did, two or three times a year, always without warning. I wasn't alert enough to see the signs, but maybe there were no signs. How could I not have seen this? I'm sure people will think I was blind, but Harvey was an occasional binger, not a daily user. He wasn't hanging out with the downtown crowd. He was disappearing into his hole, wherever it was, and descending into his private hell. Why didn't I put my foot down and insist that Harvey get help? At the time, he was seeing an analyst, and he told me she knew all about his drug use. He assured me they were working on it. The whole business was outside my experience. I didn't know about drug users or enablers. It was easier to believe that, by making our life better, I could make Harvey happier. I decided we needed to move out of the city.

One day in late 1989, after wrapping *Goodfellas*, I told Harvey, "I'm over this city living. The kids need nature in their lives every day. I want to buy a house outside the city. Margaux and Stella deserve it. We all deserve it."

Harvey was very resistant to this idea; he'd never lived anywhere else. A weekend at our place upstate in Kripplebush was one thing. Living in the country full-time was another. But I was ready for him. "We can afford it with my money from *Goodfellas*," I reasoned. "We can keep the loft, too."

"We're not that rich," he grumbled.

Ellen Burstyn had told me about a sweet little enclave north of the city in Rockland County, called Sneden's Landing. It was home to many artists, actors, and writers, and was tucked away from the main roads along the Hudson River. Ellen's riverfront house in Sneden's was for sale. It was out of our price range, but I'd checked and there were a couple of less expensive houses available. I made an appointment with a real-estate agent, and I told Harvey we were driving up that weekend to look at houses.

He glared at me. "So you've already decided."

It was true. I had. I was taking charge of our lives for the sake of the girls. Harvey thought living outside the city was comparable to being sent into exile, but TriBeCa was beginning to feel like exile to me.

We drove up that weekend. We crossed the George Washington Bridge and came up along the Palisades Parkway, a scenic two-lane highway where no trucks were allowed. We clocked in at an easy thirty-five minutes. When we turned down the main road into the village of Sneden's Landing, no signs welcomed us. This little gem was hidden in plain sight. The girls and I were immediately charmed by the fairy-tale town, where lush foliage surrounded the quaint homes along narrow roads. It was like entering the set for the musical *Brigadoon*. Lots of gingerbread-style Victorian houses. Lots of trees and woods, leading to a hundred-acre nature preserve.

Remarkably, Sneden's Landing had remained an insider's find for decades, in spite of its lineage as a bohemian writers' and artists' colony and its proximity to Manhattan.

The real-estate agent met us at a glorious house at the bottom of a winding lane. She was charming and enthusiastic about the property. "These houses on the Palisades cliffs are one of a kind," she raved. "The one I'm showing you isn't on the river, but it's private and has over an acre of land. The owners have completely remodeled it. It's a steal at half a million."

Harvey snorted. We drove up a steep incline and parked in front of a lovely white clapboard. The house was spacious, with several bedrooms and a huge family room facing a wooded backyard. The master bedroom looked out at the river beyond. The view was seasonal—what real-estate people like to call "winter water views." Come spring, when the leaves returned to the trees, the view would be gone.

It was a very nice house, but it didn't speak to me. "I don't know," I said. "I think we need to look at some other places."

"I could show you Ellen Burstyn's house," she suggested. "Personally, I think it's one of the best locations on the Hudson."

"It's too expensive for us," I said, "but I'd love to see it. Do you mind, Harvey?"

He obviously thought it was a waste of time, but he agreed. We all piled back in the car.

We drove down a long lane, past several lovely estates, as the agent explained that this "gem" we were about to view was at the southern edge of Sneden's, built right into the rock face of the ancient Palisades, high above the river. A long private road, barely wide enough for a single car, wound through the woods leading to an iron gate. Once through the gate, we bumped along over a rugged gravel entry and entered the property. It was a woodland paradise, with a tree-covered hill to the right, and a large expanse of forested land winding down to the river, which seemed to be miles below. The house was nestled like a prize into the side of the hill.

"Built on a rock. I like the symbolism of that," I said to Harvey, gazing around in wonder. I'd wanted nature, and this was nature plus. "It's beautiful."

Harvey was looking over the edge of the steep hill, down at the water. "Yeah, it's a great place," he said. "If you're a goat."

"Let's go inside," the agent suggested. We followed her through a trellised, wisteria-covered entrance into the upper level. The house was filled with light, and the bedrooms led out to decks with breathtaking views of the river. The master bedroom had a wood-burning fireplace, as did the den, which opened onto a circular stone stairway that led to a terraced garden and a nature preserve. A waterfall burbled gently over the hillside. It was magical. Delighted, Margaux and Stella scampered down to take a look.

The lower level featured a massive living room facing the river, with a large deck and side entrance to the patio. The sunlit kitchen overlooked the nature preserve. Just outside, a handcrafted stairway wound down through the woods to the water. It was simply the most beautiful and inspirational place I had ever seen. We stood on the deck and watched a single sailboat drift by on the river below, the silence surrounding us. This place felt like a healing house. I thought it was a space where a family could thrive.

I turned to the agent with regret. "I love it," I said, "but it's way out of our price range." In fact, it was double the price of the previous house we'd looked at. We headed back to the city, agreeing to keep looking. But it was hard for me to get Ellen's house out of my head.

The following week I got a call from the agent, telling me that Ellen might be agreeable to renting the house with an option to buy. It would require a leap of faith on our part—the hope and expectation that we could actually afford to buy the house in the near future. What if we moved to Sneden's Landing, loved it, and then had to move out?

Harvey and I discussed it long and hard. Finally, he said, "I know it's what you want. Let's do it."

I was elated, and our leap of faith would pay off. Within a year we owned the house.

We moved in that summer, and registered the girls in the local school system. Margaux would be starting in the middle school, and Stella in kindergarten. Registration brought the usual confusion over names. I can assure you they weren't used to encountering such a jumbled lineage in Rockland County. There was Margaux ("That's spelled with an *aux*, not an *o*") Guerard, and

Stella Keitel. I was Lorraine Bracco. No, Harvey Keitel and I were not married. "I see," said the registrar, but her face, impassive, implied the faintest hint of shocked disapproval at our bohemian ways. Welcome to the suburbs.

We arrived in Sneden's Landing on the front wave of a population boom. The river villages of Rockland County spread north along the Hudson, and they appealed to young families who wanted to be near the river without paying the higher price tag of Westchester County. Piermont, the town immediately north of Sneden's Landing, had been a factory town until the early 1980s, and plans were under way to replace the hulking waterfront shells of the old factories with condominiums. Main Street Piermont was as charming as a movie set—and that's because it *was* a movie set. In 1984, when Woody Allen chose Piermont as the setting for *The Purple Rose of Cairo*, he rebuilt the façades of the buildings along Main Street to give them a sweet, old-world charm.

I should point out that when I say we "moved in," it was a little more complicated than that. We didn't hire a moving van and ship our belongings north. The TriBeCa loft remained mostly intact, and we set out to decorate our Sneden's house in a country style, piece by piece. It wasn't a formal house like some of the neighboring mansions. The kitchen was tiny (fine with me because I wasn't a cook) and there was no separate dining room. We didn't even have a separate guest room. As Margaux once noted, "It's so cozy that if you sneeze, someone at the other end of the house says, 'Bless you.' "

The timing of our move was difficult because I was working a lot—which meant being away for weeks at a time on shoots. I treasured those rare weeks when I could be home with Margaux and Stella, working on the house. We'd explore the flea markets and antique stores in the surrounding villages, buy fresh produce and baked goods at the farmer's market, and simply enjoy getting to know the area. Once we got over the shock of being in a place that was within walking distance of absolutely nothing—and forget about ordering takeout!—the kids and I loved Rockland County.

As for nature, we had plenty of that. Of course, I hadn't been around nature much, so I had to get reacquainted. One day while the girls were at school, I looked out to see a baby raccoon curled up on the back patio. I didn't know enough to realize that this was a very bad sign. For one thing, raccoons are nocturnal, so if you see them during the day it means they're probably sick with rabies or something. The other thing is that if a baby raccoon is alone, its mother has to be looking for it. But all I could think of was that the girls would so love to see this baby. So I got out a small crate, poured a little puddle of Coca-Cola in a dish, and set it inside the crate. When I put it on the porch, the baby raccoon scooted right in and began lapping up the liquid. I clicked the cage door shut, and left to pick up the girls at the bus stop.

"I have a surprise at home, a big surprise," I sang out when Margaux and Stella stepped down from the school bus. Stella danced excitedly around me, while Margaux just looked at me with a raised eyebrow. She was at an age when Mommy's surprises had to be treated with healthy skepticism. For good reason, too.

When they saw the cute-as-a-button little raccoon, it was love at first sight. "Oh, let me hold him," Stella cried.

"No, no touching," I said. "I just wanted you to see him. I'm going to release him back into the wild."

At that moment we heard a piercing shriek that sounded like "Eeeeee . . . eeee."

"That's a mean sound," Margaux said. Mom was coming.

"Okay, back in the house," I ordered. I opened the cage door and we ran inside. Sure enough, a huge, not so cute raccoon came lumbering out of the bushes, shrieking with fury. She stuck her head in the cage, took a sip of Coca-Cola, and grabbed her baby. Then she turned and gave us the evil eye before they both disappeared into the woods. That was a close call.

I loved nature, but obviously I had a lot of learning to do. The wooded areas surrounding our property were home to a large variety of animals—most of which were not for petting. In addition to the raccoons, there were skunks, foxes, wild turkeys, groundhogs, and deer. Giant hawks circled the treetops. Mallards and geese drifted by in the water below. A family of elegant osprey lived in the treetops across from my bedroom, and I would watch them fish in the river.

It was beautiful, and it wasn't just nature in the abstract. The Hudson River below us was also a living thing. I woke up every morning and the first thing I saw was the river, a piece of art in motion, made of incredible grays and blues and violets. It was a dynamic meditation, a sight that never failed to bring on a rush of gratitude just to be alive.

It was thanks to Margaux that I became involved in helping to keep the river alive. Margaux came home from middle school one day and announced, "Mom, the river is dying."

She was so intense, so serious, I had to smile. "Tell me about it," I said.

She repeated the lesson she'd learned in school, about the toxic wastes that made the river so foul and polluted that it could no longer sustain populations of edible fish. Margaux increased our awareness of environmental issues. I wanted to make a difference, and when my friend John Hoving introduced me to Bobby Kennedy, Jr., and his dedicated organization, Riverkeeper, I knew I had to get involved. I decided that if we were going to live on the river, we had a responsibility to be its guardians.

I had hoped that finally getting out of the city and into the countryside would be good for Harvey. It would give him room to breathe, give us a chance to be a real family. I thought I could make things better by giving him a beautiful sanctuary deep in the woods. But the tension built up in that house, too. It crackled through the rooms, and lived in the walls. There were two distinct lifestyles being lived. In one, the girls and I were having the time of our lives. We were free from the confines and the choking density of Manhattan, and we were elated. I loved the chaos of domesticity—kids, animals, the happy noises of laughter and play filling the house. The big table in our family room was constantly cluttered with remnants of Margaux's homework and various arts and crafts projects. Friends were always coming in and out. But it wasn't like that for

Harvey. He loved Sneden's Landing, but he couldn't allow himself to be happy there or anywhere else.

The essential difference between Harvey and me was that he viewed life as an epic battle, and I viewed life as a search for joy. It had taken me a long time, but I was starting to get the picture: Harvey wasn't happy unless he was struggling. Struggle was good. Struggle was deep. My attempts at lightheartedness annoyed him. I was constantly saying, "Relax, Harvey. Lighten up, Harvey." Why shouldn't he? We had a really good life—two beautiful girls, a wonderful home, rewarding work. Harvey thought that my disinterest in joining the epic battle for artistic suffering was a sign that I lacked substance, that I wasn't facing reality. You were either a deep, suffering artist or you were a happy-go-lucky civilian. Which was I?

I learned to avoid certain topics of conversation because they provoked him. Harvey would get preachy. His way of thinking was the only way. He would fight me in a conversation until I was exhausted, demoralized, and didn't even care anymore. Finally, I'd give up and just "yes" him. He was relentless.

Harvey had a way of making me feel guilty for wanting to be happy and laugh. I found that he was attracted to other intense types in the business, who would fuel their angst with liquor and drugs, and converse for hours about the deep, dark nights of their souls. When we were out with these people, I could tell that I embarrassed Harvey. He thought I was too stupid to be miserable, too unaware to be morose and intense.

"There's something you don't understand," he'd lecture me. "I'm a marine . . ."

"Harvey, you are not a marine. You haven't been a marine for thirty years."

Ignoring me, he'd continue, "When I was seventeen years old, just a young, scared marine recruit, a drill instructor said something that has stayed with me my whole life. He said that the thing every human being feared most was the darkness—the unknown. And he told us he was going to teach us to know the darkness, so we wouldn't ever have to be afraid. I never forgot that. And ever since then, I've been asking myself, what is darkness, and how do I learn to live with it?"

"Oh, you've got darkness down pat, Harvey," I'd say sarcastically. "It's the light you can't stand."

Harvey could be very loving, and there was a side to him that was extremely appealing. He had a great personality, and when he was in a good mood, he'd have us all rolling on the floor with his humor and wit. But he was also quite demanding and full of rules for the girls and me. Preteen Margaux was beginning to buck against his rigidity. She was a good girl, and she resented the way he punished her for breaking a silly infraction, like turning on the TV before she finished her reading. He was always trying to inspire the kids to read, read, read, but he did it with a heavy hand, and his intensity was a turnoff for Margaux.

That rigid, critical side of Harvey began to be much more in evidence those days. In our early years together, I'd been a complete pleaser, but I was changing. For one thing, I was tired of trying to please a man who couldn't be pleased. For another thing, I was growing stronger, and I was less willing to put up with his ridicule. Here's a perfect example. From the very beginning of our relationship, Harvey knew that I couldn't cook. Cooking didn't interest me. As a result, I was a klutz in the kitchen. My scrambled eggs might be too runny, or the steak too well done. Harvey would stare at his plate in utter disgust, and then push it away with a grand, sweeping gesture. It hurt my feelings. He could have cooked, or we could have ordered out. There were many options available other than belittling me and ruining our evening. And I thought, why should I be standing in the kitchen with my gut clenching for fear I wasn't going to cook a steak to Harvey's liking? How did I get in that position?

Harvey could be incredibly disciplined. He worked out every day. He read philosophy books long into the night. He was even seeing an analyst, a specialist in addiction. But his self-destructive impulses, his need to "know the darkness," always seemed to have a stronger pull. As the person who loved him the most, it was very hard for me to watch, and it was even harder to live with.

I knew Harvey was happy for my success, but it seemed to me that he was in a constant state of anxiety and despair about his own career. Harvey's brilliance was something I could only aspire to, but he wasn't being sought out. His name wasn't on the short list of major male film stars, which was a source of enormous torment. He'd been irate when the studios tried to prevent him from being cast in his last two movies—*The Last Temptation of Christ* and *The Two Jakes*. Both Martin Scorsese and Jack Nicholson stood up for

Harvey and insisted on casting him. It wasn't just blind loyalty. They knew Harvey's electric presence would add an essential quality to their films. Although neither movie did that well at the box office, Harvey was universally praised in the reviews. He stood out, but he wasn't able to stick in the industry's consciousness. His phone wasn't ringing. I didn't blame Harvey for feeling let down by the business. It wasn't right and it wasn't fair. But I had no magic wand in my arsenal that I could use to lift Harvey up and put him where he belonged. He'd been my teacher and my mentor. He'd given me my career. But now there was nothing I could do to help him.

Unlike Harvey, I could separate work from life. For Harvey, work *was* life. It wasn't all mixed together for me into one big, throbbing compulsion. I knew where my art stopped and my real life started. I'm not saying that's a better way to be; Harvey was brilliant, and I didn't kid myself that I was brilliant in that way. But I did wonder what good art was if it killed you in the process, if it gnawed at you and ate you up, if it made your life a living hell. How could you be so talented, and yet not have the opportunity to express it as you wished? And Harvey's demons were hard at work.

While my career was taking off, I think Harvey felt stalled. And when his despair became too great, he would disappear. Looking back, it seems to me that the binges were becoming more frequent, and it was extremely stressful not knowing when they would occur. I became a lunatic if he was five minutes late or didn't immediately return my call. To make matters worse, his mother was dying, and on one occasion, she called the house looking for him, sounding desperate to talk to him, and I didn't know where the hell he was. I wanted to scream—I did scream—with frustration. I knew that if his mother died and he wasn't there for her, he would eat himself alive with grief and guilt. I didn't want him to have to go through that. I wanted to spare him that. I wanted to protect him from himself.

I lied to his mother, told her he was working and promised to give him the message. She'd call the next day, and I'd lie to her again.

When he finally showed up, he'd have nothing to say about where he'd been, but he would look like he'd just crawled through the fires of hell. I started not to care. I was beside myself with frustration and worry. "I'm lying to a dying woman to protect you. You said you wanted to work on this, and your analyst says you want to work on this, but it just keeps getting worse."

Wordless and staggering with exhaustion, he'd push past me into the bedroom, where he would fall onto the bed and sleep for two days.

"Come quick, kids. Daddy's home!" No, I never yelled those words. We'd all creep around, trying not to disturb Harvey as he slept off his most recent binge.

This was the story of our lives in those days—the story nobody knew. I worked overtime trying to keep everything looking good. I could feel myself getting more and more stuck in the relationship because of the kids. Had I built my life with a drug addict? How could I tell my parents? They loved Harvey, and he loved them. He'd become part of the Bracco clan. Lizzie suspected something was wrong, because she'd been there that first time, but I downplayed everything, desperate to make it go away.

I sensed Harvey's problems were getting worse, so I was willing to try anything. I agreed to go with him to his analyst, but the experience left me feeling betrayed. It seemed to me that Harvey's analyst was more of an enabler than a healer. It was such a sham that Harvey would do a line of coke in her office bathroom before the sessions. I confronted the analyst. "Is this a joke? He's doing coke in the bathroom."

She replied calmly, "Lorraine, these things take time. Harvey is working diligently to resolve his problems." She was defending him! I was disgusted. I felt desperate and abandoned. I didn't see how this was going to work.

He was always full of self-recrimination, always dejected in the aftermath of one of his disappearances. He'd say, "I can't believe I do this to myself," not seeing that he was doing it to us, too. I didn't think he was interested in fixing it.

I couldn't penetrate his wall of cold indifference. I felt that his destructive self-absorption was killing us, blocking the main arteries of our love and our connection, cutting off the blood supply that kept our relationship alive. It ate away at me and corroded my feelings for him. I cried at night, wondering what I could do. I tried to keep my feelings from the girls, but life with Harvey was becoming more and more intolerable. My stress level was so high that I wasn't even excited about all the calls for work I was getting. When producer Michael Douglas called from Germany to talk to me about seeing the rushes from our movie, *Radio Flyer,* I was so excited that I accidentally cut off an incoming call for Harvey. He came storming up the stairs and burst through the door, screaming, "Hey! My calls aren't important? Why don't you just go suck Michael Douglas's dick?" Burning with embarrassment, I quickly ended the call with Michael. He must have heard the screaming. I prayed he hadn't heard the words.

I started hoping the phone *wouldn't* ring and scripts wouldn't be delivered. Imagine that! What a crazy mentality for an actor. But I wanted things to work with Harvey, and a part of that was not making him feel that I was competing with him for attention while he was struggling to find the more substantial parts he wanted to do.

People have since asked me if I ever thought of leaving him during this period. Truthfully, I never considered it. It didn't seem possible. We were a family, we had two daughters. I loved the good man inside of Harvey. I didn't want to leave; I wanted Harvey to change. I hoped he would see what it was like to have a happy family, and the experience would erase all the bad stuff. I was naïve and ill-equipped to accomplish that. You can't fix another person. You can't live on hope and expect it to magically change your life. Hope is not fairy dust.

I had been cast in a leading role for a movie called *A Talent for the Game*, starring Edward James Olmos. And in the summer of 1990 I took off for Idaho for a few weeks to shoot the film. It was a relief to escape the brutal real-life drama I had been living on the home front, and to immerse myself in a scripted screenplay. It was a wonderful true story about an over-the-hill baseball scout named Virgil Sweet, who discovers the latest pitching phenom living quietly on an Idaho farm. Edward James Olmos played the scout. I would be playing his girlfriend, Bobbie. I liked the idea that it was a fun little movie. No heavy lifting, no searing drama.

When I arrived on the set, I was kind of hoping Eddie wouldn't really remember me. That *Miami Vice* fiasco was better forgotten. But he greeted me with a big smile, saying, "Lorraine, how nice to see you again."

Eddie's warmth and good humor were contagious. Everyone on the set loved him. He was so upbeat and extroverted. He strode through each day with a purpose. He spent as much time working on humanitarian causes as he did on acting, and he was interested in making socially conscious films. In 1989, while he was still starring in *Miami Vice*, Eddie had been nominated for an Academy Award for Best Actor in *Stand and Deliver*, a wonderful true story about a teacher who inspires an East L.A. classroom filled with disenfranchised tough kids, mostly Mexican-American gangbangers, to pass the advanced placement calculus test. Eddie really believed in that story, and believed that even the most hopeless kids had a future if we cared enough to give it to them. "Education," he often said, "is a vaccine to violence."

It was wonderful having lively conversations with someone about things that were bigger than just ourselves. I hadn't realized how much I'd been craving that. I had grown so tired of navel-gazing, of constantly trying to look deep inside of myself for all of the answers. Eddie brought out my natural altruistic spirit, the realization that I could do more than just exist on this planet, that I could reach out and make a profound difference in other people's lives.

Eddie seemed to like me. He was nice to me. I basked in Eddie's sweet concern, his optimism and honesty. He was so filled with hope. He poured himself into the upbeat spirit of the role, and I found myself grinning when I watched him work. The movie was fun for him because he was a huge baseball fan. He told me that as a kid he'd been obsessed with baseball—and for a time even thought he'd make a career of it. Baseball had been his escape from the poverty and violence of East L.A., and from his dysfunctional family. "My parents split up when I was eight years old," he told me, "and I found that I could lose myself in baseball. I played every day, because when I was out in the field or at the plate hitting that ball, I wasn't thinking about my troubles or my family."

I had never known a man like Eddie before. He was so strong and secure in himself, yet bursting with a genuine concern for others. His friends would call him selfless. I couldn't help but compare his ebullient, open personality to Harvey's dark, brooding demeanor. It was literally the difference between night and day.

It's such a cliché in the film industry to say that actresses fall in love with their leading men, especially when they go off on location together. But guess what? I began living and breathing that stupid cliché. It wasn't love, really; not then. It was more like a mutual admiration. I was drawn to Eddie because he was so easy to talk to, so comforting to lean on, so accepting of me for who I was. He didn't need me to be deep and brooding, all dark and intense. He liked my upbeat spirit, and my willingness to laugh at myself and others. I felt as if my life force around Eddie was allowed its full measure of fire. I was allowed to feed on the sun and *shine.* I didn't have to subdue myself and keep my feelings tamped down to fit the needs of my mate.

I can't justify having had a romantic affair with Eddie during that time. It was my weakness and my need for loving approval that I acted on, and it was wrong. I took full responsibility. I never felt that I was driven to do it by Harvey's behavior or my unhappiness. I wasn't trying to get back at him. There is no other way to explain my actions than to say that I caved in to a feeling.

When Eddie and I parted at the end of the filming, I was feeling grateful for his love and kindness, but at the same time I was sick with guilt. I was afraid I'd screwed up so badly that I'd never be able to recover. I'd let down my moral guard, and I was ashamed of myself. I had to remember who I was, and who and what I was committed to.

"I've got to go home and try to make my life with Harvey work," I told Eddie. "I have the girls to think of." He understood, but he was sad to see me go. Flying back to New York, I was uncomfortable. I knew how much I wanted to work on my relationship with Harvey, but I was worried. He had shattered my trust in him, and I had answered back with shattering behavior of my own. I had never cheated on a man I was in a relationship with. It didn't feel right. I was desperate, in spite of everything, to keep my family together.

Harvey had psychic radar that was so powerful it was positively eerie. He knew something was different the moment I walked through the door. He looked deeply into my eyes as he bundled me in his tight embrace. I saw him studying me, reading me, squinting his eyes, and nodding to himself. The tension between us had not lessened in my absence, but now there was a new dimension to it. I did my best to avoid his scrutiny.

He battered me with questions about the shoot, and in particular about Eddie. What kind of guy he was, whether we hit it off.

"It's hard not to hit it off with Eddie," I said. "He's a really nice guy."

Harvey nodded his head knowingly. "A nice guy, huh?" That's all he needed. "You slept with him, didn't you?" he demanded.

He was angry and threatening, which only caused me to shrink away from him. "What the hell are you talking about?" I said. He indicated that he'd "heard things." I denied it. I was determined to deny it until my last breath. It seemed to be the wisest course of action. I didn't know what Harvey would do if I told him. We were incapable of having a discussion about our problems, or of working together to solve them. I wasn't about to confirm his suspicions and give him the chance to bombard me with accusations. My affair with Eddie had to remain my secret.

He kept after me, pushing and prodding about my relationship with Eddie. I kept telling him there was nothing. I hadn't had any contact with Eddie since the shoot. We hadn't even talked on the phone. "Why don't we work on *our* relationship?" I said to Harvey, pleading for a change of direction. I didn't like where this discussion was heading.

I don't know if Harvey actually believed there was anything between Eddie and me, or if he was just afraid I was getting stronger and less willing to put up with his bullshit. He was very controlling. Sometimes around Harvey I felt like a little mouse being pursued by a determined cat—like there was no chance. He was going to corner me, badger me, for a long time, and then eat me up. He wanted me to know that he could lift me up, but he could also smack me down. I was tired of it. I didn't want to live like that anymore. I wanted to break loose.

I wanted to have fun. I wanted to laugh. I had always been a big laugher, but that wasn't so true anymore. I got it into my head that maybe I could laugh vicariously by acting in a comedy. People were always telling me I should do comedy because I was so funny, but for some reason directors preferred to cast me in extremely *un*funny roles. Cop's wife, mob wife, bad mother. When Heather called to say that Mel Brooks was casting for a comedy, called *Life Stinks*, I thought, *Aha! Here's my chance*. It was a classic Brooks story line: A rich businessman makes a bet that he can survive on the streets of Los Angeles for thirty days. In the process he falls in love with a homeless woman. Heather arranged for me to audition for the role in L.A. I could do a funny homeless woman. Yeah, definitely.

Like most actors, I worshipped Mel Brooks. If he thought you were funny, it was like the Good Comedy Seal of Approval.

I auditioned for Mel, and he watched me without expression, then declared, "You're not funny."

I was flabbergasted and not a little insulted. I almost grabbed at him over the table. "I am too funny!" I roared.

"No you're not."

"Yes I am!"

"Not."

"Am."

"Not."

"Am."

A long silence. We stared at each other.

"I am funny."

"No."

"Am."

Two kids going back and forth. Now, *that* was funny. I started laughing, thanked Mel and left. I still thought I was funny, though. And then he cast Lesley Ann Warren. I was indignant. Since when was *she* funny?

In September 1990, *Goodfellas* was released to great reviews, and the congratulatory calls started coming. I was as proud of that performance as anything I've ever done. But there was a chilling reminder for me in playing the life of Karen Hill. Stand by your man no matter what? Was that doing the right thing? Harvey was possessive, and he thought he had a right to have his family be completely supportive and by his side, no matter what he did.

At least he was working again, and the roles were solid. Ridley Scott cast Harvey as a cop in *Thelma and Louise*, and Warren Beatty wanted him to play the Jewish gangster Mickey Cohen in *Bugsy*. We were both working a lot, and I thought the work might save us from banging heads and losing each other.

For once, our dance cards were full at the same time. As the year came to a close, I learned that I'd been cast as the female lead opposite Sean Connery in the movie *Medicine Man*.

I was on top of the world and I didn't even know it. When the Golden Globe nominations were announced in December and I was nominated for *Goodfellas*, I didn't really understand the significance. Harvey explained that they were big—that they could be a precursor to the Oscars. He was so proud of me. He threw a small party for me in Sneden's Landing. Al Pacino was there. So were Vic Argo, Toukie Smith, Heather, my parents, and the kids. The river shimmered in the cold December sun as we all ate cake. It was a very sweet day.

Then the Academy Award nominations were announced in January 1991. I was by myself in L.A., filming *Radio Flyer*, and a phone call from Heather woke me early one morning with the news that I had been nominated for Best Supporting Actress for *Goodfellas*. I know that actors always say they don't expect it, they're totally shocked, and all that other nonsense, but you need to know this: in my case, it was really true. As proud as I was of that performance, I was stunned to have been acknowledged by the Academy in this way. It was a confirmation of any actor's wildest dreams. I was blubbering by the time I called Harvey and the girls and my parents. Flowers and fruit baskets began to arrive in New York and L.A. I'll say this for Harvey; he was proud of me that day, and genuinely happy for me. He knew that this was an incredible honor, and that we had worked really hard to get there.

Goodfellas had also been nominated for Best Picture, and Marty for Best Director. Joe Pesci got a nomination for Best Supporting Actor. De Niro was nominated for Best Actor, not for *Goodfellas*, but for his brilliant portrayal of a catatonic man restored to life in *Awakenings*. In my opinion, he was so good in both of those roles that he should have been nominated twice. I was also disappointed that Ray, who so embodied Henry Hill, had not been nominated. He deserved it.

I wanted to savor this amazing moment, but I didn't want to go overboard. I was sensitive to Harvey's personal frustration, and I didn't want to do anything—including celebrating this extraordinary success—that might unleash the demons. Harvey's take on the Oscar was pretty clear. "The Oscar doesn't mean shit," he said. "It's the craft that matters."

He understood that an Oscar nomination was a great boon to an actor's career, but it didn't matter as much as the opportunity to do the work itself. Awards are nice, but they don't take the place of doing meaningful and satisfying work.

A hot fudge sundae with all of the fixings is yummy; the maraschino cherry on top is just decoration. You still get to eat the sundae whether the cherry's there or not. That was the Oscar. It was the cherry on top. It didn't make the sundae any better; just more festive.

Of course, that cherry could guarantee you roles you might never have had the opportunity to play, and the chance to be paid well for the work. That was the real difference between the cherry and the Oscar. Oscars don't come in bottles filled with syrup. An Oscar means you've arrived at a point of time in your career that may never be the same again.

So Harvey was right. The craft matters. But the Oscar opens doors that may have been closed before to allow you to work at your craft. The Oscar is the cherry on top. And I always loved the color red.

Six · Free Fall

Psychologically, a secret is a heavy load that leads to feelings of guilt, which further burden the mind.

· Dr. Jennifer Melfi

MARCH 1991

I was dangling from a harness 120 feet above the ground, in the middle of the Mexican jungle, and I wanted to scream, "Somebody get me out of here!" If I hadn't been so petrified, I might have noted what a perfect metaphor it was for my entire life.

I was in the middle of a five-month shoot for *Medicine Man*, the movie that was supposed to save the rain forest and spark a romance onscreen to rival the old Tracy/Hepburn chemistry. It was a very tall order.

Medicine Man was the story of an eccentric, reclusive biochemist, Dr. Robert Campbell, played by Sean Connery, still the sexiest man alive at sixty-one. He was in the Amazon rain forest, doing cutting-edge cancer research for a major corporation, when he cut off all communication. I played Dr. Rae Crane, a brilliant biochemist from the Bronx, who was sent to check on him. They are like oil and water, then lovers—all the while finding the cure for cancer in a rare plant and battling to save the rain forest. The director was John McTiernan, who'd done *Die Hard* with Bruce Willis and *Predator* with Arnold Schwarzenegger. Sean had worked with him a couple of years earlier on *The Hunt for Red October*, which had also starred Alec Baldwin.

Naturally, I was pretty dazzled by the idea that Sean Connery had handpicked me to play his love interest. Double-oh seven? Sean Connery? James freaking Bond? Who wouldn't jump at the chance to work with him?

The movie was filmed in Catemaco, Mexico, in a lush tropical setting that simulated the Amazon rain forest. It was the real thing. Very authentic. One hundred percent humidity every day, guaranteed. Scorpions, tarantulas, and other exotic creepy-crawlies on full display.

Before I left for Mexico, I sat down with Harvey and told him that my feelings had changed. I needed time to sort things out. In a way, Mexico was a blessing because it gave me that distance. I wasn't about to leave my girls behind, though. I decided to take them with me. Being a working film actor is like living a gypsy's life, always on the go, one location to the next, and that's a very tough thing if you have kids. When I agreed to make *Medicine Man*, I had a choice: leave them home and be separated from them for five months, or pack them up and bring them with me. I'd been away from my girls so much over the last couple of years, I decided I couldn't leave them behind. I wanted them with me. There was no way I could be apart from the girls again for that long, or they from me. Naturally, there was a lot of chaos and complications involved—pulling them out of school and away from their friends, having to bring along a full-time nanny, cook, and tutor, packing our lives up and heading south. We ended up moving practically the entire household down there, and then I was hardly around. I was in every scene of the movie, and the shooting schedule turned out to be backbreaking.

Some people might criticize me for pulling the girls out of school for such a long period of time. Even with a tutor, it wasn't a normal, stable environment. I happened to think that in the long run it was more important for them to have their mother—to feel secure in the understanding that they would not be left behind, that they were wanted. I trusted that the experience would provide an education that could not be duplicated in the classroom.

The housing setup was reasonably comfortable. The girls loved the little house the production company rented us. At first, though, they couldn't understand why it was surrounded by a chain-link fence separating us from the beautiful waters beyond.

"I want to go swimming," Margaux complained, her face soaked with sweat. "I wish that fence wasn't there."

I asked about swimming, and the local workers who'd been hired to look after us broke into raucous laughter. Alligators, they said, pointing at the water. Crocodiles. "Oh. Oh! Okay. Never mind," I responded. I told the kids to stay the hell away from the fence, too. Just for good measure.

We were all a bit squeamish about the scorpions and spiders, which were the size of Frisbees, and the preponderance of tiny jumping frogs. I freaked out one day when I came back early from the set to find my daughters casually trapping giant hairy tarantulas underneath cardboard shoe boxes. "Look, Mom, they're so cute," Stella said. Nature was everywhere, and it was robust and profuse. I asked the girls to promise me that they wouldn't play with the hairy tarantulas anymore. Or decide to swim with the crocodiles. Or feed them. Or pet them. But the overall setting was truly breathtaking. A magical aura of primeval power hung in the wet, heavy air.

The town of Catemaco is known as the City of Witches, and our arrival there coincided with an annual convergence of witch doctors, shamans, and natural healers from all over the world. The magic of the shamans was even incorporated into the film.

Still, I had to wonder. Five months in the jungle: was I out of my mind? What had I been thinking to expose myself and my children to these casual hardships and real dangers? In spite of the ever-present machine gun–toting guards, the banditos were not dissuaded. They knew how much money was on the set, especially on Fridays, when the local crew was paid in cash. On one occasion, the accountants were held up at gunpoint. There was nothing petty about the petty cash we lost that day. Another time, a member of the camera crew was kidnapped and held for ransom. The ransom was paid, and he returned to work, a little beat up but okay. I always wondered how the ransom was listed on the accounting ledger.

The jungle was an indelible learning experience. It was also a taste of hell. I found myself thinking that the person who said a woman could have it all—career, home, family, love life—should get kicked in the ass. You can't have it all. You can only sacrifice one thing for another. There will never be having it all. You either give yourself to this, or you give yourself to that. It was just a matter of making up your mind and then sticking to it.

Sean Connery endeared himself to me forever with his tremendous generosity in the middle of the shoot. The Academy Awards were taking place in Los Angeles, and Warner Brothers had decided the logistics were just too difficult to fly me up from the jungle. I was disappointed, deflated, the wind knocked out of my sails. I resented the studio's indifference to me, the way they figured that as long as the *fellas* were there, I didn't matter, but Heather put up the biggest stink. For some reason, though, it didn't occur to me to make a big deal about it. Why is that, do you think? I guess I didn't feel I had a right. Wow. I just shake my head when I remember that feeling. And they say feminism has outlived its usefulness!

Since I had expected to attend, I'd already arranged for my dress. I had seen this dress, designed by Valentino, in a magazine. It was a white gown, embroidered in silver beads that spelled out the word "peace" in different languages. I had asked Valentino to make me a version of it, and he'd agreed. In fact, he was giving me the dress as a gift. (He also made a gift of another gorgeous dress for my mother.) Since I was going to be in the jungle, there was a big discussion about how to do the fittings. Finally, Valentino's staff in Los Angeles hit on a solution. They made a gauze pattern of my body before I left for Mexico, and they were working from that. Now it looked as if I wouldn't have a chance to wear the Valentino gown made just for me, and I wanted to cry.

When Sean heard that I wasn't going to the Oscars, he was indignant. This was an important acknowledgment, he said. I should be there.

In spite of his amazing career, Sean had been nominated only one time—in 1987 as Best Supporting Actor in *The Untouchables*—and he won the Oscar that year. Like all great actors, he had the proper perspective about winning an Academy Award. It wasn't the be-all and end-all. But he also gave the Oscar its due, and believed that if you were fortunate enough to be nominated, you should damn well pull out all the stops to have your moment in the sun. So he took it upon himself to make sure I got to Los Angeles.

Part of Sean's agreement with the producers of *Medicine Man* was a certain number of hours on a private jet that had been reserved for the film—to bring his family down or take a break. He gave me a big chunk of his air time to fly to L.A. and back for the Academy Award ceremony.

I have always said that Sean Connery gave me a chance to be Cinderella for an evening, and I'll never forget it.

McTiernan didn't protest my leaving the set, but I still had to work a half day on Saturday before I boarded the flight to Los Angeles. Once I got to L.A., I was in for a whirlwind day and a half.

I arrived in Los Angeles in the early evening and took a cab to the rented house where Harvey and my parents were waiting for me. You can imagine how grungy I felt, but I had to clean up good and fast, because we were going to a party at Barbra Streisand's house. Oh my God, my childhood idol! Barbra had tracked me down in the jungle to invite Harvey and me to a party she was giving for Irwin Winkler, the producer of *Goodfellas,* and Marty.

What could I say? I sent a message back, thanking her, and saying how much I wanted to be there, except I was flying my parents out for the Oscars, and I had to be with them.

So she wrote back, "Oh, please. Bring your parents."

I managed to make myself presentable, and off we went to an evening you could only dream of. I expected my parents to be starstruck when they met Barbra, but not them! They launched into a story about how I used to play her records in my room and sing along with my awful voice, until they couldn't stand it anymore.

"We'd be shouting, 'Turn off that God-awful music,' " my father said to Barbra Streisand.

"Lorraine ruined you for us," my mother added.

I started dragging my folks away before they could make any further choice revelations. Barbra loved it.

The next day was packed with activity in preparation for the Oscars that evening. Valentino's people brought over the dress, which fit perfectly. It was gorgeous. In place of the writing, Valentino had sewn on silver and gray beads that looked like roses. Along with the matching gloves and shoes and the stunning diamond earrings loaned to me by Van Cleef & Arpels, my transformation from jungle rat into princess was almost complete. The hair and makeup people arrived at 11:00. We had to be at the Shrine Civic Auditorium at 3:30 sharp. But when the limo pulled up at 2:15, Harvey announced, "I don't like this limo."

I stared at the mile-long black stretch limo and said, "Huh?"

"The windows are supposed to be tinted," he said. "We need to call the limo company and have them send another car."

"Harvey, it's almost two-thirty on the day of the Oscars. You're crazy to think we'll be able to get another limo in time. It's an hour drive, and the doors close at four." My voice rose at the end, and my gut clenched. *Don't do this, Harvey,* I said silently. *Don't do this.*

But he called the company and had a lengthy negotiation with someone on the other end of the line. I started yelling, "Let's go. I'm going," and I marched my parents out to the limo. Harvey came running out. "It's okay," he said. "We're going to meet them at the corner of . . ."

"No," I said. "We're not. Let's go."

I won that tussle, but it irritated me to no end that Harvey had to be difficult even on the most important day of my career.

Walking the red carpet was a whirlwind of pictures and interviews. Finally, we were seated. We were in the front row—my father, my mother, Marty, me, and Harvey, all in a line. It was thrilling to be so close to the stage. After Madonna performed "Sooner or Later" from *Dick Tracy,* which later won the Oscar for Best Song, I cheered enthusiastically. Madonna was my old buddy from *Goose and Tomtom,* and I just loved her. As she left the stage, Madonna reached through an army of security guards and squeezed my knee. That little squeeze of acknowledgment really tickled me.

During the long commercial breaks, everyone would socialize. It was like a big cocktail party without the drinks. I was having the time of my life, chatting away with people I had only admired from afar. As I was laughing and talking, Harvey suddenly squeezed my arm. "Pay attention to me," he said.

His words and his tone cut right through me. It was my moment, I was being recognized, and he was chiding me. *Pay attention to me, lady. That's what you're supposed to be paying attention to.*

I was irritated, but I locked the feeling away in a back drawer of my mind. Nothing was going to spoil this perfect night.

Being nominated for an Academy Award is one thing; that's a real feather in your cap in itself. Showing up at the Oscar ceremony and then waiting to hear whether you've actually won is a strange experience. It's thrilling and terrifying all at once. I felt beautiful and very proud that night, though, and I'll never forget the experience. No one can ever take that away.

There are two truths I discovered about getting nominated: First, you really do want to win. You want to win! That hope, that desire, is the only thing you're thinking of when you're sitting there in that auditorium. And the second truth is, it really doesn't matter if you lose to somebody else. Either way, you actually do win. You were nominated for an Academy Award! It's all over in an instant, and life goes on. *Dances with Wolves* was the big winner that night, beating out *Goodfellas*. Whoopi Goldberg won Best Supporting

Actress for her performance in *Ghost*. Joe Pesci won for Best Supporting Actor, and our little gang from *Goodfellas* cheered wildly for him.

As we headed off to Penny Marshall's post-Oscar party, a Hollywood reporter called out to me, "Lorraine, how's it going?"

"It's a jungle out there!" I called back. And I really meant it, too.

By midnight, I was out of the gown, wearing sweatpants and a T-shirt I'd borrowed from Penny, and back on the plane to Mexico. My Cinderella moment was over.

It was a tough shoot. Sean and I had to attend "tree school" every Saturday to learn this complicated system of ropes and pulleys that had us bouncing along above the treetops like monkeys. But I wouldn't have minded that so much if the script had given my character half a brain.

Rae Crane was supposed to be a brilliant scientist, but you'd never have known it from the lame dialogue. The original script, the one I'd read and loved, was a lot different from the final script. Other writers had come in, and I didn't like what they had done with my character. But McTiernan was very different from the directors I'd worked with before. I felt that I was nothing more than hired help.

He always wanted something more than I was giving him, but he was unable to communicate what it was. I even took the step of calling in my own acting coach, Penny Allen, to help alleviate the frustration that both John and I felt.

It was agonizingly slow work, and the conditions were pretty awful. The heat, humidity, and stultifying closeness of the jungle drained the energy from all of us. It also played havoc with some of the sensitive equipment, further delaying our progress. It was brutal, and the film's crew wasn't having all that much fun, either. They were out there day in and day out, sometimes all night long, too, trying to do their jobs, just as we were trying to do ours; the conditions we found intolerable, they also found intolerable. Still, we soldiered on together. That's what people do when they work on a film shoot. It's like an instantaneous little family, made up of all of these diverse elements. Everyone has a job to do, the jobs are very different, and all of it has to coalesce into one main thing—being able to shoot the scene. Making a movie.

After a couple of weeks, I began to feel more comfortable. And when I could, I tried to find little ways to have fun and get a laugh. The crew was working so hard, and everyone was so grim and tense most of the time, that I felt duty-bound to try and provide some respite from the sheer grind of it all.

Sometimes I'd invite everyone over to the house on a Saturday night, and we'd eat and drink and dance to Brazilian music. We celebrated Margaux's twelfth birthday during the shoot, so I arranged a party for her. Sean may have come up with the most imaginative gift of all. He gave Margaux a twelve-year-old bottle of Scotch, murmuring in his charming way, "I don't know what little girls like." Margaux still has that bottle of Scotch, and it's one of her most prized mementos. A bottle of twelve-year-old Scotch, given to her on her twelfth birthday by Sean Connery. Who wouldn't love that?

As the shooting dragged on, I was spending less and less time with the girls, and this worried me. I'd brought them so we could be together, but the demands of the shoot kept me on set practically 24/7. I decided they needed some company.

I called my good friend Gail,* whose daughters Susie* and Kathy* were close to the girls. Kathy, twelve, was Margaux's best friend. Susie, fourteen, often babysat for Stella.

Gail was a bright, creative woman, and had been a good friend to me. I felt for her because she had endured a horrific breakup with her husband and was working hard to get back on her feet. I wanted to help lighten her load, and I thought a month's vacation might be just the ticket. Gail and the girls arrived in Catemaco, and I arranged for them all to go to the Mayan ruins for a week while I worked. Margaux and Stella were excited about the trip, and I was relieved that they would be having fun while I trudged through the endless days of shooting. I handed Gail my American Express card and told everyone to have a good time. It was expensive, but I thought it was worth every penny.

I did manage to have some fun. For one thing, I loved teasing Sean. He was the perfect foil. As immensely professional and kind as he was, he tended to be very serious. Nothing wrong with that—this guy had been the sexiest James Bond ever! What I knew

* Not their real names.

for certain about Sean was that, like me, he wasn't so comfortable living and working in the jungle. Like all of us, he was especially nervous about the creepy-crawlies that were everywhere. The scorpions, the tarantulas, the poisonous snakes posed a real danger. It was evil of me, but I couldn't resist playing with his beautiful head.

One day, when we were about to film a scene set at a camp table, I asked one of the prop guys to find me a stick. It had to be just the right length. They knew what I was up to, and I could see the barely suppressed grins spreading on the crew's faces as we started to film the scene.

As Sean was saying his first line, I imperceptibly reached over and lightly brushed the stick along the lower inside of his right leg. There was a barely detectable tightening around Sean's mouth, the slightest twinge, which I'm sure only I noticed. I said my line, then waited for his response. As he began to say his line, I brushed the same spot on his leg again. What a pro. I mean it. This guy was so good—not a sign of anything. He didn't even flinch. I waited, and then slowly moved in for the kill, tickling his leg lightly, higher and higher. Nothing. He finished his line. I moved the stick again. Again, nothing. And then . . . boom! He leapt straight out of his chair, furiously slapping at his leg, as the crew collapsed into helpless laughter. I was laughing so hard I couldn't breathe. When Sean realized the joke, he laughed, too. Believe me, a moment of laughter on a tough set is like a drink of cold water. Carefully boiled first, naturally. Sean was, of course, forgiving and a good sport, and we were able to get through the scene without any more creepy-crawlies.

One reason I teased Sean was to distract myself from how unbelievably attractive he was. What woman could resist him? I was so nervous before our big kissing scene that I was having heart palpitations. I was afraid to kiss Sean Connery. I mean, I wanted to, but I was afraid I'd be hit by lightning or something. I was so nervous, we had to do fifteen takes. And Sean was looking at me like, what's wrong with you?

Sean's a big man, and I didn't have that much experience kissing big men. For some reason, the men in my life had always been short. And big men have a way of towering over you, cocking their heads and swooping down. Every time Sean started to do the move, I'd burst into a giggling fit, like I was thirteen years old. He was getting pissed off, so I pulled myself together, and he finally succeeded in planting his lips on mine. We had to do a number of takes. It was a tough job, but someone had to pucker up.

The shoot finally ended in May 1991. Home sweet home! Back to my house built on a rock. I swear, after making *Medicine Man*, I was thinking I never wanted to do another movie again. I wanted to nest, and the late spring on the Hudson River was pure heaven. I was thirty-seven, going on thirty-eight, and it was time for me to find that peace and stability I craved. I wanted my life to be about family for a change. I wanted it to be about silliness and fun. I wanted my girls to have a normal life, and also have a ball, and wherever that fun was, I wanted to be available to drive them there. To do that, I had to be around, and I was looking forward to being around that summer, just like a regular mom.

Harvey had once asked me if I had that fire in the belly, the burning desire to achieve real artistry as an actor, and I said yes. Yes, I did. I wanted it. But I think we were talking about two different things. I wasn't willing to be consumed by the fire. I didn't have that kind of ambition. You can't have peace and the flame. One is antithetical to the other.

More and more, I was seeing that you can't have that fire in the belly and be a nurturing mother. Children get burned by the fire of an artist's ambitions; it's the opposite of the comforting peace and security they so need. This is something that every actress—and some actors, too, I suspect—with children has to face at one point or another. I faced it in Mexico, and I learned a tremendous lesson. I wasn't willing to sacrifice my children's needs, what was best for them, for my ambitions and desires as a successful film actor.

Ambition can be a positive force, but it can also interfere with your real purpose in life. Too much ambition can cripple you, and, as unbelievable as it seems, too much success can almost be worse than too little. The business will literally eat you alive if you let it. I was determined to find some kind of balance in my life. Let other actresses jump into that fray—it wasn't for me. When I was offered the lead role in *My Cousin Vinny,* I said no; I just couldn't do it. Heather was stunned, but she knew I didn't have the physical or emotional strength to take it on at the time.

My life with Harvey was unraveling at a rapid pace, and I was so unhappy. Our unfinished business sat in the middle of the room like a gargantuan elephant. Once and for all, it would have to be addressed. In spite of all of my pleading and cajoling, Harvey never really believed I would take a stand against his drug use, which was destroying our family. He was wrong, though. I was determined to make a change—I didn't want to wake up in five years and be feeling this same misery, or worse.

The extremes of my life were laughable. Yeah, I was this film star, Lorraine Bracco. The Academy Award nominee. The fabulously sexy Sean Connery's movie love interest, soon to be on screens worldwide. Impressive, huh? Big fucking deal. Behind closed doors, beyond the eye of the camera, my life was a big mess.

It was insane. After all this time, Harvey was still nagging me about Eddie Olmos. "Reality check, Harvey," I'd say. "I've been in the freaking jungle for five months."

He continued to badger me. It was an illness, this obsession, and I'd finally had it. "You want to know the truth?" I screamed one day, sick to death of him. "You really want to know the truth? Yeah, I slept with him. All right? Are you happy, Harvey? Are you satisfied?" I started sobbing. I cried out of hopelessness—I had already been condemned in Harvey's mind, and could never make it right. He would never hear me. He didn't care what I had to say. He didn't even want to know. I disgusted him. The sight of me revolted him. I cried because I had done the one thing I knew would doom us forever: I had told Harvey the truth about Eddie.

For once, Harvey was speechless. He turned and walked out of the room, and he kept walking, out the door. He drove away from the house. And it was over. I was done fighting for this relationship, for the girls or for me.

In the coming weeks, Harvey moved all of his things back to the TriBeCa loft, and the news started to leak out that we'd split up. I knew what Harvey was telling people, because word got back to me. He railed against me, saying I'd betrayed him—I'd wounded him in the one way no man could stand to be wounded.

Harvey always made our split about Eddie. He told people I had left him for another man. I had put a stake through the heart of his machismo. He portrayed my brief infidelity as the destructive source of our woes. To hear Harvey tell it, we were a happy little family brought down by my single act of treason.

If I'd expected our breakup to bring a certain peace and closure to life, I was dead wrong. Once we broke up, he just seemed angrier.

"How do you think Stella will feel when she hears that her mother's sleeping with other men?" he screamed at me.

"Harvey," I said, trying to keep my voice level, appealing to a reason I wasn't sure existed behind his wild brown eyes. "Don't you dare."

"She shouldn't know?" he taunted me.

"We're adults here," I warned.

I didn't even try to explain to him that our breakup was not about Eddie. I hadn't even spoken with Eddie. Harvey could be the injured warrior in public, but I would not allow it in my house.

His rage was flammable. I imagined it spreading through the industry, burning the bridges I had worked to build. I feared Harvey would try to destroy my career.

When I look back on it with more perspective, I realize that things might have gone differently if I'd had more understanding, if I'd had more insight. I wish I had handled everything better with Harvey. I was not thinking clearly. I could have made it easier. I could have been stronger—if not for my own sake, then for the sake of the children.

I wish Dr. Melfi had been around in those days. The analytic therapy she practices is all about getting in touch with the injuries of childhood, and I've learned a tremendous amount through her about the keys that might have unlocked Harvey's struggles. I sensed he'd always felt that his childhood was the source of his lifelong struggle to belong and to fully express himself. But he never saw a way out of that bind. It was as if he were stuck with a burdensome genetic predisposition. But, as Dr. Melfi reminds Tony Soprano, "Genetic predispositions are only that, predispositions." The point is, people can change and they can grow, even if they've had rotten childhoods. They can see the light. They don't have to be stuck in blame and anger.

My attitude was, everyone's got problems. You learn from them, you live with them, you move on. It's a choice you make if you want to have a happy life. Look, was my family sometimes dysfunctional and nutty? Trust me, there were fights, there was screaming, there was yelling, there was pot-throwing. But at the end of the

My parents, Sal and Sheila Bracco, with my brother, Sal, a year before I entered the picture. (BRACCO FAMILY ALBUM)

Mom was thrilled when I arrived in 1954. Now she had her little girl to dress up in frills and lace. (BRACCO FAMILY ALBUM)

Even as a baby, I led with my mouth. Here I am making my point to Mom and Sal. (BRACCO FAMILY ALBUM)

Lizzie was a little doll. Everyone doted on her and called her "the baby," even as she grew up.
(BRACCO FAMILY ALBUM)

For fun, my high school friends and I did mock photo shoots in my backyard. Our props for this clever shot were a mirror and a foot of snow.
(BRACCO FAMILY ALBUM)

"I don't know what it is, but I like it." Wilhelmina saw something special in me.

(BRACCO FAMILY ALBUM)

For Salvador Dalí, I agreed to curl up in a bathtub with another model, draped in jewelry. He didn't mention the five hundred escargots until we were already in the tub.
(PERSONAL COLLECTION)

Proud father Jean Poniatowski at his daughter Marie's 2002 wedding in Morocco. I have had a wonderful lifelong relationship with Jean. (PERSONAL COLLECTION)

Fashion shoot in the middle of traffic. Champs-Elysées, 1976.
(PERSONAL COLLECTION)

Margaux, Daniel, and me on holiday in Arcachon, France.
(PERSONAL COLLECTION)

Mom flew to Paris when Margaux was born in April 1979. (BRACCO FAMILY ALBUM)

Margaux and Stella were adorable at Lizzie's 1987 wedding. (BRACCO FAMILY ALBUM)

Margaux and Stella loved Oscar and Sneden's Landing. (PERSONAL COLLECTION)

Harvey and me in the early TriBeCa days.
(PERSONAL COLLECTION)

Sean Connery and me on the set of *Medicine Man*.
(PERSONAL COLLECTION)

Who could have imagined I'd be doing the red carpet walk at the Oscars as a nominee for Best Supporting Actress, wearing a dress personally made for me by Valentino?
(JIM SMEAL/WIREIMAGE.COM)

Harvey and Stella.
(PERSONAL COLLECTION)

Harvey holds newborn Stella while Margaux awaits new teeth.
(PERSONAL COLLECTION)

Eddie and me, newly married. (PERSONAL COLLECTION)

Margaux's high school graduation in 1997, at which Eddie gave an inspiring speech. From the left, my friends Amy and Matt State, my dad, John Hoving, me, Mico, my mom, Tammy, Eddie, and Brandon, with Stella and Margaux up front. (PERSONAL COLLECTION)

David Chase and me at the Peabody Awards luncheon in New York, on May 22, 2000. *The Sopranos* won for its first season. (© SYGMA/CORBIS)

New York Mayor Michael Bloomberg skipped the Columbus Day Parade when organizers wouldn't let Dominic Chianese and me march with him. But he took us to a fabulous Italian lunch in the Bronx. (© SPENCER PLATT/2002 GETTY IMAGES NEWS)

Stella and me at the HBO Emmys party in 2000, when I was nominated for Best Actress. (PERSONAL COLLECTION)

I joined my sister, Elizabeth, and her husband, Aidan Quinn, for the premiere of his movie *Michael Collins*. They have been married for almost twenty years. (© EVAN AGOSTINI/1996 GETTY IMAGES ENTERTAINMENT)

Margaux and me at her 2001 graduation from NYU. I was so proud, I cried like a baby. (BRACCO FAMILY ALBUM)

The May 2003 USO lunch where my mom produced Glenn Miller's autograph, which she had kept for fifty years. (D'ARLENE STUDIOS, INC.)

Here I am with Sal Jr., Lizzie, and my mom. (BRACCO FAMILY ALBUM)

Celebrating in 1999 with Jimmy Gandolfini. (PERSONAL COLLECTION)

At a 1998 Riverkeeper benefit with Bobby Kennedy and John Hoving. (PERSONAL COLLECTION)

New Year's Eve 2005—me and my girls! (PERSONAL COLLECTION)

day, my parents sat on the couch and they snuggled. I realized that Harvey had it rougher than I did, but it all boiled down to the same choice—keep reliving the disappointments, or get past them.

But I was nowhere near the place where I could realize these truths, much less get Harvey to understand them. Instead, I hurt him. I was stupid and immature and, I guess, a little bit desperate. When I ended it with Harvey, when I spilled the beans, I didn't consider his state of mind—how betrayed he might feel, how angry he might get, and how much he might still want to exert some form of control.

Regrets? I've had a few.

I didn't think I would hurt him that much. I didn't think he really cared in the long run. I was very wrong.

Through lawyers, Harvey and I carved out a legal agreement that I would have custody of Stella, but he would see her frequently, as his schedule permitted. We'd consult each other on every important issue and behave like reasonable, responsible adults. We decided to go together to a highly recommended family therapist, Dr. Harvey Corman, to talk about how we could best assure Stella's well-being. Okay so far.

But during our first meeting with Dr. Corman, it seemed that, in Harvey's mind, the only issue was my infidelity and how to break the news of it to Stella. He appeared too angry and hurt to see that our breakup was a long time in the making, and that the best thing we could do for our daughter was to figure out how to move on peacefully.

Dr. Corman discouraged Harvey from talking to Stella about my affair with Eddie, but Harvey kept insisting that the truth was best for everyone. He brushed off my pleas, accusing me of only wanting to protect myself. There was just no reasoning with him. He often said, "You cheated on your daughters and me," as if they were a package that I'd destroyed.

We had wanted Harvey to maintain his relationship with twelve-year-old Margaux, but that didn't work too well, either. She accompanied Stella on a weekend visitation into the city, and returned vowing to never go back—and she never did. She said that Harvey had spent much of the time screaming, and it had been awful. From then on, little Stella would make the trip alone.

"Mommy, why can't Margaux come with me?" Stella whined each time she got ready to go to Harvey's. It was hard enough for a young child to understand why her daddy didn't live with us anymore. It was very hard to explain to her why Margaux wasn't part of the visitation system. We'd always been *one* family, and while Harvey wasn't Margaux's biological father, he'd been the father figure in her life for the last eight years. But now everything had changed.

In August of 1991 we planned for Stella to spend three weeks with Harvey in L.A., where he was filming a movie. I had hoped it would be a good break for her before she started kindergarten in the fall. Margaux was in Paris visiting her father, and I flew out to

California with Stella. When we arrived at the house he was renting in Malibu, I immediately saw that this wasn't going to be a cordial exchange. Harvey was happy to see Stella, and gave her a huge hug and kiss, but after she'd run off to her room, he started in on me.

"Harvey, keep it down," I said, worried that his yelling would upset Stella. I knew I had to get out of there before he really erupted. Seeing me just brought out the worst in him.

I found Stella, and kissed her. "You have a good time, honey," I said brightly, faking a smile. She was happy to be in California, and for once she didn't seem to notice the tension.

Harvey followed me out to the car, badgering me all the way. He was full of questions, mostly about Eddie.

"I don't want my daughter around that man," he growled.

"Harvey, Stella has never even met Eddie. Cool it, all right?"

I started to get into the car, but Harvey clamped a hand around my arm and yanked me out. He started shaking me, screaming obscenities. I sensed he was spinning out of control. I was afraid he would hit me. I pulled loose, furious, and got back in the car. He yelled after me, "She's staying with me now. You're not getting her back."

I figured it was just talk, but when the end of August came, Harvey called and announced that he was keeping Stella and registering her in school in the city.

"Harvey, she's already registered in Rockland County. You need to bring her back."

"Make me," he shouted, slamming down the phone.

By this point I had hired Manhattan attorney Jack Zulack to

represent me, so I put in a call to him. He talked to Harvey's lawyer and called me back, informing me that Harvey said he wouldn't give Stella back until a court ordered him to.

"That's ridiculous," I said. "We have a legal custody agreement."

Unfortunately, legal agreements are only as good as the willingness of the parties to go along with them. Jack was reluctant to get involved in a lengthy court battle over custody, and so was I. The lawyers were already engaged in a complicated and frustrating effort to reach three separate agreements on custody, child support, and the disposition of our shared property. Harvey seemed determined to make things difficult every step of the way. He finally returned Stella, but only after my lawyer put the pressure on.

I was working overtime to hold everything together. I had to think of the girls.

I needed a strong, reliable nanny, and Ruth Bergman was recommended to me. She had previously worked for Ellen Burstyn. I liked her immediately. Ruthie was a plump, cheerful grandmother, who had a master's degree in early childhood education. She was exactly what we needed, and the girls loved her. If it weren't for Ruthie, I don't know what Margaux would have done. I had been so worried about how to give Margaux what she needed while being tied in knots over Stella's custody. Ruthie was there for Margaux in every way, and I was more grateful for that than I could say.

Seven · Revenge, Served Hot

Do you think making hamburger out of me will make you feel better?

· Dr. Jennifer Melfi

Six-year-old Stella looked at me with wide eyes. "Mommy, are you having sex with Eddie Murphy?" she asked.

"*What?*" I gasped.

"Daddy says you're having sex with Eddie," she replied.

Arghh! Sometimes I just wanted to pull out my hair. Despite our therapist's strong advice, Harvey had told Stella that her mother had been having sex with another man, identified only as "Eddie." Stella had never met Eddie, so she made an assumption and figured he must be talking about Eddie Murphy. How was I supposed to respond?

Stella was very upset, perfectly mirroring her father's high anxiety. Mostly, she was confused. One can only imagine how a little kid processed this kind of information. I suppose that Harvey could not discern what was appropriate for a young child to be exposed to, in spite of Dr. Corman repeatedly telling him not to talk about our conflicts in front of her. Stella seemed like some kind of guinea pig for Harvey's peculiar brand of child rearing. While he was filming *The Bad Lieutenant,* Harvey got Stella hired for a brief scene as one of the lieutenant's kids. He didn't consult me; he never consulted me about what Stella did when she was with him. Harvey later assured me that Stella wasn't exposed to any of the ugliness of *The Bad Lieutenant*—and it was an ugly, violent film, with Harvey playing a bad cop who descended into hell.

The problem was, Harvey felt obligated to *explain* to his tender little daughter just what he thought it meant for a man to descend into hell. He sat Stella down and told her all about his character's horrific behavior—his drugging and sex and godlessness. And what was six-year-old Stella to learn from all of this? How was she supposed to absorb this kind of information?

I was burning up the phone lines to my lawyer. "Jack, what can we do to stop Harvey from talking to Stella about adult matters?" I asked. "Can we call anyone?"

Once again, Jack regretfully gave me a lesson in the law. There was no instant fix. I could take Harvey to court, but that would be an extremely lengthy and expensive process. Any charges I made would be met with countercharges. It was all hearsay; words and intentions could easily be warped. The law is an adversarial system, with a presumption that there are two legitimate sides to every story. Both sides have equal weight until the family court judge makes a decision. In the meantime, Stella would suffer.

"I don't believe it," I said. "You're telling me that a child's father can discuss adult matters with her, and no one will step in to stop it?"

"Believe it," he said grimly. Then his voice softened. "Listen, Lorraine, the courts have limitations, and that's not all bad. We don't want them to have free rein to interfere with families. There's a reason for the process. Unfortunately, people get hurt. At this point, the best thing you can do is to keep detailed records of everything that happens."

I had never been so frustrated in my life. Silly me, I'd always thought if things got too bad, I could take legal action. Instead, I was powerless because Harvey was Stella's father. And even as I demanded action, what really made me sick was that I knew how much it would devastate Stella if she was separated from him. I didn't want that, either. I just wanted him to stop exposing our little girl to the burden of adult problems and worries. It was a completely warped way of thinking.

I asked myself, was Stella safe with Harvey? I thought she was. Of course, I wasn't *there,* but one thing I knew about Harvey was that he wasn't just hanging out with Stella in TriBeCa. He had a full contingent of caretakers, cooks, and housekeepers and, thank God, Vic Argo. This gave me some sense of relief. I didn't have to worry that Harvey would disappear and leave Stella alone. If he was continuing his binges, he was doing it on his own time.

When Harvey introduced another woman into the mix, it got more confusing for Stella. I heard that Harvey's new girlfriend was a twenty-year-old aspiring actress working as a waitress at the Tribeca Grill. Harvey brought her into Stella's life, and Stella was naturally confused by everything that was happening. She started to act out. She was having sleep disturbances, crying jags, and behavioral problems. Sometimes she refused to talk to Harvey when he called. Of course, he blamed me.

In December 1991, there was a little party at Stella's school to celebrate her sixth birthday. I brought cupcakes, and Harvey showed up. We joined the class in singing "Happy Birthday" while Stella beamed and blushed. Harvey left and I stayed to clean up. When I walked out to the parking lot in back of the school, he was standing in the shadows, lying in wait for me. We were all alone and I felt ambushed. Harvey got right up in my face, screaming, "You took my daughter away from me. You robbed me, you fucking cunt."

What was he so pissed off about that day? Who remembers? The harassment was constant. It doesn't matter anymore. What *does* matter is why I allowed him to menace me for so long. Was I so full of guilt and self-loathing that I thought I deserved this?

Harvey was telling anyone who cared to listen that Eddie had moved right in, replaced him in his own home, but that wasn't true. Eddie was in Los Angeles directing *American Me*, a penetrating look at East L.A.'s gang culture. He was completely absorbed in his work. We would often talk on the phone, though, and hearing Eddie's voice was the best kind of therapy for me. But we weren't together the way Harvey thought. I hadn't left him for Eddie, I'd left him because I could no longer tolerate his behavior.

You know, people can and do get past a partner's infidelity. They choose to work it out for the sake of the children. Not Harvey. We'd been apart for only a few months at this point, but it seemed like years. Harvey hadn't been sending me any money for Stella, and he stopped paying his share of the mortgage for Sneden's Landing. He had a "make me" kind of attitude. Our joint counseling with Dr. Corman was a shouting match. Corman's office was the only place I felt safe talking to Harvey. I sometimes wondered, though. Was it good that I was fighting back when it only inflamed him? On the other hand, where would I be if I backed down?

Harvey's rage was scary. He seemed obsessed with getting back all the jewelry he'd ever given to me. He often said, "You deserve nothing." I refused to give it back, telling him that I was keeping it for the girls. It drove him crazy, that jewelry. I have no idea who did it, but the jewelry was later stolen from the house. It seemed a strange coincidence to me.

One evening, when the girls and I returned from a trip, we found the door open. The house had been robbed. Not ransacked, just robbed. All of the jewelry Harvey had given me was gone, but other jewelry, including a Rolex watch, was still there. Most terrifying, on the dining room table was a wig I had worn in *Radio Flyer* with an alarm clock sitting on top. I was terrified. I filed a police report and an insurance claim, but I never found out for sure what happened. The episode left us all deeply shaken, but I think Stella was frightened the most. In time, Margaux and I got over the experience, but it was years before Stella could be alone somewhere in the house, even if I was just in the next room.

During that time, I asked myself whether I would ever break free of Harvey's spell and find my way back to myself. When you're with a man like Harvey, you can easily lose sight of who you are.

The world seems to revolve around men like him, and I'd been spinning in his orbit for so long, I'd lost track of part of my own identity.

Harvey and I had agreed that Stella would join him in New Zealand for ten weeks while he was filming *The Piano,* and I thought it would be a wonderful opportunity for her. I was still telling myself that it was just a matter of time until Harvey calmed down. He was still with his girlfriend, and it seemed impossible that he could stay so mad at me. Maybe he'd calm down and it would blow over.

As 1992 dawned, I was relieved to put 1991 behind me. It had been a jam-packed year that veered from the highest high—Oscar night—to the lowest low—all this crap with Harvey. I'd been mentally and physically exhausted when I returned from shooting *Medicine Man* in May, but I'd never had a chance to rest and catch my breath. The months sped by, filled with lawyer's meetings, therapy sessions, and no work. At the same time, I was intent on being present for my daughters during the difficult transition. I worked hard never to let them see my anger and frustration. I wasn't a child psychologist, but I didn't need a diploma on my wall to understand that kids need to be protected from their parents' rancor. Stella needed to feel it was okay to love and be loyal to her father—that she didn't have to make a choice between us. I never spoke ill of Harvey in front of the children, yet my life was now a full-blown nightmare.

One of the best things I could do for Margaux and Stella was show them that they were part of a big, loving family, and that was easy to do during the holidays. We always spent Christmas at my parents' house on Long Island, and it was a big deal. My parents have always loved Christmas. They usually had the house fully decorated by the first of December, the first house on the block to be lit up, with a star on the roof and blinking reindeer in the yard. The Christmas tree, which occupied a customary place in a corner of the living room, was a lush green beauty and blanketed top to bottom with ornaments and tinsel. Beautifully wrapped packages were piled high underneath. Carols played in an endless loop on the stereo. My mother baked butter cookies and gingerbread men and my favorite, delicious Norwegian cookies she learned to make from a neighbor back in Brooklyn. Just being there was like getting a big warm hug.

The girls and I arrived on Christmas Eve and stayed over. Everyone was trying hard to make things seem normal without Harvey. My parents had always liked Harvey, and while he wasn't one to hang out at sports events with my dad, they got along well. Back in June, when I'd broken the news to my parents that we were splitting, they were very surprised. I knew they'd be totally behind me in my decision, but I didn't give them many details in the summer. I had never been one to confide too much in my parents. I felt it was my responsibility to handle my own problems, and they certainly didn't need to worry about me at this point in their lives. However, when I finally told them about Harvey's drug use, my dad called him a "stupid ass" for throwing his life away.

Lizzie and I had grown closer since she married Aidan and moved to North Jersey. Our houses were only fifteen minutes from each other, and we were back and forth a lot. Lizzie had temporarily stopped working to stay home with their two-year-old daughter. She was very supportive of me during this time. I see now that my reluctance to share my problems with my sister was an ego thing. I was the big sister, the one who was supposed to be in control and have my act together. I liked playing that role, even if it wasn't true.

On Christmas Day 1991, we were all together—Sal and his wife, Jill, and their two daughters, Lizzie and Aidan and their daughter, and me and the girls. At the dinner table my dad made a joke about how our family was getting overrun with women. It was true. Sal, Lizzie, and I all had daughters. There wasn't a boy in sight. "It's not such a bad idea to have more girls in the world," I said. But I have to admit that the sight of my parents and siblings—and their spouses—made me more aware of my loneliness.

After Christmas, Stella left for New Zealand with Harvey, and suddenly things were quiet. You'd have thought I'd enjoy the peace, but by now I was starting to feel a little desperate about work. *Medicine Man* would be released soon, and maybe that would remind people that I was still around. My phone had been deathly silent since Harvey and I split. It was a funny thing. Harvey was working constantly, and I wasn't working at all. I was starting to regret not going for *My Cousin Vinny.*

Ten weeks passed, and when it was time for Stella to return from New Zealand, Harvey announced that she was staying with him. Back to the lawyers. I started to get it that every time Stella went away with Harvey, it would cost me a bundle in legal fees to get her back.

Jack assured me that our original custody agreement was legal and binding, and that Harvey had no right to pull these custody stunts. Silly me. I thought a legal agreement was more than just a piece of paper. It seemed like Harvey thought he could change the rules whenever he wanted to. It was frustrating, and I'll tell you, it opened my eyes to just how little you can control another human being through the legal process.

Harvey didn't live at the house in Sneden's Landing anymore, but his presence was like a looming ghost. The feeling of dread was constant. It all came to a head on an afternoon in May 1992, when he came to the house to pick up Stella. From the moment he walked in, I could feel his rage at me. Within minutes, he was yelling; the next thing I knew, he was holding a chair over his head. He got in my face again, screaming with anger. We were in the hall; he started backing me down the stairs. I was scared out of my mind, but I begged him to get control, to get out of the house, to stop scaring the children. Margaux and Stella hid from this escalating scene in the closet. I feared that Harvey might get violent, so I grabbed the phone and dialed 911.

"The cops are on their way," I said to Harvey when I hung up. The realization seemed to snap him back to reality. He picked up the phone and made a call of his own, then quickly headed for the door. "I gotta get out of here before the cops come," he said, and left.

By the time the cops arrived, Harvey was gone, but that was the breaking point for me. The last straw. Harvey had been pushing me around ever since our separation. I was weak, so I let him. But this was the first time I felt threatened in front of the kids, and I was livid. The thought of Margaux and Stella huddling in the closet in fear made me sick. Harvey had crossed a line this time, and I had to make sure it never happened again. I knew I had to keep Harvey away from me, but I didn't know how. One of the cops gave me papers and suggested I get a restraining order preventing Harvey from coming near me. I took the papers, but I never filed them. I was afraid. I didn't want to do anything to make Harvey angrier. Always, in the back of my mind, was the memory of the gun I'd found on the high shelf of a closet in the TriBeCa loft some years earlier. It was a huge mistake not to get a restraining order. I shouldn't have let my fear stop me.

When one of the cops suggested I contact the Rockland Family Shelter, I thought he was nuts. I was hardly a battered woman. I didn't understand the concept of emotional battery—the fear and menace that were just as destructive as broken bones. I agreed to talk to a counselor at the shelter, mostly to check my perceptions. I was beginning to think I was crazy. Unlike most of the women who sought help there, I had the financial resources to protect myself. But my emotional bank account was empty.

I received one piece of invaluable advice from the shelter's director: I had a right to set boundaries. She suggested I make arrangements for transferring Stella back and forth that didn't involve Harvey coming to the house. The chance of emotional outbursts was too great. Ruthie took over the details of transferring Stella to Harvey's and back, and I refused any further face-to-face meetings. Eventually, I cut off phone contact as well, and my lawyers informed Harvey that for the time being, our communications would be through the lawyers or by fax. It was a matter of self-preservation, and it was very empowering.

It was a tough stance for me to take, and it took me far too long to take it. I guess I didn't think I had a right to my dignity. But once someone said, "Hey, wait, why are you putting up with this?" I saw things in a clearer light. Was I so guilty that I thought I deserved to be belittled and threatened on a daily basis? The answer was no. I was just so sick of his bullshit. And with that, I physically cut Harvey out of my life.

My real relationship with Eddie took a long time to develop. It grew out of the charred embers of my breakup with Harvey—but it was not the cause. Eddie and I were treading very carefully, taking things slowly.

Eddie was extremely concerned about the effects of our relationship on Margaux and Stella. In his mind, the children always came first, and this was evident in his own life. He had two sons with his ex-wife Kaija Keel—Mico, twenty, and Bodie, sixteen—and two adopted sons—Michael, twenty-one, and Brandon, twenty. Eddie had married Kaija in 1971, and over the years they'd grown apart. After she left him, their four sons had continued to live with Eddie, and he had always been the primary parent. They were fine boys. Although Eddie and Kaija's split had been less traumatic than mine and Harvey's, Eddie was sensitive to how difficult separation was for kids. It jolted their sense of security in the world, and the adults had an obligation to minimize the damage and help the kids feel secure. From his mouth to Harvey's ears!

Like a soothing breath of normalcy, Eddie and his sons filled the space that Harvey had vacated. It took more than a year for me to even introduce Eddie to the girls, but as our two families got to know each other, I began to feel a surge of hope. This was the warmth and support I craved. People who laughed and loved, without the murderous rages. With the approach of summer 1992, I was feeling better than I had in a long time.

Best of all, our children were crazy about one another. Eddie's boys had never had sisters, and they doted on Stella, and kidded around with Margaux in that familial way that reminded me of the way my brother and I were growing up. There was laughter and fun and sweetness whenever Eddie and the boys were around. We'd been missing that in our lives.

I relished the feeling of being a big, happy family. It was the first time we had all been together. I had finally been cast in a film, *Scam*, a Showtime made-for-TV movie, which was shooting in Florida and Jamaica that summer. Eddie and I decided to rent a big house at Golden Beach, near Miami, and bring all the kids—his four boys and my two girls. I also invited my friend Gail's two girls, Susie and Kathy, to come along. Gail was in the process of moving and she appreciated having the girls cared for. I brought Ruthie along as a nanny. Ruthie was like a member of my family. She was mature and wise, and the kids adored her.

The beach house was fantastic. Eddie's boys were very nice and very cute, and this big gang of rambunctious kids was having a blast, swimming, sunning, playing guitar, and eating me out of house and home. They all learned to scuba dive. The weather was beautiful, and everyone was having a great time. At the end of July Margaux was scheduled to visit her father in Paris, and she invited Kathy to go with her. Ruth was taking Stella back to New York to be with Harvey. That left Susie. "What do you want to do?" I asked her. "Do you want to go back with Stella?" Susie begged to come with us while we finished the film shoot in Jamaica. I agreed.

Susie sighed blissfully when it was time to leave. "This was the best summer of my life," she told me. "Thank you so much!"

We were all feeling lighter and happier those days. Fun had been reintroduced to our lives, and a real relationship was developing between Eddie and me. This was a stable, adult relationship—not the crazy love of my misguided past. In August, Stella and I flew to Los Angeles to attend an event in Eddie's honor. Harvey called three times in one day demanding to talk to him. He was livid at the thought that Stella might be enjoying her time with Eddie, or coming to view him in a positive light. "She should know what a shithole he is," Harvey growled. When he learned that we took Stella to a Mets/Dodgers game, he became apoplectic. "Eddie deprived me of the opportunity of taking my daughter to her first ball game," he raged. "I wanted to buy my daughter her first hot dog." In the eight years I had known him, Harvey Keitel never once went to a baseball game.

It sounded so juvenile, but it was more than that. Harvey was demonstrating extreme possessiveness—a sense of entitlement that went beyond normal parental love and edged over into mania. Why couldn't he look at his daughter and say, "This is Stella. She is a unique individual"? Why could he not see her as more than an extension of himself or of me? Why couldn't he simply be glad she had fun at a ball game? It was exhausting for Eddie and me, and it made Stella anxious. She loved her father, and she wanted to please him, but she knew that by now, Eddie was a bad word in Daddy's book. She was tormented by the pressure to make a choice.

In the fall of 1992, I persuaded Eddie to become involved in Bill Clinton's presidential campaign. I believed in Clinton and Gore, and I knew Eddie could be influential in the Latino community. Eddie and I threw ourselves into the Clinton campaign. I enjoyed being involved with a man of such substance, someone who cared about what was going on in the rest of the world. He wanted to make a difference, and I admired that.

One day in September, Gail stopped by for coffee. She was excited about a catering business she wanted to start. Gail was very talented, and her food baskets were gorgeous. I had bought many of them myself, and recommended her to others. While we sat, she asked me if I'd be interested in investing in her business. Well, anyone who knows me knows that my first reaction to new possibilities is always to look into them. I never say no. So I told her, "I might. Why don't you send me the papers, and I'll talk to my accountant."

Gail beamed. "That's great, Lorraine. I think this could really be big."

The papers arrived a couple of days later. I was a little taken aback when I saw that Gail wanted me to invest $75,000. Geez! Maybe she thought I was rolling in dough.

"Seventy-five thousand dollars?" Eddie shrieked when I told him about it on the phone that night. "For food baskets?"

"Well, it's more than just food baskets," I said. "Gail is a single mother. I'd like to help her out, if I can. Gail's a good friend."

"Lorraine, get a grip," Eddie said. "That's an outrageous amount of money. If you want to make an investment and help your friend, give her a few thousand bucks. But don't go overboard here."

I decided that Eddie was right. I had to control my impulse to be a big people pleaser. I wrote Gail a nice check, and put it on my desk with the intention of mailing it later. But I was preoccupied with other things and forgot all about it. I'd been cast in Gus Van Sant's movie *Even Cowgirls Get the Blues*, and I had exactly two weeks before I left for filming in Oregon to become a cowgirl. I had never ridden a horse or cracked a whip, and my character had to do both. She also had long monologues in French and English. I could find a place to ride in Rockland County, but where the hell was I supposed to learn whip cracking? I doubted that I could find a trainer for that in New York City.

I was wrong. Gus's production team in New York found the closest thing to a whip trainer on the Lower East Side. They hired an S&M artist to give me lessons. I actually got pretty good at it. My whip-cracking coach kidded that if the cowgirl thing didn't work out, maybe I could find a gig as a dominatrix.

I took Margaux and Stella with me to Oregon. We had a great time on that shoot, riding horses on the set and enjoying the stunning vistas. Eddie's boys came up, and Eddie even filled in as an uncredited musician at a barbecue scene in the movie. Everything worked out smoothly.

Stella discovered horses on that shoot. Everyone on the set was amazed at the ease with which this little girl took to riding. "You're a cowgirl wannabe," one of the crew said to me, laughing. "But Stella is a cowgirl in the making." It was the beginning of what became an enormous passion for her.

Best of all, it looked as if Harvey was getting on with his life. Stella was in good spirits during this period. Before we left for Oregon, she came back from a weekend visit with Harvey bubbling with excitement. "I'm going to have a sister," she announced.

"Oh, really?" I said.

"Daddy said I'm going to have a sister."

It turned out that his girlfriend was pregnant. It sounded like Harvey was enthralled with the idea of playing daddy once again, and I thought that was fine, and it was especially fine if it meant that he would stop obsessing about me.

The impending birth of Stella's baby sister would consume her for weeks before and after Oregon, and she was over the moon when the baby was born. Unfortunately, the story wouldn't have a happy ending. One day, months after the birth, Stella returned from a weekend visit with Harvey dejected, her face somber, her voice shaking. "I don't have a sister anymore," she blurted. Big tears rolled down her cheeks.

I pulled her into my arms. "Honey, tell me. What is it?"

"Daddy says they had a blood test, and it proved Daddy isn't the real daddy, so now the baby can't be my sister anymore."

I didn't know what to say. I was furious that Harvey had not told me so I could have been prepared to help Stella. I just hugged her. How do you explain this sort of thing to a little girl?

"Mommy," she sniffled after a while, "did you have the blood test?"

"What?" I drew back and looked into Stella's concerned face.

"You know, the blood test," she insisted. "To prove you're my real mommy."

I returned from filming *Even Cowgirls Get the Blues* on the Monday night before Thanksgiving, after being away on the shoot in Oregon for six weeks. Eddie was already there, and would be returning to L.A. that evening to spend the holiday with his sons. We were having a nice time together. Margaux and Stella were very relaxed around Eddie. He was great with kids. There was no yelling. It was all easygoing, and it was nice, a slice of real life the way it's supposed to be. It had reached the point where we all missed him when he had to go back to L.A.

Tuesday morning, a phone call from Gail woke me up early. Her voice was tight and angry. "You need to come over here immediately," she said.

"Gail, what's wrong?" I said, alarmed by her tone.

"Just get over here." When a friend calls and they sound like that, you worry.

I hurriedly dressed and drove over to Gail's house. When I walked in the door, her face was contorted into an angry mask. She didn't say a word. She just handed me a letter. It was from her daughter Susie. I scanned the words, not quite comprehending what I was reading. The gist of it was that Susie was accusing Eddie of having touched her sexually when we were in Florida during the past summer. The incident supposedly happened while they were watching TV in the bedroom one night when I was on the set.

I stared at Gail, dumbfounded. She told me that she had contacted a lawyer and was looking into their options. I don't remember what I said.

My head was spinning. I took the letter, stumbled out to my car, and drove home.

When I got home, Eddie and Ruthie were in the kitchen, making coffee. They stopped talking when they saw my face. Eddie told me later that I looked as if someone had died. I handed the letter to Eddie, and a look of shocked disbelief swept over his eyes and face as he read it.

His eyes locked with mine. "This is a shakedown," he said quietly. I had never seen him so angry, but it was a calm, controlled anger. This was deeply disturbing.

Ruthie's anger was more explosive. As she read the letter, she was yelling. "I was there every minute. What is she talking about? I ask you, if the girl was so traumatized, why did she beg—I mean *beg*—to stay with us and go down to Jamaica? She was having the time of her life."

I started rereading the letter. It seemed to me to be too well crafted. I wondered about that, too. It didn't sound like something a fifteen-year-old girl would write. Was it possible, as Eddie suggested, that her mother had put her up to it? Was it possible that Susie had misinterpreted Eddie's warmth for something else? Eddie was a very physical guy, full of affectionate hugs and kisses. But this? This was outrageous.

The whole thing smelled bad. But I was a mother, and the first thing I had to do was protect my daughters. After a shocked Eddie left that night for L.A., I sat down with each of them, and we had a couple of extremely uncomfortable but specific conversations. I was obligated to know if anything had ever happened with my daughters that made them feel in the least bit uncomfortable around Eddie. Had he ever done anything? Anything? No, no, and no.

I called Dr. Corman. "What can I do?" I asked. He suggested that I talk to Susie privately, and question her carefully about her allegations. This was serious business.

Gail agreed to let me speak alone with Susie, and we had a lengthy conversation. I asked her extremely detailed questions, as Dr. Corman had advised, but her answers seemed too vague and they didn't seem credible to me. The fact that she and Eddie were alone in the bedroom watching TV could have been seen as inappropriate, but it was a giant leap from that to sexual misconduct.

I also didn't understand why Susie insisted on staying with us, instead of leaving when the other girls did. If she was so scared, she had an excellent opportunity to leave with Ruth and Stella. But I never sensed a hint of anxiety. She had begged to stay with us. When I pointed that out to her, she had no answer. I felt that something was definitely not kosher.

I was even more shocked when Gail told me she'd had Susie's letter since mid-October.

"And you didn't tell me until almost Thanksgiving?" I asked Gail in horror. "You think Eddie molested your daughter, but you didn't tell me about it immediately, when you knew he was with me and *my* daughters? You contacted a lawyer before telling me?"

She gave the lame excuse of not wanting to bother me while I was filming the movie in Oregon. I was deeply hurt by her betrayal.

Eddie was devastated by the allegation. He had always lived his life with such integrity. He simply could not believe it. Back in Los Angeles, he sat down with the boys and told them about it. It was a very emotional discussion. Bodie started crying. "It's all my fault," he blurted out. "I was hanging out with Susie. Maybe . . ."

"No!" Eddie cut him off. "This is not your fault. Don't ever think that. It's something else. I just don't know what."

For the sake of my daughters and for my own peace of mind, I knew I had to pursue a thorough personal investigation. I had already taken Dr. Corman's advice and spoken with both of my girls as well as Susie. I wasn't willing to rely on anyone else for answers. In the meantime, I felt it would be best if Eddie and I didn't see each other for a while. I decided I had an obligation to explore Eddie's past. I talked to many people who had known and worked with

Eddie, and it became glaringly obvious that this was not a man who would go after a young girl. In Eddie's entire life, there had never been even a hint of an allegation like Susie's—in spite of the fact that Eddie had a houseful of kids, with his son's friends and girlfriends coming and going and playing in the pool. You don't just suddenly become a child molester at the age of forty-five. If that is your tendency, it's not something you can hide. Susie's allegations didn't ring true, and I was torn apart by the thought that Susie might be being used by her mother to get to me and Eddie. I wondered whether Eddie's suspicion could be true, that this was a shakedown of some kind. Remember, Gail was a good friend, or so I thought. Could a good friend betray me?

One morning Gail showed up at my door. She told me that they had spoken with Linda Fairstein, who headed up the sex crimes unit at the Manhattan D.A.'s office, and that she found Susie believable.

"Really." I stared at her coldly.

Gail went on to say that Linda Fairstein couldn't intervene because it wasn't her jurisdiction. If they chose to make a report, it would have to be done in Florida, but they had decided against it.

"Let me get this straight," I said. "You are saying that Eddie is a child molester, but you're just going to drop it? You're just going to let it go?"

She defended the decision, pointing out that it would be expensive and complicated to pursue the matter in Florida.

"Florida?" I said, incredulous. "If someone molested my daughter, I'd go to the fuckin' moon to get them."

Gail replied that they just wanted to forget the whole thing. I later found out from Eddie that Gail was seeking a settlement on the advice of her brother-in-law, a D.A. in the Bronx who was acting as her attorney.

I shrank away from her. "Gail," I said again, "if you believe that Eddie molested your daughter, you have an obligation to pursue this. Don't you care about protecting your daughter—or my daughter, or anybody's daughter, for that matter?"

Her answer? "You have to stop seeing Eddie. He shouldn't be around your girls."

Gail insisted that she was only looking out for me and the girls. She repeated her demand that I never see Eddie again, suggesting that if I didn't do as she said, she might have no choice but to tell Harvey.

Gail knew how terrified I was of Harvey, and how emotionally abusive he had been to me. I was furious. Did she think she could tell me how to live my life, using Harvey as a threat? I would not be pushed around by Gail or by anybody else.

I looked at the woman who had supposedly been my friend, and I saw red. Here was someone else trying to control my life, and I just wouldn't have it.

I opened the front door and motioned for her to leave. I said, "Have a nice life, Gail."

That was it. Our friendship was over. After I "broke up" with Gail, everyone kept telling me they'd always known she had an angle. "I never trusted her," my mother said, and my sister Lizzie agreed. So did Ruth and others who were around my house a lot. "Well, why didn't someone tell me?" I complained. But I probably wouldn't have listened. I was naïve about people. It didn't occur to me that a friend might take advantage of me, and I tended to go overboard—not because I was such a wonderful, generous soul, but because I was willing to help people who needed help. I was beginning to see that only the people I let into my life could hurt me.

My biggest mistake in all of this was that I didn't go to Harvey and tell him immediately myself. But I was petrified of him. Harvey's potential for rage terrified me. His blind hatred of Eddie terrified me. I figured that someday he'd probably find out, maybe in the far distant future. At this particular point in our lives, though, I wasn't about to add any fuel to Harvey's fire.

Eddie heard from Gail's lawyer. They wanted $750,000 to make the whole thing go away. I thought it was despicable. How could you settle for money if you really believed someone had done what they were accusing Eddie of doing? For his part, Eddie had always believed it was a shakedown, and now here we were.

"I've consulted my lawyers," Eddie said. "They are advising me to pay these people something."

"No way." I was outraged. "No way, Eddie."

"Look, Lorraine," he said, "My lawyers are concerned that if this goes public, I'll spend the rest of my life fighting the allegations. It doesn't matter that they're lies. They'll have a life of their own. It will destroy my career and my reputation."

"Won't people say that paying money is like an admission of guilt?"

He sighed wearily. "That's the point, darling. People won't say anything, because it will be over."

I never would have paid them a fucking dollar, and I told Eddie that. "If it were me, they'd have to put a gun to my head and march me to the cash machine," I said. "But you have to do what you have to do. I know you didn't molest this girl, Eddie. I know you don't have that in you. But if you think your lawyers know best, go ahead. End this nightmare."

Eddie ultimately settled, paying them $150,000, and it came with the signed and sealed promise of their eternal silence. It was sleazy, it was wrong, and it was an ordeal, but at least it was finally over.

Or so I thought. It was inevitable that Harvey would find out about what happened with Gail. But it took about a year until I got the dreaded phone call. The damage was done, and that's when my real troubles began.

Harvey moved swiftly through his lawyers to have our custody agreement amended. He had two demands: The first was that Stella not be allowed in the presence of Eddie or his sons. The second was that our nanny, Ruth, be fired, on the grounds that she had not told Harvey about Susie's allegations.

"Can he do that?" I asked Jack Zulack. "Can he have control

over whether or not I have a relationship with Eddie? Can he control who I hire as my nanny?"

Jack told me that, technically, Harvey couldn't impose restrictions on a voluntary custody agreement. The courts weren't in the business of saddling custodial parents with stipulations. "He's not asking for custody," Jack said, "so it's doubtful that any court would amend the agreement as stipulated."

Jack brought in a Rockland County attorney, Sandy Dranoff, to represent me. He also assigned one of his best attorneys, Pamela Sloan, to work on my case. Pam was a brilliant lawyer and a real fighter. I liked her immediately. She wasn't the least bit intimidated by Harvey or his lawyers. And she had confidence in me.

She explained that the allegations against Eddie were peripheral, not directly related to Stella. Furthermore, the allegations had remained just that. No charges had ever been filed against Eddie. No investigation was in motion. Gail had not even filed a child abuse complaint. Essentially, Harvey wanted to try Eddie for molestation without the benefit of evidence or a legitimate legal process.

Pam filed a countermotion, and she also requested a gag order. In light of Harvey's antipathy for Eddie, she and Jack felt it was important that we put a lid on Harvey's ability to spread unsubstantiated rumors that might compromise Eddie's career and reputation.

Harvey's lawyers responded to the request for a gag order with a new flurry of filings, highlighting the public's right to know. I was seething. "The public's right to know?" I bellowed over the phone to Pam. "Explain to me why a man who loves his child would want to see her private life all over the tabloids."

"Don't worry," Pam soothed. "I'm sure the judge will establish a gag order."

And he did. But that didn't really stop Harvey, who relied on a collection of surrogates to keep the whispers alive. Items would appear on Page Six in the *New York Post*. Reporters would call the house trolling for tidbits. Harvey was making a sham of the gag order.

One day my sister Lizzie called me. An actor friend in Los Angeles who'd been working on a movie with Harvey had phoned to ask, "What's the big problem going on with Lorraine and Eddie?" She said that Aidan had heard rumors, too. I hadn't said a word to my family about this, hoping it would go away. I told Lizzie it was nothing.

Some gag order. The news was leaking out—if not directly from Harvey, then from his surrogates. I felt sick, angry, and alone. The whispering campaign was happening behind my back, and all my old friends—or the people I thought were my friends—were silent. No one called me up and commiserated. No one offered support, or let me know they were on my side. How had I grown so isolated? Where were my friends now that I really needed them? That's when I realized that for almost a year I had been withdrawing, not confiding in anyone, not letting people into my house. Partly, it was due to my suspicion of others and my concern over public disclosure. But mostly it was shame and fear. Everything was spiraling out of my control, and I closed myself off and waited for the looming D-day when I would face Harvey in court.

Eight · Justice, Schmustice

Rage is a big, loud, flaming self-distraction from feelings that are even more frightening.
· Dr. Jennifer Melfi

JANUARY 1994

The truth, the whole truth, and nothing but the truth, so help me God. That's what the courts are for, right? Yeah. In your dreams. Once Harvey rode into town as the avenging father and launched a fight over the conditions of Stella's custody, all hope for truth and justice flew out the window.

Harvey contended that Stella was at risk because she was living with a child molester. It didn't matter that no charges had ever been filed against Eddie, no criminal court had been involved, no investigation had taken place. It was his chance for revenge.

It was a happy day, I thought bitterly, when Harvey heard about the allegations against Eddie. It seemed to me that Harvey should have wanted to know if the allegations had any basis in fact—if they were reasonable, given Eddie's sterling reputation and character. But I didn't think Harvey was interested in hearing another side to the story.

Women who have fought custody battles are in a special club, and now I was a member. If you've been through the whole thing with the lawyers and the family courts, the justice system will never be the same to you. If you don't have enough money to fight for your children, if you don't have the financial means for a protracted legal battle, you're in a world of trouble. You end up signing your house over to attorneys so you can keep fighting to hang on to your children. You end up with your life in a shambles. How does that make sense? We made some lawyers very wealthy. We literally spent millions of dollars fighting for custody of Stella. Sadly, it's easy to cripple someone in court if they don't have money or the stamina to go on.

Let me say here that I believe family courts have an important purpose. I've been involved in the Rockland Family Shelter for many years, and I've seen the results of women and children who are victimized and abused, physically, sexually, and emotionally. I admire the work of Safe at Home, the foundation started by Yankees manager Joe Torre. Joe courageously went public with the story of the abuse he suffered as a child, and he decided to commit himself to helping other children escape that nightmare. I believe it is absolutely essential that we protect all children from abuse, and the family courts are one of the means we have to do that—to legally separate children from parents who are causing them harm. Unfortunately, the family court system doesn't always work so well, and this is especially true when a parent is willing and able to jam up the works with expensive lawyers who keep the fight going, beyond any consideration of what is best for the child.

I came to believe that the family court system was a despicable way to deal with most custody cases. I approved of mediators, psychiatrists, therapists—but did this really belong in court? Did it belong in the public arena? It was all about psycho parents and innocent children.

The standard in family court is "the best interests of the child." But how do you determine that? How do you decide who is a better parent? How do you find the truth when facts are in dispute? Custody battles are often about everything *but* what is best for the children. They become an ugly game, fed by the desire to wound. Jack Zulack once told me he could look at the stacks of case files on his desk, and he could tell you who the psychos were by the amount of paper they filed with the court. He said he'd never seen a pile as high as Harvey's.

With the custody case scheduled for a hearing in Rockland County Family Court in early 1994, Sandy and Pam questioned me closely about my relationship with Eddie.

"Are you considering marriage?" Sandy asked.

I shrugged. "We've talked about it. It's what Eddie wants. And the kids are always bugging us to get married."

"And you?"

I sighed. "Oh, I don't know. I love Eddie, but there's so much to deal with right now."

Sandy put it to me straight. "If you're planning to get married at some point, I'd advise you to do it now," he said. "It will improve your position with the court. It will be much easier to fight this case as a stable family unit."

Whatever it takes, I thought. I called Eddie. "Hey, you wanna get married?" I asked.

"Are you serious?" He was shocked. He'd asked me to marry him several times, and I'd always said I didn't want to get married.

"Eddie," I said solemnly, "we love each other, the kids are happy. Let's be a family and fight this thing together."

The wedding took place January 28, 1994, in a small ceremony in New York City, with our six children in attendance. Eddie's boys and my girls were all delighted. It was frigid outside, but the warmth in that room gave me hope that we could survive this ordeal. In the photograph, featured in the Styles section of the *New York Times,* we are beaming with happiness.

Two weeks after the wedding, Eddie was back in Los Angeles, and I was heading for Toronto for a month to film the television movie *Getting Gotti*. I played the lead as Diane Giacalone, who was—get this—a lawyer! I couldn't get away from the long arm of the law those days. Specifically, Diane Giacalone was the assistant U.S. attorney who first tried John Gotti, and I enjoyed playing the role. I was able to summon up all of the righteous indignation brewing inside me. I also felt I could learn a lesson in patience from my character. She worked for years to build her case against the Teflon Don.

Margaux and Stella were able to visit me during the shoot, and we took a little time to explore Toronto, a beautiful city. (It's not

Brooklyn, of course. That was one of my pet peeves about the film industry—the number of projects that were being shipped off to Canada because it was cheaper. Whatever happened to "Buy American?")

Although we were newlyweds, Eddie and I wouldn't see each other for several months. Our marriage was long distance, and it always would be. Harvey was convinced I had plans to move to California with the children, but I had no such plans. I had promised Harvey in our original custody agreement that I would not move out of state before Stella was fourteen, and I kept my promises. Besides, California wasn't my kind of place. I never felt very comfortable there. I was a New Yawker through and through. I returned to Sneden's Landing and prepared for the opening of the custody case in April.

We showed up at the Rockland County Family Court, in New City, where our case was being heard by Judge Bernard Stanger, an elderly, dour-faced judge. Harvey and his lawyers sat on one side, and I sat with my lawyers on the opposite side. The tension in the room was choking. I felt as glum as the judge's face.

Harvey's rage had a volcanic force, and he spewed ash and molten lava all over the courtroom in his attempt to convince the judge that he was Mr. Mom. It was his darkest role to date. He had actually convinced himself that Stella would be better off in his custody. As he would arrogantly—and melodramatically—write in the court papers:

> I entered into the custody agreement most reluctantly, as I myself wanted custody of Stella, but concluded like the true mother of the baby that King Solomon threatened to cut in half, that a bitter court battle over Stella's custody was not in our child's best interest.

Give me a break.

That was Harvey through and through, building himself up into some epic character. Well, as far as I was concerned, the court case should have been over the minute my lawyer asked Harvey what grade Stella was in at school. He didn't know. He didn't even have the foggiest idea. I wanted to jump up and shout, "Your Honor, I rest my case." Obviously, this was a father who wasn't that involved in his daughter's life. But no. The judge ignored the obvious disconnect. He allowed the case to go on. He did, however, appoint a law guardian to represent Stella's interests. This is commonly done in custody cases, and in theory it's a good idea, but as I looked at the man who would ultimately hold Stella's fate in his hands, I wondered if I could trust him. Did he have hidden biases and attitudes that would make him more inclined to see things from Harvey's perspective? I didn't know, and I couldn't control it.

Susie's allegation against Eddie was the sum total of Harvey's case. It was the reason we were there. Harvey wasn't fighting me because he said I was a bad mother, or because Stella was harmed or neglected in my care. It was all about Eddie. Based upon Susie's unsubstantiated allegations, Harvey claimed that Stella was at risk of being molested as long as Eddie was in my house. Susie had to submit to questioning, and my heart ached for her, because no young girl should be subjected to that kind of interrogation. I wondered, listening to Susie's testimony, how anyone expected the truth to come out in Rockland County Family Court, when no investigation had been conducted in Florida. It seemed like a sham to me—and very, very sad.

Meanwhile, Harvey was busy trying the case outside of the courtroom. He seemed to prefer to air his dirty laundry in the press and in public, holding court in his favorite restaurants, surrounded by his cadre of supporters, where his voice could be heard railing against Eddie. In contrast, Eddie was the picture of control, even though it was his life and sterling reputation that were being dragged through the mud. "I have never, ever, molested or abused anyone," my husband told the court.

"Harvey doesn't care whether any of this is true," Eddie told me privately. "This is a vendetta."

Sadly, I had to agree.

When Judge Stanger found Harvey in contempt of court for violating the gag order, it didn't even matter. The damage had already been done. The word was already out.

One weekend during the first year of the custody fight, while Stella was in the city with Harvey, I received a message on my answering machine. It was my little girl's voice, but the words shocked me so much that I had to sit down and catch my breath.

> Hi, Mom. This is a joke. Don't get upset. Dad taught me . . . You bitch. You fucking bastard. Bye, Mom. You fucking bastard. Fuck you. Bye-bye.

I started crying. This was so wrong. I wanted to call 911 and have my daughter rescued that minute. Instead, I called my lawyer, who instructed me to remove the tape from the machine and hold on to it. Then I called Harvey. I was shaking. Lucky for him, he wasn't home. I slammed down the phone without leaving a message.

Harvey would later try to laugh off the entire incident, saying it was just a joke. He said that when he was little, older kids used to give him money to call their parents and say swear words. He thought it was funny. Ha-ha-ha. I didn't think it was funny, and I didn't think the court would think so either.

"Play this tape for the judge," I demanded, when I handed it over to Pam. "Something has to be done."

"Don't worry," she soothed. "The tape will be a part of the record."

"What does that mean, part of the record?" I asked. "This should be played for the judge—now!"

Pam gave me another lecture about "the process." She was trying to reassure me that in the long run, we had more than enough evidence to win the case, but I wanted action in the short run, and I wasn't going to get it.

My guilt and sorrow were enormous for the toll this was taking on Stella, who was now seven. As the custody fight wore on, her visitations with Harvey were becoming more and more difficult. Stella was not being cooperative. In the hours before the car service was scheduled to arrive, she'd have a tantrum, tearing up her room. "I won't go, I won't go," she'd scream.

"Come on, honey," I'd cajole. And she'd sob, "I don't want to go there."

After this happened a couple of times, I called Harvey. "You know what?" I said hotly. "I can do a lot of things, but I cannot push this child out the door. I cannot carry her to the car. Tell me, Harvey, what's going on there that she's so hysterical about visiting?"

Later, we found out why Stella was reacting as she did. Harvey had taken to interrogating her. He did everything but put her in a room with a bare light bulb dangling over her head. *"Where's Eddie? What's your mother doing? Eddie's a bad man."* When I finally found out what had been going on, it made me sick.

Whatever good feelings I had ever had for Harvey were being squeezed out of me, drop by drop, because of what he did to our daughter. He wanted to get back at me? Okay, I could take that. But to hurt Stella? It was unconscionable.

My motherhood was on the line. It was surreal that during the first year of the custody fight, I was filming *Basketball Diaries*, a movie where the mother's choices were so torturous it bruised my soul to play her. The movie was based on the true story of Jim Carroll, a young man who descends into the nightmarish world of heroin addiction. Leonardo DiCaprio played Jim, and I played his mother.

For me, the most poignant scene in the movie comes toward the end, when Jim stumbles to his mother's house, desperate for money to feed his habit. He pounds on the door, calling out to her, telling her he needs money, that it's not what she thinks, he won't use it for drugs. She opens the door slightly, keeping the chain on. He pleads with her, and she is dying inside.

"Mom, will you hold my hand," he cries, and she does, reaching through the narrow opening. Then she releases his hand and pushes the door shut.

She's his *mother*—oh, I felt that so deeply playing the role. She wanted to give him money, to hold him, to make him better, but she knew he was beyond her help. It was so hard to fathom—that your child could need you desperately, and you would have to *choose* to turn away.

Weeping, she picked up the phone and called 911, as her son screamed, "You don't know what you're fucking doing to me. I'm in pain. How can you do that to your son? You bitch. You fuckin' bitch."

Every time I read the script and rehearsed the scene, I longed for it to have a different ending—and that's what I think the audience wanted, too. Not for her to give him money so he could continue to kill himself, but for her to heal him, help him, protect him. She was his mother.

Playing that role took a lot out of me. The irony was that I was becoming something of an expert at playing lousy mothers onscreen. In 1992 I'd played the mother in *Radio Flyer*, Richard Donner's film about two boys who are terrorized by their stepfather while their oblivious mother works two jobs to keep the family afloat. That was also an emotionally draining role. I'd beg Richard to allow my character some protective spirit. "She should know what's happening with her sons," I'd insist. "She should try to protect them." But it wasn't in the script.

It was beginning to feel like directors were thinking, "If you need a lousy mother, call Lorraine." I knew that I had to believe in myself in order to fight for my children, but I was reminded of how fragile our connections are with the ones we love most, how even when we do our very best, no parent is perfect. Mothers aren't omnipotent. We're all flawed, and we can't always control what happens to our children.

It was a sobering realization. But I was going to fight for my children, and I wouldn't let anybody get in my way.

Though I was hoping to have the custody battle over by Christmas so we could enjoy the holiday, Pam called me in November with bad news. "Judge Sanger died," she said.

"He died?" I repeated. "Geez, that's terrible." The truth was, the old judge hadn't looked so sharp lately. I felt bad for him, but it didn't immediately occur to me that his death would have such a big impact on the case.

"Lorraine, brace yourself," Pam said quietly.

"What? What's wrong?"

"I'm afraid we have to start the case over before a new judge," she said.

"Pam," I said urgently, "that's impossible. We can't go through any more of this. Please, someone has to talk sense to Harvey—beg him to stop."

I was desperately afraid for Stella, who was growing more withdrawn and weepy. I couldn't bear to see how her bright, imaginative spirit had been ground down, and I feared for her mental and emotional health. She had started seeing a wonderful child psychologist, a compassionate and caring woman Stella seemed to like. But Harvey had made even that difficult. He barraged the therapist with angry phone calls, insisting that if she was doing her job, she'd be telling Stella about Eddie's supposed molestation. Stella's therapist tried to explain that it wasn't appropriate—and, in fact, the real issue was Stella's sense of confused loyalty. Harvey didn't agree. He contended that honesty was the best policy, no matter what.

My own strength was draining out of me, and I wasn't sure I had enough stamina to go on. One particularly low day, I said to Pam, "I don't know. Maybe Stella should live with Harvey. At least the fighting would stop."

Pam nearly slapped me upside the head. "No," she said. "I don't care how bad you feel. This isn't about you. It's about protecting your child."

I'd forgotten for a moment. She was right. I had to keep going.

Nine · Nuclear Meltdown

What happens to a tree that's rotted out?
· Dr. Jennifer Melfi

JANUARY 1995

One night, Stella curled up beside me on the couch and clung to me. In a tiny voice, she whispered, "Fight for me, Mommy. Fight for me."

"Don't worry," I said, stroking her hair. But I couldn't say those words with full confidence. Harvey's court papers may have sounded like a high-minded defense of the nuclear family, which he claimed I had destroyed, but Harvey was the one who was going nuclear. He refused to listen to reason or adopt a perspective that would move the case to a resolution. I felt the court had allowed him remarkable leeway, and now that we were back at square one, who knew what to expect? Meanwhile, he continued to play games. And this had been going on for years.

One day when Stella was about nine, she arrived home from a visit to Harvey's carrying a big, long package. Eddie was in town, and we were relaxing in the living room when she came in with a smile on her face. "Look, Eddie," she said. "My daddy sent you a present." She looked hopefully from Eddie to me. "See, Daddy's nice," she said. Her face was glowing. She was so excited that Harvey had sent Eddie a present.

With some trepidation, Eddie opened the box and we peered inside. It was a machete, with a large curved steel blade that must have been two feet long. Stella had carried it home.

"Daddy said you'll know what to do with it because you're Mexican," Stella said happily.

Eddie didn't let on that he was shocked. He thanked Stella effusively, and never let her know how he really felt. Only after she had left the room did he let his anger show. He was horrified and heartsick. He stared into the box with an expression that said, *What the hell am I doing with these people?*

The stress got to all of us. But what really pushed me over the edge was when Stella started to get sick. I couldn't have imagined that the ultimate casualty of this ugly battle would be Stella's health.

On January 20, I was at the Sundance Festival for the premiere of *Basketball Diaries* when I received a call from Ruth. "Stella's very sick," she said urgently, and I could tell by her tone that this wasn't just a case of the sniffles. "She's burning up. I called your mother. She's on her way over. If we can't get the fever down, we'll take her to the emergency room."

"I'll be on the next plane," I said, throwing clothes into my suitcase. All thoughts of the premiere disappeared. I caught the last flight out of Utah and was home the following morning. I walked into the house to find my mother, my sister, Margaux, and Ruth all hovering around Stella's bed.

"The fever is down," my mother said with relief. "The doctor thinks it might just be a bug, but this little one gave us a scare."

I sat down on the bed next to Stella, and kissed her pale face. She clung to me, and her teeth started to chatter. "I'm cold, Mommy," she said weakly. I asked Margaux to get my white silk comforter and I snuggled underneath it with Stella until she fell asleep.

It seemed the worst was over, but the next day Stella's fever spiked again. She had been asleep when I heard a pitiful mew, wounded and sickly, coming from her room. I found her half asleep, tossing and turning, her bedcovers a jumbled knot. When I laid my hand on her forehead, she felt hot. She looked at me through bleary eyes. "It hurts," she croaked. I tried whatever I could to bring her fever down, but every movement made her scream out. "The sheet hurts!" she cried.

Finally, I called Harvey, and for once we were on the same team. He behaved in a decent, adult manner. We decided to bring Stella to a doctor in New York City, and he immediately sent her to Mount Sinai Medical Center, where she was admitted. I stayed by her side twenty-four hours a day. At one point, Stella's fever was so high—a dangerous 107 degrees—that the nurse thought the thermometer was broken.

"What do you think is wrong with her?" I asked, my eyes burning, my voice hoarse with exhaustion and dread. I stayed in a chair near Stella's bed for the rest of the night, dozing off, waking only when another nurse or technician would come by to check on Stella's temperature, or take yet another blood sample.

I kept being told they wouldn't know until they had run all of the tests. Stella's official diagnosis was "a fever of unknown origin"—and there we were. I wanted to be told something I didn't already know. It was a process of elimination. Was it a flu bug? Some horrible blood disease? God forbid it was some kind of cancer, like a leukemia. An infection? A weird, unknown parasite? No one knew. And that was without a doubt the worst part. Because how do you treat something, how do you make someone better, if you don't know what to treat? I kept a vigil by my fevered little girl's bed, barely containing the hysteria that was rising up in me. Her condition seemed to grow worse with each passing day. Her legs, shoulders, and back were stiff, and her body was covered with a rash. It had become increasingly painful for her to move. She told me that the blankets hurt, eating hurt, swallowing hurt. Everything hurt.

I felt completely helpless. Not knowing what was wrong with Stella was a nightmare. When you know the enemy, you can at least begin to plan a counterattack. But we knew nothing, and each day we knew more and more of nothing. Test after test came back with no conclusive result. I pleaded with the doctors to give me information, but I could see what was happening. Because they'd already run so many tests and still remained baffled and were unable to offer a definitive diagnosis, they had decided to clam up. They were reluctant to say anything that might spark my already horrific imaginings with medically fueled nightmarish scenarios.

Everyone came running when they heard, and I was relieved and grateful to have the support. My parents were there. Eddie flew in from L.A. Harvey paced the hospital corridors, agonizing. Through it all, Margaux was a gem, though she was terrified to see her sister so sick. She was a truly caring big sister, and my greatest ally. It somehow brought the three of us even closer than we'd already been, and we were already close. As much as I appreciated all of the support, though, what I really wanted was answers.

Stella's illness had temporarily sucked all of the oxygen out of our animosity. Harvey and I were actually able to sit in a room and talk to the doctors like concerned parents. We presented a united front.

The doctors thought it was important to explore every nook and cranny of our family medical histories in order to rule out hereditary factors. We answered a thousand questions about our families, but when we came to Harvey's father, he became uncomfortable, and said to me privately that he knew his father was not his biological father.

I thought it might be part of the puzzle that made Harvey who he was. He had experienced things in his childhood that I couldn't imagine, and perhaps he'd carried his lack of trust into adulthood. I wondered if, deep down, Harvey believed that all women were unfaithful. I wondered if my unfaithfulness had traumatized him so much because it confirmed his fears that the women he loved would betray him. I wondered what it did to him to discover that his girlfriend was carrying another man's baby. I have to say, I felt sorry for Harvey that day.

When the diagnosis of Stella's condition finally came, it left me completely baffled.

Through a process of elimination, the determination was that Stella had become afflicted with something called systemic juvenile rheumatoid arthritis.

Arthritis? I didn't understand. How could a healthy nine-year-old girl suddenly have arthritis?

And that began my education in the mysteries of autoimmune disease. Rheumatoid arthritis, I learned, is a severe and chronic inflammation of the joints. It happens when a person's immune system goes into overdrive. It's sometimes triggered by an underlying infection.

The way the doctor explained it to us, it's an extreme overreaction by the body. "If you think of the immune system as the body's military, whose job it is to hunt down and fight infections, this would be like the army destroying an entire city to hunt down one terrorist," he said. "They may get the terrorist, but they leave the city destroyed and in flames. That's what's happening here. The immune system is overreacting and trying to mow down everything in its path. It's causing this systemic inflammation in the membranes surrounding the joints, causing severe pain."

He was less clear about what caused an autoimmune disease. What would make Stella's immune system start acting crazy like that? But he did ask if Stella had been under any particular stress recently.

Oh, boy. "You might say that she's been unusually stressed," I replied. "Are you telling me that stress can cause this?"

He knew what was going on in our lives, and he stopped short of saying that stress had caused Stella's illness. But he did say, "The best thing you can do for Stella is to reduce the amount of stress in her life."

I wholeheartedly agreed. Meanwhile, the doctor tried every type of anti-inflammatory drug on the market, to very little avail. He finally began a course of steroids, which had miserable side effects but worked. Slowly, Stella's appetite returned, the fever abated, and the pain eased. Over the next few months, she started to get better.

"The good news," her doctor reassured me, "is that systemic juvenile rheumatoid arthritis often doesn't continue into adulthood. But this has been a severe attack."

He was right, but I didn't mind at all. The important thing was she was going to get better. Stella recovered, but it took her a long time to get her strength and her spirit back.

The doctor had recommended physical therapy to loosen up Stella's stiff joints. I wanted to find something that would be fun for her—that wouldn't feel so much like therapy. I longed to see that old sparkle back in her eyes. Knowing how much she loved horses, I suggested that learning to ride and groom horses would be great physical therapy because she'd want to do it. For once, Harvey agreed with me about something, and he even offered to pay for it. I signed Stella up at a nearby horse farm, and she couldn't wait to get to her riding lessons. She was happy to spend hours every week working in the barn and riding. She developed an incredible passion for horses that was amazing to watch. It filled her life, shutting out the sadness and worry that had consumed her during the court fights. Finally, this was something that belonged to her. No one could take that away. She thrived.

One day Stella arrived home from the barn carrying a little black ball of fluff. "This is Crack," she announced. The kitten was strange-looking. He had blazing eyes, and when you petted him, big tufts of fur came off in your hands. Margaux looked at him doubtfully. "There's something wrong with that cat," she said.

Crack was a natural mouser. He happily stalked and killed every last mouse within two acres. Every time he killed a mouse, he'd drag it to the door and let out a throaty yowl of fierce hunter pride, and we'd come running, oohing and aahing with praise for our great protector. Unfortunately, once Crack had decimated the mouse population, he started in on the previously happy chipmunks and bunnies, and this was more problematic. One day we found Crack yowling at the door with yet another gift, only this time it was the eviscerated remains of a baby bunny rabbit. Stella loved animals, and baby bunnies were so cute. She cried for hours. She had nightmares about that bunny. It was a hard lesson for her. Nature is wonderful, of course; it can also be unforgiving and cruel. Over time, having proved his prowess as the great hunter, Crack grew to be a lazy ball of fur, and he stopped chasing everything but his dinner bowl.

Stella had always been a great animal lover. We soon had two big, lazy Labs, and then Stella fell in love with a spunky little Jack Russell terrier she saw at a horse show. Stella called him Chandler, after Matthew Perry's character on *Friends*.

Margaux made a terrific observation. "Chandler has a Napoleon complex. He thinks he's a big dog."

But he made us laugh, and it felt good. As she was learning to ride, Stella spent hours outside teaching the dogs to jump over barriers in the driveway. To this day, Chandler is an impressive jumper.

Harvey didn't think a dog's life was so amusing. Now, when he sent faxes scheduling Stella's visits, he included big block letters and exclamation points: "No dogs!" But Stella stubbornly refused to be separated from her menagerie; sometimes Harvey would have to suck it up and accept an extra four-legged visitor or two. In a funny way, the dogs gave Stella a semblance of power that she had never felt before, a bargaining chip. "Love me, love my dogs," she proclaimed. Her spirit was back.

I consciously set about making our home a happy, stable environment. I didn't want my daughters' waking moments to be dominated by worries about the custody trial, or by Harvey's dark anger. Laughter was our medicine, and I served it daily. In the morning before breakfast, I'd throw open my closet and let Margaux and Stella choose their favorite high heels to wear to breakfast. As they toddled down the stairs, giggling, I reveled in the sounds of normal girls having fun. I kept reminding myself that this was what life was all about.

While Stella fought her way back to health, we began Custody Battle, Take Two, before a new family court judge, in early 1995. Judge Elaine Slobod was a no-nonsense woman, with a thick crown of dark hair and a stern but thoughtful disposition. By the time she came into the case, the documents numbered in the thousands of pages. In addition to rehearing all of the testimony, she would have to plow through a staggering historical record. It would take another year and a half before she ruled.

Time after time, I went to court, always on my own. My only accompaniment during those difficult hearings was the necklace of Tibetan turquoise beads that Stella had made for me. It was my talisman. I never went to court without it. Still, the endless hearings were damaging to my soul.

"Stella will be grown up, married, and have kids of her own before this case is settled," I grumbled to Pam. Pam ignored my griping and told me that Slobod was a very good judge—very thorough. She also reminded me that Stella's law guardian, who had been involved since the beginning, would be writing a report, and his view would carry great weight. "He speaks for Stella," Pam said. "His motivations are seen by the court as pure."

We received a copy of the law guardian's report in the summer. Only four pages long, it was succinct and sharply worded:

> Petitioner . . . makes an emotional appeal to this Court by convicting Edward Olmos of sexual abuse and placing him within the purview of what is now known as Megan's Law . . .
>
> . . . these laws provide the community with information on convicted sex offenders, and thus are totally inapplica-

> ble in this case . . . Petitioner's brief is a blatant attempt to deflect the true focus of this case.
>
> . . . a determination now that Harvey Keitel would be the appropriate custodial parent would be improper, given the evidence presented to this Court, his lack of parenting skills, his exposure of Stella to age-inappropriate circumstances, and his unique philosophy on child rearing . . .

"It's all good," Pam said. When Judge Slobod's ruling came down on September 5, 1996, she followed the law guardian's recommendation, but added plenty of commentary of her own. The ruling was in our favor. I would retain custody of Stella. For the first time in three years, I felt as if I could breathe.

Judge Slobod's ruling was lengthy. While she recognized that Harvey was devoted to Stella, she was clearly concerned with the stability of his home environment. For the first time, he was being held accountable for his obsessions. The judge wrote:

> Unquestionably loving and giving, some of his conduct with or involving his daughter not only with respect to the husband, but in his general perception of what is in the best interests of a young daughter, have been unquestionably inappropriate. The record will reflect such things as encouraging his young daughter to use vulgar and gross language towards her mother; discussing sexual matters blatantly inappropriate for a young child; and prematurely cre-

ating false expectations in this young girl regarding the anticipated birth of a baby half-sister. These and the near obsessive badgering regarding the mother's husband do not project the image of a father with the ability to establish and maintain a healthy environment for a pre-teenage child.

However, Judge Slobod also imposed some conditions that I thought were absurd. The most devastating was her ruling that neither Eddie nor his sons could be alone with Stella. That was pretty tough. How do you arrange that when you're living in a house as a family? The answer is, you work it out. Thank God for Ruthie. But we'd never lived together as a family, anyway, and I wondered if we ever would. Eddie and I were together with the kids only sporadically. Our long-distance marriage was becoming increasingly distant. I didn't know how much this had to do with the court case, but there was no question that the allegations against Eddie, being repeated over and over in court and—thanks to Harvey—in the press, had taken a toll on what we were trying to build together. You can't have a full relationship with a man if the first guy won't leave the room. Sometimes it felt as if Harvey loomed over us.

Judge Slobod also ruled that Eddie was required to seek therapy regarding sexual molestation. What was that about? *Just in case?* How humiliating, considering that Susie's allegations had never been fully investigated. Eddie was willing, in part because he believed a psychiatrist would clear him of the stain that the false charges had brought. But again, without the allegations being proven or explored on their own in a legitimate setting, the family court decided to treat them as if they might be true. The first psychiatrist recommended by the court threw up his hands after one session with Eddie. "I can't do this," he said. "I don't understand the task here." How do you treat a man who is not a molester for being a molester?

Judge Slobod was clearly frustrated by Harvey's and my inability to communicate, and she sternly admonished us to do better in that regard. Harvey's side tried to make it my fault. "She refuses to give him her personal phone number!" they harrumphed. "He wants to have lunch with her and Stella to talk about school, and she says no." "She doesn't call him when she hires a nanny." On and on they went. I had two responses. First, Harvey did not have my phone number because I would not subject myself to his abuse. A phone call with Harvey was a day-killer—it didn't matter what the topic, there were always threats and vulgarities. I regretted not having pursued that restraining order in 1992. If I had, maybe Judge Slobod would have understood how battered I felt by my contact with Harvey. But there was a larger issue, too, that went to the definition of custody itself. When the custody agreement stipulated that I would inform and consult with Harvey on important decisions related to Stella, I did not believe it meant that he could tie me up in knots every day of my life. I didn't have to get his permission to hire a housekeeper, or to take her to visit friends, or to schedule a sleepover. He always wanted to know exactly who was watching Stella when I was not home. Some days it felt like he was living there, the flurry of faxes was so constant.

The whole experience and the court's ruling concerning Eddie were exhausting to our young marriage. How do you survive that as a couple? Any hope we had of normalcy, let alone happiness, was damaged. Eddie began working more and more in L.A., and I have to say it was a kindness. If he wasn't living in the house, at least Harvey couldn't interrogate Stella about whether she'd been alone with him in a room.

Harvey, of course, appealed the custody decision, and back to court we went, over and over again. I couldn't get Harvey out of my life, or out of Eddie's life. There was never any closure. Harvey took me to court for everything—and I mean everything. I believed that the constant legal filings were Harvey's way of trying to cripple me—to ruin me financially and emotionally. It made me contemptuous of the legal system, because the system allowed it. Even after I presented extensive documentation to show that Harvey was badgering Stella, it took the court years to issue a ruling forbidding Harvey from interrogating Stella about my private life with Eddie. He took me to court because he didn't like the tutor I'd chosen, because he didn't like the school. He hated her therapist. He took me to court because I owed him a couple of thousand dollars on my share of medical expenses—and it cost him more money than I owed him to do it. He took me to court on the outlandish charge that I had violated the gag order by telling Stella's therapist what had transpired. The lengthy legal papers drawn up by Harvey's lawyers were filled with personal attacks. They were ugly. Pam couldn't get over it. "I have never seen such personal animosity reflected in a court document," she said in astonishment. On a couple of occasions, she asked Harvey's lawyers to tone down the language. It's as if they had been possessed by his rage. You'd think there would be some way to stop it, but the sad fact is, if someone brings a charge, it has to be answered, and then a judge has to rule. It's the way our country works. A judge has no ability to say, "I never want to see you back here again."

I had no idea how the system worked until I was in the middle of it. Like many people who are involved with the courts for the first time, I began the process full of trust, but as time went on, I grew hardened. I earned my $2 million law degree through years of bitter lessons. When a ruling went in our favor, my relief lasted only as long as it took Harvey to appeal. Then around we'd go again.

When the appellate court finally upheld Judge Slobod's decision to award me custody of Stella, I held my breath, waiting for Harvey to launch another appeal. I couldn't believe it was really over. It took a while for my lawyers to convince me that we had finally won. Even then, I couldn't feel overjoyed. The victory was tainted by years of strife. Our little family was damaged. My marriage to Eddie was hanging on by a thread. How could it be otherwise? It takes time and effort to build a strong foundation for a marriage, and my energies had been devoted to saving my children. Could Eddie and I now pick up where we'd left off years ago? I honestly didn't know.

The arrival of a peacock in our backyard may have been a sign that things were looking up. At first, I thought it was a wild turkey. Wild turkeys roamed freely through our part of Rockland County in scattered families, waddling and cackling as they scampered up the hillside. But this was no turkey. This was definitely a peacock. The girls and I stared out the window in awe. The dogs joined us there, ears perked up with interest. *Ah, what have we here?* Chandler, my alert little Jack Russell terrier, pressed his nose against the sliding glass door in the kitchen and raised one paw, signaling his preparedness to investigate further and, if necessary, do battle.

"Mommy, he's crying," Stella said, referring to the peacock's call. "He needs some food. He's hungry."

"What do peacocks eat?" I had no idea.

"We could give him some bread," suggested Margaux, looking through cupboards. She pulled out a bag of rice cakes. "It's all we have," she said. "Rice cakes are breadlike."

Stella started to pull open the sliding door.

"Whoa! Hold on," I cried. This peacock wasn't petite. It was enormous. Possibly dangerous to nosy terriers and rambunctious children.

"Do you think it's someone's pet?" Margaux asked. "Maybe we should put up signs: 'Found. One peacock. Call this number.' "

That's what we did, but there were no takers. I finally called Bobby Kennedy. "Hey, Bobby, I have a peacock in my yard. Is that even possible?"

He laughed. "Leave it to you, Lorraine." Bobby knew everyone in the environmental community, and he was able to arrange a more secure home for our colorful visitor.

Life went on. Stella grew stronger. Margaux and I watched over her. The leaves fell from the trees and the weather turned cold. We kept warm in our house built on a rock. Like it, we weren't going to move.

Ten · Calling Dr. Melfi

If you're really ready to commit to mental health,
I say great, let's get going.
·Dr. Jennifer Melfi

OCTOBER 1996

There's a price to be paid for everything. All the years that I spent fighting to protect my children, to see Stella through her illness, to make my new marriage to Eddie work, and to hold on to my home, took an enormous toll on me. The raw energy required for these battles kept me going as much as they wore me down. I was forced to fight or declare defeat, and I chose to fight. There was a frantic purpose to my life, and even during the grimmest periods, I always knew there was an end in sight. But I couldn't do everything. I wasn't really taking care of myself. I was emotionally bankrupt, a condition that matched my financial state. And that's where I found myself in late 1996, emerging from a dark tunnel after years of constant battle. Unfortunately, I didn't emerge into the light of a bright new day, but into a gray gloom of exhaustion and despair.

I wasn't really myself anymore, that was for sure. Where once I had been open and loving, the doors to my heart and my house were now closed. My former friend Gail's breach of trust, Harvey's endless legal challenges, Stella's illness, and the slow crumbling of my marriage to Eddie—all of it made me reluctant to let anyone else inside. I just couldn't bear the pain of further betrayals, or the weight of new catastrophes. I froze the world out, and it prevented me from gaining a healthy perspective. The phone had become my enemy. Its ringing would pierce me, its sound knifing into my guts. Would it be my lawyer with news of yet another court challenge? Would it be my accountant, letting me know that the numbers didn't add up again that month? Would it be a doctor with another worrisome test result for Stella? Would it be one more person wishing to take advantage of me, or to ask me for some favor that always came with strings attached? After years of treading water and barely keeping my head up, I was sinking.

My finances were in the toilet. For the first time in my life, I was unable to meet my obligations. My tab for the ceaseless court battles was approaching $2 million. Maybe Harvey could afford that kind of expense, but I surely couldn't. My lawyers were very understanding, but they wanted to be paid—and, God knows, they deserved to be paid. The bills were piling up and the collection agencies were calling, and in the meantime, I wasn't getting work. I was behind on my taxes. I felt humiliated and distressed. It may sound very obvious, but it is very embarrassing to be broke. I'll never forget the time I went to lease a car, and the guy looked at me red-faced and said, "I'm a big fan, Ms. Bracco, but I'm afraid your credit doesn't check out."

I was barely hanging on. The IRS had a lien against my house, and my lawyers were preparing to file suit to collect the money I owed them. I was sinking. Finally, my accountant, Bert Padell, suggested I consider filing for Chapter 11 bankruptcy. It was the only way to save the house. I felt totally defeated. I had my daughters, but was I going to lose everything I'd worked so hard for? The answer seemed to be yes.

Declaring bankruptcy was a big shock to the system. The day I walked into the bankruptcy lawyer's office on Lexington Avenue, I was feeling as low as I've ever felt. As I approached the office, I saw a van sitting in the street, emblazoned with the words "Sad but True." I thought, *Yeah, that's me.* The experience of declaring Chapter 11 bankruptcy was complex and expensive, but it forced Harvey to finally settle our joint real-estate holdings. The price tag was high. Believe me, it costs plenty to be officially declared broke.

My marriage was as good as over by now, although Eddie and I wouldn't officially separate until 1997. There it was; another flop. I was a lousy role model for my girls when it came to relationships. *Woulda, coulda, shoulda*—that was me. I could wallpaper my house with a list of the mistakes I'd made, and I could wallpaper all of Rockland County with the court papers I'd accumulated.

There was so much anger surrounding my life, it was beginning to feel like a curse. All of the fighting, all of the lawyers, all of the tumult and the commotion, all of the emotions that were exposed and then left to fester like open wounds—it was a hellish period. The darkness that seemed to surround us all for far too long culminated in this moment, when I could barely feel anything anymore. I felt I'd won the battle but lost the war.

Depression doesn't always have an obvious trigger, though mine did. For some people it just happens, and you have to be able to recognize the signs. It's not just the blues, or a couple of weeks under the covers. The most remarkable thing about my depression was how normally I functioned. I could have gone on like that forever, at a low hum. I could keep doing everything I was supposed to do, without fully being there.

During the years when I was fighting for control of my life and my children's lives, I had always said, "I'm not going to let anyone hold me down and push me into a damned box. No one controls me. Not Harvey. Not Gail. Not the courts. No one." And I fought my way out many times. But now I felt trapped in that box, and it seemed to me that it was my own hands that had swung the hammer and nailed the lid on tight.

It never occurred to me that I couldn't fix this. I'd use my head and break free. I thought, "I'll take a yoga class. I'll start exercising. I'll be okay. Better than that, I'll be great!" But you've got to be motivated, and my motivation was shot. It didn't last. Then I started hanging out at the local Barnes & Noble, in the self-help aisle. Interestingly, my instinct wasn't to escape through drink or drugs or sex. My escape was to read books! There was lots of good advice in the self-help aisle. Remember, I spent so much time there, I practically got my own chair.

I read a lot of great books, and enjoyed discussing them with my friend John Hoving. It was like having my own private book club. We'd talk about M. Scott Peck's *The Road Less Traveled,* Joseph Campbell's *The Power of Myth,* and Gary Zukav's *The Seat of the Soul.*

What of my dreams in those days? And what had happened to my career? I thought I didn't have much of anything left—dreams or a career. I really felt over the hill, all used up. I was only in my forties, but I felt eighty. It didn't help that the industry was treating me like I had the plague. While Harvey's career had thrived after we split up, mine had stalled. I had encountered so many problems—after all of this, who was going to offer me a role in their $75 million movie? While Heather was still trying to manage my career, my longtime agency, CAA (Creative Artists Agency), dropped me.

Margaux used to say to me, "Mom, you never give up. You shoot for the moon." I had been spending a lot of time up at Margaux's school, helping put on their musicals. I really enjoyed helping with those productions, and I loved watching Margaux sing and dance. She'd watched many times as I got passed over in auditions, or received bad reviews, or weathered whatever the next big disappointment had been, and I'd just barreled on ahead. She saw me as unstoppable. That old spirit may have been crippled, but it hadn't completely died. If I couldn't run, and I couldn't walk, I'd just crawl along for a while. That's what I was doing when *The Sopranos* came into my life.

In a sense, Dr. Melfi rescued me. As I've said before, it wasn't that being cast in this great role, in this great series, suddenly cured my depression. Depression is not cured by good things happening to you—which is why it's so hard to get a handle on. My depression responded to real treatment, not the glimpses of psychotherapy people have seen on TV.

But it was certainly serendipitous that Dr. Melfi came into my life at that particular moment. As my own therapy progressed, I watched my character open a dialogue, shared by millions of television viewers of *The Sopranos,* about the struggle for morality, courage, and happiness—all within the context of being imperfect human beings. Dr. Melfi forces us to think about things we may not have considered, and to ask ourselves important questions. And she does it all as a terribly flawed person herself. I've had psychoanalysts tell me that they were horrified when Melfi took a couple belts of hard liquor before a session with Tony Soprano. How unprofessional! How wrong! How could she? But a lot of people got it. It rang true, because everybody knows that even doctors have failings. It made her real. Melfi is admirable in that respect, because she keeps trying to do good, even though she's broken. If Dr. Melfi was just sitting on her high horse spouting psychobabble, she wouldn't be such a powerful character.

I've learned a lot from Dr. Melfi, and Dr. Melfi has learned a lot from me, because I've tried to infuse her character with the integrity I saw in my own therapists. In fact, it was the one thing I insisted on when I first talked to David Chase about the role. I said, "You have to promise me that you won't make a mockery of therapy. If you want to make Dr. Melfi a psycho-killer sex addict, I can't do it." David assured me that he was deeply interested in Melfi's character, because she was the voice of conscience in the drama.

Even though I was still battling my own depression as I prepared my scenes for the first season of *The Sopranos,* I threw myself completely into the role. As always, I practiced my lines rigorously, memorizing every word and inflection. David Chase liked to do read-throughs with the whole cast, but I knew my weakness when it came to reading out loud.

The problem was finding someone I could trust to practice my lines with me. We were all sworn to secrecy, and I had to choose someone I was absolutely certain would not breathe a word to anyone about the show.

Of course, I chose my mother.

Mom was happy to help. My parents had moved from Westbury to North Jersey, and were living in a cozy house not far from me in Sneden's Landing. Mom and I rehearsed in the afternoons—she played the role of Tony. She was good at it, too, although some of Tony's lines shocked her—and even shocked me when I heard them coming out of her mouth. Sometimes she'd stop mid-sentence and gasp, "Oh, does he have to use such language?"

"Mom, just read the line." I'd laugh, and we'd forge ahead.

My parents were thrilled with my new role. I was playing an educated Italian-American woman.

The Sopranos did have its critics over the years, mostly from organizations that decried the stereotyping, labeling David Chase a self-hating Italian-American. The largely Italian-American cast didn't share the sentiment. We understood that what David was portraying was not an onerous Sicilian stereotype, but a slice of American middle-class life. David wasn't saying that all Italian-Americans have mob ties. For example, Dr. Melfi and her family and friends aren't in the mob; it's completely foreign to them. There's a reality that is portrayed in *The Sopranos*, but it's not the only reality. David has always liked to push the envelope. When he did *I'll Fly Away*, the television drama depicting a southern town in the 1960s, he showed some white bigots. But his point was not that all southern whites were bigots.

What really bothered my dad was what he thought was the disrespectful behavior of the Soprano kids. "If I'd talked to my parents like that, they'd have thrown me out the window without opening it," he grumbled. That was probably true. But, for better or worse, Meadow and A.J. are pretty typical American teenagers.

Thanks to Mom, I felt ready when it was time to play the scenes.

When we gathered for our first reading, it was a little bit like the first day of school. Some old friends, some new ones. I knew Michael Imperioli, who plays Christopher, because he was in *Goodfellas*, where he played Spider, the poor bartender who gets shot by Joe Pesci's character. Tony Sirico, who plays Paulie Walnuts, was also in *Goodfellas*. Vincent Pastore, who played Big Pussy, was in *Goodfellas*, *Basketball Diaries*, and *Riding in Cars with Boys*. Most of the rest of the cast I'd never met, though. Everyone was very friendly and a little excited. Jimmy Gandolfini and I chatted each other up. We'd be spending lots of time together in that therapy room, and we needed to feel comfortable with each other. David showed me the set for Melfi's office. It was round. "It looks like a womb," I told Jimmy, which made him laugh.

We all got settled with our scripts around a huge square table for the read-through. David Chase, Chris Albrecht, the president (now chairman) of HBO, and Ilene Landress, the producer, hung back to listen. There were about fifty people in the room, and we were charged up. I had the first line of the first show. It was "Mr. Soprano?" That's how the show opens, with Dr. Melfi coming to the door of her waiting room to greet Tony.

David liked to do read-throughs to listen to the words in character. It is an exhilarating experience for a writer to finally hear his script come alive in the voices of his chosen cast. He didn't want us to act, just to read. There was reaction, of course—laughing and the tension of anticipation. But it was very straight. An hour around the table, followed by platters of food brought in by the caterers.

The read-throughs became an important connection point for me because they were the only time I got to be with most of the other actors. I'd always sit next to Jimmy and get to hang out with characters Melfi would never meet in a million years. Remember, Dr. Melfi does her scenes almost exclusively with Tony, and occasionally, Carmela—except when she sees her own shrink, Dr. Elliot Kupferberg (played beautifully by Peter Bogdanovich).

From the very start, shooting the pilot, I was impressed by what a well-oiled machine David and Ilene ran. I'd heard about the craziness that went on with some TV shows, with rewrites at three in the morning—*You're dying, you're not dying.*

I'll tell you one thing. On *The Sopranos,* you always get advance notice when you're going to get killed. It's horrible! David calls you in and tells you you're going to get whacked or whatever, and I've heard from those who have been there that your instinct is to get down on your knees and beg for your life. Nobody wants to leave this show. During the first year, if your character was getting killed off, David would take you out to a "Last Supper." Now, you get killed first and taken out to dinner second, so the press doesn't catch on.

We cried when Big Pussy got it. The worst was Drea de Matteo, who played Christopher's girlfriend, Adriana. That was awful. I was sitting there with the script right in front of me, and I was *still* praying for a different ending.

I have always had trouble sitting still, and I was extremely conscious of that as I sat across from James Gandolfini when shooting our first scene of *The Sopranos* together. As Dr. Melfi, I was required to be physically and emotionally still. Melfi was the embodiment of therapeutic calm. In the beginning, it felt like a stretch for me as both an actress and a woman. Ilene Landress joked that they might have to Krazy-Glue my butt to the chair. I felt as though all of my recent trials and tribulations were permanently etched on my face. But Melfi was calm, so I would be calm.

Beneath that stillness, I was searching for the truth, the essence of Jennifer Melfi. As an actor, I get to create a backstory to her life.

Luckily, I had been in therapy—and I'm a great mimic. I worked with the costume designer to decide on her look for each day. I knew I wanted to project the image of a polished, intelligent, professional woman. The hair and makeup people and I would work together, too.

The very first scene in the pilot opens with Tony Soprano sitting in Dr. Melfi's waiting room, staring in confusion at a sculpture of a female nude. It's not the sort of thing one would expect to see in a psychiatrist's waiting room, but I fought to get that sculpture included. It's the work of the incredible artist Robert Graham, and I thought it reflected Melfi's aesthetic sense. I wanted it known that Melfi wasn't a stiff cardboard cutout of a therapist. She was a living, breathing, vital woman, with interests outside of her office.

Tony doesn't really know what to make of her. Melfi is educated, refined, an intellectual. Tony is a thug. He's not a stupid thug, but he's not an educated man, either. He's crude and rough, and Melfi is caring and smooth. They come from different planets. That's probably why Tony is so attracted to Melfi: she represents the forbidden fruit. She's a passionate, caring woman, but with real intellect, someone who is neither frightened by nor attracted to a gangster. Tony's power holds some appeal for her, even though I'd say that she's repelled by it, and ultimately by Tony, too. She knows that what he does is evil. He and the mob represent everything that she personally rejects as wrong in our society.

It's inevitable that Tony Soprano has sexual thoughts about Melfi, and he even tells her, "I'm in love with you." She calmly responds that the love isn't real. It's transference, and it's a sign that they're making progress. Viewers who witness constant examples of Tony's violence and infidelity outside of Melfi's office may rightly wonder what kind of progress she's talking about.

How many years now have people been telling me that Melfi and Tony are going to get it on someday? I guess since the first season. I can see why people would think that is a possibility. Jimmy Gandolfini portrays Tony Soprano beautifully, and he's been able to make Tony sexually appealing. Trust me, nobody asks how his therapy is going. As Tony Soprano, he maintains a certain kind of charm and neediness within the framework of being a deadly killer and a conscienceless prick. What James Gandolfini does with Tony is an example of a great balancing act by a great actor. He brings Tony to life.

What makes the scenes between Melfi and Tony work is the powerful human X factor that Jimmy and I have. The scripts are brilliant, but the real magic ingredient is the chemistry that occurs between us when we are together in that room, living fully in that moment. To have an experience like that is amazing and always surprising. It's why I love acting.

Sometimes I'm so mesmerized I find myself breaking out of character, and just sitting there watching him, as though I've become a part of the audience. Believe me, I don't permit myself to do that often, but James Gandolfini is a very compelling actor. It's a pleasure to work with him, and he's one of the reasons I love the craft of acting. He raises the game of everyone around him. It's a rush to work with someone that good. It's like when you have a tennis partner who is better than you, and it improves your play. Some scenes are so smooth, I feel like we're Serena and Venus, lobbing the words over the net.

Tony Soprano's attraction to Jennifer Melfi isn't just physical. I think what really turns him on is her intelligence. He sees her intellect as a kind of a power he doesn't have, and he's drawn to it. He wants Melfi because to have her is not only to have her submit to him sexually—which he fantasizes about all of the time—but to have her accept that she wants Tony, too. That's what really makes Tony Soprano excited. That's what he really wants.

Tony is obsessed with Melfi because he wants power, and he's used to getting what he wants, even if it's self-destructive. He doesn't comprehend that if he got what he craved, it would destroy their relationship, as well as any possibility that Melfi might actually help him.

Outside of his therapy sessions with Dr. Melfi, maybe the most educated woman Tony deals with is his daughter, Meadow, who is trying to balance being the child of a gangster with being a "normal" Ivy League college student with a life away from her family. The question remains as to whether Meadow will ultimately be able to separate herself from her family, get away from them emotionally and physically, and make a life for herself in a moral universe.

Melfi has no intention of ever giving Tony Soprano an inch in any of her dealings with him. She has correctly assessed that if you give a guy like him an inch, he'll take a mile . . . and then he'll take your arm, your leg, everything. There's no stopping a guy like him.

He's a monster. But this is a truly compassionate woman. That's why she allows him to return to their therapy sessions, although it ended badly the first time around.

Dr. Melfi truly believes that she can help this evil man. If she doesn't show him forgiveness, if she doesn't lead by example, then how will he ever learn forgiveness? The type of analysis she practices searches for the source of a patient's struggles in the wounds of his childhood, and she recognizes that Tony was gravely wounded—and as an adult continues to be wounded by his mother. Here's a man whose own mother conspired to have him killed. Melfi posits the question: how can you know love, or show love, if you've never received love from your own mother?

Viewers find Tony Soprano fascinating. They're intrigued by the possibility of his redemption. In a sense, Tony is the portrait of the charming bad boy that women are so drawn to. In the scenes with Dr. Melfi, he is outside his violent persona. His vulnerability is touching. And Dr. Melfi is the caregiver, something he's never had from his mother. He confuses her care for lust, because he doesn't know how else to process it. She is showing him a different way of being with a woman, and viewers hold their breath wondering what will come of it.

Nancy Marchand, who played Tony's mother, Livia Soprano, was one of the few cast members who was not Italian-American, but that didn't matter. Livia was sort of an Everymother—an Every-*bad*-mother, that is. Nancy played her so convincingly that her scenes provoked both chills and laughter. I can't tell you how many people have said to me that Livia was a reincarnation of their own mother, grandmother, or mother-in-law. In Livia, David Chase created the core psychological drama of *The Sopranos* and the centerpiece of Tony's therapy with Dr. Melfi. Livia was the emotional underpinning of the show. She was the reason Tony was in therapy—to face down, once and for all, the mother who had ruled his psyche. It was a scarier prospect than having ten armed goombahs at the door. The fact that she conspired to have him whacked in the first season was the least of it. She'd been "whacking" him his entire life. As Dr. Melfi pointed out, "If she tried to have you killed a year ago, believe me, in your childhood she's inflicted serious psychic injuries that are still there."

You could see that Jimmy savored every scene with Nancy. They were completely in tune, and he was achingly convincing when he declared repeatedly in the second season, "She's dead to me."

Nancy Marchand was a pro's pro and a very classy lady. In fact, though she usually played classy ladies in film and on TV, she thoroughly enjoyed playing against type. She'd laugh that it was the only time in her career where the job of the hair and makeup people was to make her look *worse*.

During the second season, we all knew that Nancy had lung cancer, but she was so strong and confident that she made us believe she'd beat it. We were shocked and devastated when she died suddenly before we began shooting the third season. There was never any question about Nancy being replaced by another actress. She embodied Livia so completely that no one could take her place. Besides, David told us, people still have to confront their mother issues even after a mother dies, especially if there are a lot of unresolved conflicts. So when Tony tells Melfi, "She's dead. Our work here is done," she sets him straight. To the contrary, their work was only beginning.

I believe it was Nancy Marchand's incredible performance in the first two seasons of *The Sopranos* that kept the viewers coming back for more. They could see that this wasn't just your ordinary mob drama; it was a family story they could relate to. And if they, ordinary law-abiding citizens, could see something of themselves in Tony Soprano, maybe he was redeemable after all.

So, is there hope for Tony? I would say that there is always hope. The therapist-patient relationship is very sacred, and if you find the right person, miracles can happen. This faint possibility that even a guy like Tony Soprano can be redeemed keeps viewers coming back for more.

Good and evil. Life and death. Reality commingling with fiction. With *The Sopranos*, I had reason to hope that I could get back on my feet financially, but I was still fighting for a foothold emotionally. Every time I thought the worst was over, I got dealt another blow.

There's a famous line in *Godfather III*, repeated in *The Sopranos* by Silvio Dante (played marvelously by Steve Van Zandt): "Just when I thought I was out, they pulled me back in." That's the way I felt when I received new court papers from Harvey, appealing the court's decision to award me custody of Stella.

This time, he claimed that Stella was in extreme danger when she was around Eddie, based on rumors that members of the Mexican Mafia, a California prison gang featured in Eddie's 1992 movie, *American Me*, had threatened Eddie's life. His "evidence" was that two lieutenants in the Mexican Mafia were murdered after appearing in the movie.

Eddie assured me that the rumor of his life being in danger was ridiculous. "Believe me," he said, "there were bigger turf battles that caused those men to be murdered than my movie. This appeal is grabbing at straws."

"Whether it's ridiculous or not, the lawyers still have to be paid," I sighed. Here we went again.

In court, Eddie took the stand and withstood another barrage of questions from Harvey's lawyer about seemingly irrelevant details of the Mexican underworld. He repeated to the judge that he was in no danger from the Mexican Mafia. In fact, he said, looking pointedly across the courtroom at Harvey, the only time his life had ever been threatened was in phone calls "from Mr. Keitel." The judge threw out the motion.

The irony of this latest trudge through the legal system was that Eddie and I rarely saw each other anymore. He was busy with a variety of different projects in Los Angeles, and I was in New York. The stress of the court fights, compounded by my depression and Harvey's unabated wrath, had doomed our relationship.

Harvey just wasn't giving up, and neither was Gail. If she had once envied me my life of privilege, she was doing her best to put an end to it. The legal bills were astronomical. Harvey and Gail had been talking to each other, and that was distasteful and seemed inappropriate. Reports that they were seen dining together at Elaine's with Geraldo Rivera in 1997 kept the rumor mill alive.

"When will it end?" I wrote Harvey, believing the real answer was "never." When Margaux's school asked Eddie to be the keynote speaker at her high school graduation, Harvey sent blistering letters and copies of court documents to the superintendent of the school district, protesting their choice of an alleged child molester. They called me, and I explained that there were a lot of ugly words, but no charges. Eddie spoke beautifully at Margaux's graduation.

On some level, I understood that Harvey believed he was taking a stand for good versus evil, but it felt like revenge. His ability to judge Eddie fairly was warped by his own wounds. It was sad, as was Gail's obsession. Unbelievably, she actually wrote me a note accusing me of "ruining" *The Sopranos* for her because I was in the show.

When I switched to a woman psychiatrist in 1999, it was because I was ready, finally, to look at my relationships and try to figure out why I was attracted to certain kinds of men who ultimately didn't give me what I wanted and needed, and I thought she might shed a different kind of light on these issues. Dr. Sullivan asked me to think about what the important men in my life might have had in common.

"They're all short," I joked. She didn't laugh. Well, okay, this was serious. I already knew that. If I joked, it was to cover up how extremely difficult it was to spread out my mistakes on the table and examine them.

There were four men with whom I'd had significant relationships—Jean, Daniel, Harvey, and Eddie. Jean I met when I was young and intoxicated with the idea of Prince Charming. His sophistication and confidence elevated me, and made me feel like a woman, not just a girl.

I suppose I fell for Daniel on the rebound, and with him—at least, in the beginning—I didn't have to try so hard. He enjoyed my youth and my silliness. I didn't have to dress up for him. He liked the fact that I was a model. I was a beautiful prize to him. Little more was expected of me. He didn't challenge or judge. We had fun. I doubt that we would have married if I hadn't been pregnant, and I like to think that I'd have seen Daniel more realistically with time.

Harvey is the only man who ever swept me off my feet. Our attraction was electrifying, but it was his generosity, loyalty, and willingness to make a commitment that really touched me. He was strong when I thought I needed someone to be strong, but although he was willing to give me the world, he wasn't willing to see me as an equal. As I grew stronger myself, I started to resent that.

Eddie came along at a point in my life when I was extremely needy, and he showed me that love didn't have to be a burden. But once again, here was an older man leading me from darkness to light. With the exception of Daniel, they had all been older men, and they had all in a sense rescued me.

Dr. Sullivan asked what it was I felt was missing in myself that I repeatedly sought in strong, older men. Did I fear I couldn't make it on my own? Did I feel unworthy of being taken seriously for myself? Deep down, did I still feel like the ugliest girl on the bus who needed to live in the shadow of men whom other people admired?

The idea of unworthiness struck a chord with me. I was loved and cherished by my parents as a child, but nobody had great expectations of me, and God knows I didn't have them for myself. I was the classic "average" person in my own mind, and if certain special people like Mr. Horowitz and Wilhelmina hadn't seen something in me, I never would have recognized it myself. Dr. Sullivan helped me see that I learned to rely on others to lead the way and identify my dreams for me. And if they ultimately disappointed me, well, that was inevitable, because nobody else can make you whole.

This was one of the breakthroughs in my therapy. As we talked about what it would mean for me to enter a relationship as a whole person, not out of need, I began to see a possibility in my future that hadn't been there before.

"What do you want the most in life?" Dr. Sullivan asked me one day.

"Peace of mind," I replied. As I said it, I was thinking of Dr. Melfi, and the way she had brought herself to such a full realization, at a time when she was broken.

There is a primal moment in season three of *The Sopranos* when Dr. Melfi is confronted with a choice between the forces of good and the forces of evil. Actors live for scenes like this. It involves Dr. Melfi's brutal rape in the stairwell of her office building's parking garage. When David sat me down and told me that Melfi was going to be raped in an upcoming episode, I was very upset. "David, I don't understand," I said angrily. "I am the only decent person here. Why would you want to hurt me randomly? I don't deserve this." Notice how I'm talking in the first person? I was talking about Melfi, but in that moment it was *me*. I took it very personally. I went home that night just horrified, even though David tried to calm me down. "Read the script," he urged.

A few days later the script arrived, and with much trepidation, I sat down to read it. It was ugly and violent and just as horrible as I'd imagined. But when I got to the last page, the light dawned. I got it. I understood. It wasn't about the rape per se. It was about the crucible of Dr. Melfi's life—whether she was going to be a moral person or succumb to Tony's evil world.

I called David. "I think it's brilliant," I said. "I understand what you're doing here. But it will be hard."

I had no idea how hard. Shooting the rape scene was a more physically violent experience than I could have imagined. I felt the degradation. My body burned with pain when I was slammed down in the stairwell. It was so realistic that I tore the bursal sac in my shoulder and was in real pain. I had to have laparoscopic surgery to repair the damage. It wasn't just me—doing that scene was traumatic for the whole crew. Many people on the set cried during the filming. The brutality was absolutely necessary. It was not gratuitous; it was real. So much of the violence we see on the screen—especially on television—is airbrushed so that it doesn't appear as gut-wrenchingly awful as it is. I think that's a disservice to society, because violence against another human being is despicable and it should be seen as despicable. You should be revolted.

After the rape, Melfi's face is bruised and swollen, and she's walking with a cane. She looks diminished, older. If you've never been the victim of a violent crime, you can't imagine it. You're in shock. How could this happen? But the worst is yet to come, because Melfi is then raped again by the justice system. The rapist is caught, but he is released on a technicality, destroying all hope of justice. Melfi is devastated. Bruised and battered, still using a cane, she returns to her practice. She tells Tony that she has been in an accident, but she fantasizes about siccing Tony on her rapist, and admits to her own psychiatrist, "There's a certain satisfaction knowing I could have that asshole squashed like a bug if I wanted."

Melfi's world is shattered by the realization that playing by the rules doesn't mean a thing. She has always believed in the system, and now it has turned its back on her. During a session with Tony, she breaks down weeping, and Tony rushes to comfort her. He stares into Melfi's eyes, and it's like he's picking up the scent of her moral vulnerability. "Is there something you want to say?" he asks.

Time seems to stop as Melfi battles with her soul. She need only speak the word and Tony will mete out the justice she was denied by the legal system. Finally, she opens her mouth and answers in one clear syllable: "No."

This was an extremely powerful scene, and I felt completely drained after we filmed it. It was so *real*. But I felt victorious, as if I myself had made the tough moral choice.

Before the rape episode aired, I warned my parents and children. "The episode this week is very harsh," I told them. "Something happens to Dr. Melfi, and you should be prepared. But I want you to know that I'm okay. I'm not hurt."

My father called me up after he saw that episode, and his voice was shaking. He said, "I was standing up in front of my television screaming, 'Tell him. Tell him!' " Many people wanted Dr. Melfi to get revenge. They, too, were shouting at their TVs, "Tell him!"

It is very gratifying as an actor to evoke this kind of passion in viewers—to allow them, for a brief time, to experience the character's thought processes and to suffer her moral dilemma along with her. However, I wondered what it meant that so many people wanted Dr. Melfi to get revenge. Did they understand that telling Tony would have been selling her soul to the devil? It troubled me, and I discussed the viewers' bloodthirstiness with Dr. Glen Gabbard, a psychiatrist who later wrote a book called *The Psychology of the Sopranos*. Glen said that, on some level, people respect the kind of outlaw moral code of Tony Soprano, and they don't want Dr. Melfi to be ethical. The idea of revenge seems so sweet! But he also said that they are ashamed of their feelings. Ultimately, I don't think the audience really wanted to see Dr. Melfi join Tony's world.

When I heard that the American Psychoanalytic Association wanted to give me an award for my portrayal of Dr. Melfi, my first response was, "What, are they crazy?" But they insisted that

Dr. Melfi had made a big impact on a lot of people. In fact, since Tony Soprano started seeing Dr. Melfi, they estimated that twice as many men were seeking therapy as before.

In December 2001, I was invited to speak to a meeting of the organization, and I was awed that hundreds of psychoanalysts were gathered to hear what I thought. Imagine that. Why did these professionals think so highly of Dr. Melfi—and, by extension, of me? When I stood up to speak, they cheered loudly. I had to tell them honestly, "I am so *not* Dr. Melfi." I also told them how lucky I felt to have been given this incredible role, for whom David Chase and his writers had written such meaningful words. But in creating Dr. Melfi, I had also brought my own life experience to the table. For the first time, I spoke openly about my own depression, and how much therapy had helped me.

The awards the association presented to me and to the Emmy-winning writers and executive producers of *The Sopranos,* Robin Green and Mitchell Burgess, looked like diplomas. It almost made me think about hanging out my shingle. We participated in a rousing discussion of the show. Many of the therapists commented that their patients frequently refer to Dr. Melfi to gauge the progress of their own therapy. And many of them felt that Melfi does a pretty good job, considering that her client is a mob boss and her skirts were too short.

At the end of the session, the sex therapist Dr. Ruth Westheimer stood up in the audience, and asked me, in her heavily accented speech, "When are you going to sleep with Tony?" Everyone laughed.

"If you're talking about Dr. Melfi and Tony, I hope it doesn't happen," I said. "Let him dream on." Then I added jokingly, "As for James Gandolfini, well, I can only say that he once sent me a bouquet of flowers in the off season, and the note read, 'I miss your legs.'"

I was standing in line at the grocery store one day when a woman smiled at me like we were old friends. "Hi!" she said brightly. "You look so much better. I didn't know how you'd ever get over it."

"Get over what?" I asked.

"The rape," she replied in a whisper.

I was starting to set her straight when her hand flew to her mouth and she groaned. "Oh, I'm so stupid. What was I thinking?" She was embarrassed because she had confused me, Lorraine Bracco, with my character, Dr. Melfi. I assured her that there was no reason to be embarrassed. It happened all the time.

It's a point of pride for me that ordinary people walk up to me and feel they can relate to me in a personal way. I'm glad they're touched by Melfi's struggles, and it pleases me to no end that my character helps them to wrestle with important topics. I can't tell you how many times rape victims have approached me, trying to make a connection. It's humbling. I, Lorraine Bracco, was not raped, so I can't tell them I feel their pain. But I understand when they express gratitude that we didn't sugarcoat it.

Eleven · Stark Naked

There is no cure for life.

· Dr. Jennifer Melfi

DECEMBER 2000

A major snowstorm hit New York the day before New Year's Eve 2000. In the days following the New Year, enormous snowdrifts had mounded into hard white crusts surrounding my house in Sneden's Landing. I sat at the big table in the family room, looking out across the frozen stretches of the Hudson River and Westchester County beyond. I had a roaring fire going. Crack was snoring, nestled beside me on my chair, and the Labs were snoozing on the rug. Even the usually feisty terrier, Chandler, was stretched out, dozing languidly in the quiet room. I was concentrating on my journal, which I'd started keeping to record my thoughts, ideas, and hopes. With the New Year coming, I guess I was in a reflective mood, thinking about what I wanted to have happen in my life. I believed it was up to me, but I was also looking for a little help from the heavens.

The Sopranos had received lots of acclaim, I loved the work, and I was beginning to enjoy my life again. The girls were doing well—Margaux in college, and Stella in high school. I had gotten strong enough to believe that I had a bright future—that was a big step out of the quagmire of depression. The question remained as to what direction that future would take.

I had been in therapy for a while, and as I progressed, I'd stopped taking the antidepressant that had been so crucial to my recovery. It's a myth that once you start taking a medication like Zoloft you need to stay on it forever. If you're ready, and the doctor weans you off the dosage gradually, you can be perfectly fine. I was. I didn't miss a beat.

It's all about striking the right balance. In my experience of being treated for depression, there were two stages. In the beginning, the medication was front and center and the talking took a backseat. Later, the talking was most important, and the medication was a backup.

You can't just take an antidepressant and go on your merry way. Talk therapy is a necessary part of the treatment. The less depressed I became, the more receptive I was to looking at myself honestly. And the more I looked, the more I learned. You're never too old to learn.

I realized that one of the mistakes I had made in the past was never really thinking about what I wanted. I had always just gone with the feeling. That had been a liberating, exciting, but sometimes dangerous way to be, since feelings often don't tell you very much about what's necessarily right for you, or whether what you may be feeling at that time will bring you lasting satisfaction of any kind later.

Eddie and I had finally called it quits after essentially living apart for years. We parted amicably, and we've remained friends, but I've had to acknowledge that it was a mistake to marry him. I jumped into marriage at the most chaotic moment in my life. It wasn't that I didn't love Eddie, because I did and still do. But we both deserved better. Being with Eddie was a comfort, but a marriage has to be built on more than a rescue fantasy.

In the future, I determined that I was going to decide exactly what I wanted, and I was going to approach those decisions with the wisdom gained from all those roads that I have traveled, even when I wandered off the path. I wanted to achieve a place where I could enjoy full disclosure—I needed complete knowledge and total understanding before ever giving myself over to anyone or anything else. There'd be no more blindly throwing myself off cliffs just to see how deep the water was at the bottom. Instead, I planned to start making it a regular habit to take a good long look at myself and see what was shaking. And I wanted the same honesty from anyone I decided to make a part of my life. No more hidden agendas, no more fame games, no more graciously taking whatever came my way.

I didn't want my happiness to be conditional—dependent on a man, on a job, on my looks. That's such a trap, because so many of the externals of life are beyond our control. Endings happen. I didn't want to be sitting around saying, "Boy, those were the days. I was happy when I was doing *The Sopranos* . . . I was happy when my kids were home."

My spirits were lifting, and I was looking forward to the future before me as I ascended higher and higher. As I moved forward in my life, I intended to always know which direction I was traveling in, and how I was getting there. I felt that I was truly in charge of myself again, and I was not going to lose sight of that. I was getting my spirit back. It felt wonderful.

So I was making a list and checking it twice, knowing that my inner Santa would find me not naughty but nice. I was taking control. I was starting over.

High on my list was to be free of financial burdens in the new year. Thanks in part to *The Sopranos*, I had almost paid off my huge debt. What had once seemed impossible was now a reality. I had always believed that I could do it, and it made me proud that I'd been able to hang on and make it possible. I added to my list the desire to be free within myself—to get back out there into life, and to be less afraid of just going with the flow and letting things happen. To just try and have some fun. Be thoughtful, but have fun. Time and tension had shut down the kid in me, and I wanted it back.

I stared out the window at the beautiful, silent river, and I thought about love. I had been alone for more than five years, and that had been fine. I'd needed to focus on my children and my work. But the girls were getting older. Margaux was about to graduate from college, and Stella would be out of high school in a couple of years. They would be off living their own lives, and I would have to decide how I wanted to fill my empty nest. I wondered if I still had the capacity to love and be loved. I wanted to feel close to someone again. I wanted to connect. I had been shut down for a while, but I was ready to open up. So I put it on the list, asking the universe to help me learn to love again. And finally, I asked for the qualities in my life that would feed my soul. Little did I know, as the year 2001 broke, that, like all Americans, I would need an extra helping of soul food.

On September 11, 2001, I was at the Canyon Ranch in Tucson with a group of my friends when I heard about the terrorist attacks. I cannot describe the feeling of helplessness, being apart from my kids and the rest of my family. But also how I hated the terrible feeling of being apart from my city. I should have been there, and now I was stuck, with no way to get home. Stella was safe in Rockland County, but she was hysterical about Harvey, who lived downtown, only a few blocks from the World Trade Center. He called her as soon as he could, and we were all relieved to learn that he was at the Toronto Film Festival. I felt for Harvey. Not only was he separated from his home, his daughter, and the city he loved, he was also apart from the woman who was about to give birth to his son. For nearly two years Harvey had been seeing Lisa Karmazin, a California ceramic artist, and their baby was due in late September.

Margaux was the only one of us who was in the city that day. After graduation, she'd gotten a job with Bobbi Brown Cosmetics and rented an apartment on the Upper West Side of Manhattan. That morning she was in midtown, doing a photo shoot. She called me, sobbing. "You aren't here," she cried. "You aren't here to see what's going on."

Margaux felt the loss of the World Trade Center deeply. When she was a little girl we'd had a nightly ritual of gazing out at the Twin Towers from the window of our loft. Margaux always argued that one of the towers was taller than the other and, of course, as seen from the angle of the bedroom, she was right! The towers had been a part of the landscape of her childhood and now they were gone.

But she regained her composure pretty quickly, and her altruistic instinct kicked in. She lived across the street from a police station, and she wanted to help out, so she went to the supermarket, stocked up, and started making piles of sandwiches for the rescue workers. She returned to the supermarket the second day, but there had been no bread deliveries, and the shelves were pretty bare. She called me in Arizona, saying, "I want to help, I'm trying to do the right thing." She told me that she'd put her name on a volunteer board because she knew CPR, and she was willing to go down to Ground Zero and help. I wasn't crazy about the idea of Margaux being anywhere near Ground Zero, but she was an adult now, and she would make her own choices. I told her I was proud of her and begged her to be careful. But the days passed, and no one called her to volunteer. She felt helpless, a feeling shared by millions of other

New Yorkers, and by the rest of the nation. Firefighters, doctors, and emergency workers flooded into New York from all over the country, and cots were set up at the Javits Center. Anticipating huge numbers of casualties, triage centers were set up both at city hospitals and in outlying suburbs. They were ready, willing, and able. But there was no one to save.

I was finally able to fly home five days after 9/11. I'll never forget looking out the window of the plane, when we were still fifty miles away, and seeing the smoke curling up into the sky, like a grim beacon identifying the site. Our plane flew above lower Manhattan to circle around and land at JFK Airport, and everyone on board grew silent as we crossed the empty skyline where the towers had stood. The man in the seat next to me put his head in his hands and cried.

We all walked around in a daze during those first weeks. Everyone was extra polite, even normally churlish New Yorkers. We lived in a shared pain. Jimmy Gandolfini organized a visit to the Javits Center, and a few of the cast members went down to thank the rescue workers who had no one to rescue. Many of these people talked to me as if I were their therapist, and I felt incompetent to help and vaguely fraudulent. There was nothing I could do for them except listen.

Margaux and I went to Ground Zero and helped with the food service. We were set up a few blocks from the site, and the stench was terrible. John Hoving took me over to where the organization Safe Horizons had set up by the piers. There were hundreds of photos and notes taped and pinned to the walls, put up by family and friends of the missing. I talked to a few of the people who were still wandering the area looking for information about their loved ones. When the unthinkable happens, you crave hope, and that's what I saw in their faces. They craved hope. So many people were willing to believe that their missing loved ones had suffered amnesia from the shock or injury and were wandering the area, or were in a hospital, unconscious, with no identification. None of these hopes were realized, and it was the saddest thing I've ever seen.

Life went on as we tried to rebuild a sense of security within ourselves. Stella was about to turn fifteen, and she was growing into a strong, spunky teenager. Her health was good, she was riding competitively and loved it, and I thought she'd come through the trials of her young life with remarkable courage.

Stella's relationship with Harvey was still fragile, and now that she was asserting herself more, they had their spats. It was a good day when she didn't come back in a fury after seeing Harvey. But after 9/11 Stella had a happy distraction when Lisa gave birth to a boy on September 25. She was excited about her half-brother, Hudson, and she liked Lisa.

One day in early October, Harvey called Stella and said, "I just got married."

"And you didn't tell me? You didn't wait for me to be there?" She was hurt that he hadn't shared the day with her, and she was surprised by the suddenness of it, but she approved of the marriage. "That's okay, Dad," she told him. "With the baby, I think it was the right thing to do."

I was downstairs while Stella was talking to her father, and suddenly I heard a scream from her room. I raced up to see her flinging things and raging.

"Stella, Stella, what's wrong!" Her face was red and tear-stained. I didn't have any idea what was going on. It took me a while to get the story out of her. Harvey had called from Israel, where he had just married Daphna Kastner, a woman he'd met just weeks earlier at the Toronto Film Festival. He hadn't married Lisa. He'd embarked upon a whirlwind, post-9/11 courtship with an Israeli woman Stella didn't even know, just as Lisa was delivering his son.

Stella was inconsolable. She felt betrayed, and sickened by the thought of what Lisa must be going through. "How could he do that?" she asked, again and again. I had no answer for her.

Michael Bloomberg was elected mayor of New York City less than two months after the terrorist attacks. Mike and I had become friends through our daughters' horseback riding, just two interested parents. Although I was a lifelong Democrat, I thought he was just what the city needed after 9/11. This was a guy who inspired confidence. He wasn't a career politician but a coolheaded businessman, who was dedicated to making a difference for the city. That first year was a huge challenge for Mike. Everyone was calling Rudy Giuliani "America's mayor" because of the incredible way he handled himself during the attack. But Mike was the one who had to pick up the pieces and get the city running again—not just economically, but emotionally.

In the fall of 2002 Mike called and asked if I wanted to march beside him in the Columbus Day Parade, then accompany him to lunch at a fabulous Italian restaurant in the Bronx. He also invited Bronx native Dominic Chianese, who plays Uncle Junior on *The Sopranos.* We both accepted. New York's Columbus Day Parade is a major event, not just for Italian-Americans, but for the whole city. With the wounds of 9/11 still fresh, even after a year, the parade took on a special meaning of solidarity and pride.

I understood perfectly that Mike's invitation had more to do with Dominic's and my contribution to the city than with our roles on *The Sopranos*, considering that he'd never even watched the show! That understanding wasn't shared by the Columbus Citizens Foundation, the parade's organizer, who viewed the invitation as a glorification of the mob. They announced their intention to go to court to block the mayor from inviting us.

"They can take you to court over this?" I asked Mike, amazed. He assured me that they could. I laughed. "Usually I date a guy before we go to court," I said.

It was ridiculous to confuse me with my character, and it wasn't that funny. Like other Italian-American groups, the parade's organizers were too carried away by their emotions to grasp the essential reality that *The Sopranos* did not glorify the mob at all. I mean, have you ever seen such a miserable group in your life? Their marriages are in the toilet, they have drug problems, their lives are hanging by a thread. Please!

A federal judge sided with the Columbus Citizens Foundation and barred the mayor from inviting anyone to march with him in the parade, so I called Mike. "It's okay," I told him. "I don't need to march in the parade. You have to do what's best for yourself."

Mike didn't like being pushed around. "No," he replied. "I invited you and Dominic to walk with me in the parade and then to have lunch. If we can't walk in the parade, we'll just have lunch." And for the first time in memory, the mayor of New York City did not march in the Columbus Day Parade. However, our lunch on Arthur Avenue in the Bronx was a lot of fun. Dominic brought his guitar and serenaded us with Italian love songs.

It is a classic nightmare that actors have. You're standing on a stage in a crowded theater, the lights go up, and there you are: stark naked. Only it wasn't a nightmare. It was real. I was forty-eight years old, and there I was, baring it all to a Broadway audience. Had I finally lost my mind? Had I been hitting the plastic surgery mills? Neither. The body was 100 percent mine, with all of its curves and imperfections. The role was Mrs. Robinson in Terry Johnson's Broadway adaptation of *The Graduate*. It was during a 2002 hiatus from *The Sopranos,* and I'd shed Dr. Melfi's prim suits to transform myself into one of the world's most famous seductresses of young men. It was a liberating moment.

When I first saw Mike Nichols's film *The Graduate,* starring Dustin Hoffman and Anne Bancroft, I was in high school, and there was so much then that I didn't understand about life. I was puzzled why the young man, Benjamin Braddock, would even be attracted to a woman old enough to be his mother, when he had a gorgeous young girlfriend—the mother's daughter!—his own age. I knew nothing about being a woman then, and less than nothing about sexual power, or the wielding of that power.

But by the age of forty-eight, I think I pretty much had it down pat. I realized that the power of expressed sexuality is enhanced by the confidence that comes with age and experience. That is, if you allow it to be.

But like all of my favorite roles, what I really loved about Mrs. Robinson was her complexity. She was an interesting, if flawed, character. Mrs. Robinson is a very lonely, bitter woman. She's miserable in her marriage and in her life. She drinks too much, and she plays cruel games with people. Why does she do this? Because she can, and because she just doesn't give a damn.

Mrs. Robinson appears to be a strong, sophisticated woman who gets what she wants. But the whole point is that she doesn't have what she really wants in her life. Maybe if she'd been born in another era, she would have divorced her husband twenty years before, and sought a new, more meaningful life for herself. Maybe she would have found a way to be happy. But she never did. As she grows older, she's reduced to being a manipulator. She seduces Benjamin Braddock to satisfy her need to dominate and control. She's a desperately lonely alcoholic with a powerful sexual appetite and a desire for some adulterous excitement. Seducing this young man, having him do her sexual bidding, has a twofold purpose. It pleases her to cuckold her clueless husband, and it pleases her to have as a secret boy-toy the very man her daughter is far more appropriate for. She is furious when they begin dating. She is, without a doubt, the most manipulative character I've ever played.

I'll tell you one thing about Mrs. Robinson, though. She understands the pure sexual heat that an older woman can radiate if she wants to. She decides that she wants that young man, and she is going to have him. When I was performing in *The Graduate*, the part of Benjamin was being played by a twenty-year-old actor named John Lavelle. John was wonderful. It was clear that he had not had as many sexual experiences as I had. There's a scene in the play where Mrs. Robinson is undressing, and she says to Benjamin, "Why don't you watch?"

So, in rehearsal as Mrs. Robinson, I slowly took off my shirt, and stood there in my bra. As Benjamin Braddock, John just stared, in shock. It seemed like a genuine reaction. It was a pretty hot moment onstage. I exerted my sexual power over him, and I have to admit that it really scared me, too.

Of course, when I played Mrs. Robinson, everyone wanted to know if I was terrified about doing the nude scene. Maybe I should have been, but, God help me, I really wasn't. For one thing, the lighting was incredible. The soft blue light that bathed the stage could cover a lot of sins. We should all have our bodies lit this way. And the scene was quick. If you blinked, it was over. It was more like a nude *moment*. It wasn't really about the nudity, anyway. It was about the sexual control that was happening in that scene. It was very intense. I don't think anyone really cared if my ass was sagging, and I'm proud to say that I am what I am.

I turned fifty on October 2, 2004. I joke that fifty is the ultimate "F" word. But the truth is, it didn't feel that way to me. I was happy on my birthday, as if I'd crossed over to a better place. Really. I'm not kidding.

I don't think I've lost my power as a woman—in fact, I think I'm just beginning to come into my own. As an "older" woman, I think I'm even better than I ever was. I've come to terms with aging, and I've chosen to remain fully alive in the moment, as the real me. Every woman reaches a point where she must make a choice about whether she is going to embrace her age and appreciate its gifts, or live in fear and desperation as her youth fades. Maybe it's harder for actresses, because our physical appearance and our youthful demeanors are so crucial to getting work. It's a tough, competitive business, and I know that people have come to expect good-looking performers on the screen. Thank God they're still writing the occasional role for less than perfect people, or else an awful lot of really good actors would be out of work. My choice is to be myself, happily and confidently. I don't care what Hollywood or anyone else thinks.

Do I ever feel desperate about growing older? Honestly? Yeah. When I was full of fear in other areas of my life, when I was depressed and thought my life was down the toilet, and all my chances were used up, yeah, I felt old. But do you get the difference? I wasn't depressed because I was getting older. I felt older because I was depressed.

Once I beat the blues and started to get my life back, started to feel like myself again, I felt like I could take on the world and do just fine. Old? Ha! I was smarter, juicier, and better than ever. It took me a while to get there, though.

Professionally, an actress has to face reality. No actress my age is getting swamped with scripts. Sean Connery was a hot leading man at sixty-plus, but so far we haven't seen that with a woman. I hope we will in my lifetime. When you do come across a part that has legs, so to speak, it's such a thrill. A Dr. Melfi, or a Livia Soprano, for example. Seeing strong, mature women on the screen gives the lie to the idea that women have an expiration date of thirty-five or forty. I'm not paying my hard-earned money to buy into that program. You know, there's nothing new about the obsession with youth. It's built into our DNA. But that doesn't mean we have to roll over and play dead.

These days, I don't have the time or interest to worry about not being young anymore. That's life, as they say, and life is what I cherish. I care about being healthy and having energy to follow my new dreams. I care about enjoying my family, and being able to sit back and appreciate the fine young women Margaux and Stella have become.

Here's the real point, though—the realization I've made about aging. Work or no work, relationship or no relationship, all you have in the end is yourself and your own integrity. Growing older strips off some of the veneer. It's harder to hide. You have to be awake, aware, and well read to constantly check yourself: "Hello, is anybody home?"

I know one thing. I don't want to be one of those people who jolt awake one day and say, "Oh, my God, where did the years go?" I won't let that happen. Believe me, the years speed up as you get older. They whiz by. I want to experience every one of them. I want to wake up every morning with a feeling of anticipation, not knowing what to expect. I want to try things I've never tried before, although it's a more finely tuned list.

When I finally got up from the couch, after examining my life, both my bad choices and my good instincts, my failures and my successes, I felt stronger, empowered, and hopeful about the future. I wasn't going to waste my time on guilt and blame and regret. I was going to be the person I was meant to be—just me, Lorraine, alive, happy, and ready to take on the world.

Twelve · Life Lessons from the Couch

Your subconscious is shouting something at you.
· Dr. Jennifer Melfi

THE PRESENT

Playing Dr. Melfi has taught me how to listen in a new way. In her sessions with Tony, Dr. Melfi addresses some of the most painful realities that ordinary people struggle with every day. Yes, it's true: even mob bosses have incorrigible teenagers, marital strife, and problems with their mothers. We are not alone, any of us, in facing these issues. Viewers appreciate and respect Dr. Melfi because they have been exposed to the reality of what ongoing therapy is all about.

I've found that a kind of transference has occurred with fans of *The Sopranos*. They seem to relate to me differently, perhaps because I play the role of Dr. Melfi. When I talk to people, they don't ask me the usual questions actresses get—you know: *How do you keep your figure? Who does your hair? What was it like to kiss Sean Connery?* (Really good, by the way.) In part, thanks to Dr.

Melfi, people seem to want something deeper, a perspective on life. As if they recognize that my ability to shape Dr. Melfi as a meaningful and sympathetic character comes from my personal experience, including some of my darkest moments.

At the age of fifty-one, I feel that I've learned many vital lessons. Believe me, it's never too late.

I've asked some hard but necessary questions in my own life: Why must we hurt each other? Why must we abandon one another? Why must so many of us always take the cheap shot and the easy way out? Do we have to? Are we bound by cultural norms that don't feed our souls? I am guilty of these things. I am guilty of lying, of infidelity. I can't change the past, but the deal I've made with myself is that I won't hurt people anymore. I will have the courage to honor my feelings sooner rather than later. It's better to live in a life that's real, even if it's difficult and uncomfortable, than to pretend. I can no longer live in a lie.

1. Be Straight with Yourself

There are few industries as filled with illusion as the movie industry. Success, celebrity, fame, and fortune are all trouble. They are dangerous traps because it takes time to find the balance. It is so easy to lose your way; it is just not normal to see your face on the big screen, to have strangers recognize you, to have to explain to your small kids why people want you to sign pieces of paper. Autographs.

Fame has changed the way most people now react to me. I'm still me, but people's perceptions of me have changed. And it's so easy to forget this—to start believing all the bullshit. Like anybody else, I want to be with people who like me for myself.

I think it's especially hard for women because you can feel elevated by being the "it" piece of ass of the moment. And the "it" factor causes so much desperation in Hollywood—or anywhere. If a woman isn't careful, she ends up compromising her dignity and her integrity. It's just not healthy.

If you go to Hollywood seeking fame and fortune and your intentions are not pure, people will prey on you with their sickness. What does it mean to have pure intentions? To be serious about the craft. The hype, the politics of the industry, the obsession with celebrity—none of that mattered to me. All I wanted to do was to be a good actress.

Our society's images of morality, as reflected in TV, movies, and music, can be soul-deadening. We live in an age where there's a warped idea of reality. Ironically, even "reality" shows are scripted. God forbid we should admit our flaws, look our age, or take responsibility when we mess up. How can we counterbalance all of the crap that is inundating us? Being true to ourselves is about knowing the difference between good and evil. It's about keeping a positive moral character. It's about living a real and ethical life.

To be straight with yourself, you have to know yourself. Therapy helped me in that way. It wasn't easy, but it was liberating. I saw the way I had depended on the men in my life to rescue me and then define me. It felt easier to be what they made me instead of doing the hard work of becoming a self in my own right. The lesson has come late for me, but it doesn't have to be that way.

Life has taught me that it is my own personal integrity that will get me through, not compromising myself, or kowtowing to others. The only thing that matters is that at night, before I go to sleep, I ask myself: am I good with me? That's my deal.

2. Own Your Life, But Don't Be a Control Freak

As Dr. Melfi tells Tony Soprano, "There is no such thing as total control." That's certainly true, but it doesn't stop people from trying. I spent most of my life trying to fix other people and to make things right, when the truth was that I had absolutely no power over the choices they made.

Control is a tough balancing act. On the one hand, you have to be in charge of your own life. On the other hand, you have to realize that you aren't the mistress of the universe.

This is an important lesson for parents. If we could wave a magic wand, every parent would do so immediately, if it would ensure that their kids had perfect lives. But we can't control our children's destinies or live our lives through them, no matter how desperately we may wish to. I had to laugh at a scene in *The Sopranos* involving Tony and Carmela's teenage daughter, Meadow. Meadow, seizing an opportunity, had hosted a drinking party at her grandmother's empty house, and the kids ended up trashing the place. Tony and Carmela were outraged, but Tony warned Carmela that they should be careful about how they chose to discipline Meadow. He said, "Let's not overplay our hand. If she figures out we're powerless, we're fucked." What parent can't relate to that?

Let me tell you, parenting is the hardest job there is. It can also be the most rewarding. I'm proud of my daughters, but sometimes I have to bite my tongue and let them make their own mistakes, knowing they have to experience the bumps and bruises of life for themselves. I hope other people will love them for who they are, and not for who I am. They are women. They're not my babies anymore.

Look, we bring up our kids to be independent, but part of us doesn't want them to be independent. There's a huge temptation to keep them needing us and being needy. But if we've done a good job, they'll fly on their own.

3. Prince Charming Isn't Coming

We all love fairy tales and romantic stories, but I've always tried to impress one fact upon my girls: Prince Charming isn't coming. He isn't on the horizon. He hasn't even saddled up his white charger. It's a shame we're still fighting that myth in this day and age, but we are. Too many young women don't prepare themselves for life, don't become their own person because they're waiting for a man to show up and complete them. It's not going to happen. Even if you think I'm wrong, and you believe it's happened for you, 99 percent of the time I'm right. There's a reason the divorce rate is as high as it is.

The whole Cinderella thing? That girl worked her ass off, okay, and it was just a fairy tale anyway. I've told my girls, sure, you can be Cinderella. Scrub the floors. Do the windows. Clean up your rooms. But please, for God's sake just don't expect Prince Charming to show up and rescue you from all of that.

Both of my daughters are smart and independent, but the myth of rescue is so pervasive that even they are vulnerable to it. I tell them, "Trust me. It's better to be self-sufficient than dependent. It's better to be a whole person, not a half a person waiting for your 'better half.' And then, when a nice guy happens to walk through the door, you won't look at him like, 'Is *this* my Prince Charming, my savior?'"

If you're the parent of young girls, you should be mightily concerned with the messages they're receiving from the mass culture. You see this neediness, this lack of independence, with so many teenage girls, even today. If they don't have a boyfriend or a date on Saturday night, they can't be happy. It's weird. We've come so far as women, as people, and yet our young girls are growing up with this myth still imprinted in them: *you need a man to be happy*. No, honey, you don't. You need to become a real human being to be happy. A guy isn't going to do it for you. You can't wait for somebody to show up and make your life perfect. Don't ever think that somebody else is going to complete you. It just doesn't work that way. You need to be complete before you can have room for someone else.

I could have hugged Margaux when she said recently, "Nobody's perfect. People are different, and that's what makes them so interesting." Quite a statement for a twenty-six-year-old! She has managed to learn early what some women never learn. There is an overwhelming drive in our society for girls and women to fit the mold of "Pretty Miss Perfect." They believe that it's the only way they can truly be accepted, to be worthy of love. But nobody's perfect. Nature isn't perfect. Chasing after a false ideal of perfection will only lead to misery. I wish the word "perfect" could be banned from the dictionary and "imperfect but honest and interesting" could become our new ideal.

It horrifies me to see seventeen-year-old girls needing boob jobs and saying, "This makes me feel better about myself." If a boob job makes you feel better about yourself, that's a tragedy. And if we as parents buy into it, instead of saying, "No, you are a beautiful and still blossoming young woman," it's an even greater tragedy.

Mothers have a big role to play here. If girls grow up seeing their mothers picking at lettuce leaves and obsessing over their weight, they're going to obsess over their weight, too. It's a fact. In my household, we tried to be healthy, but there was no starving going on.

By the way, my girls have had to learn that Daddy Charming isn't coming, either. I learned that I could only encourage them to have their own relationships with their fathers. You only get one father. The quicker you accept him for who he is, the better your life will be. They've both had to come to terms with fathers who are absent in important ways. It's been hard for me to watch, but they need to learn that they don't have to look for replacement daddies in the men they choose.

Margaux has tried very hard to have a place in Daniel's orbit, and she has usually ended up disappointed. Daniel is who he is. I've been straight with her about that, but she has to learn it for herself. Not long ago, on her way to Italy with friends, she made a special stop in Paris, and Daniel couldn't even squeeze her in for dinner. What could have been so important in his life that he couldn't spend time with his daughter—who is, by the way, his only child? Margaux has been getting this reality check about Daniel her whole life.

As for Harvey, that's a reality check, too. Here's a guy who fought me tooth and nail for custody, but now that Stella's an adult, she tells me it's hard for her to reach him. If she wants to talk to him, she has to call his office and talk to his assistant. Sometimes he doesn't call her back for days. It's tough for her. What do I tell her? I tell her that her father is who he is. Nobody can change that. I tell her she has to find her esteem from the inside. Daddy isn't going to ride in on a white steed and give her life meaning.

4. Obsession Is Not Love

Recently, when I was getting my hair done, the beautiful young woman giving me a conditioning treatment was spilling out her tale of woe to me. Her boyfriend cheated on her. He wasn't nice to her. He spent all of her money on his debts. He never told her he loved her.

Sounds like a real gem, right? I asked, "Why do you think you deserve such good treatment?"

She sighed hopelessly and said, "I don't know what it is. He's like a drug or something, you know?"

"What drug is that?" I responded. "I want to be sure to stay away from it!"

But I knew what she was talking about. These young girls get involved early on in these very intense relationships. The boyfriend becomes controlling and jealous. Jealous! Now he thinks he owns her. If I could give one big message to these girls, it's this: Jealousy is not love. Jealousy is about power and possessiveness and control. We've got to teach girls young, too. Young girls are getting into things with boys that they're not ready for. When a guy starts paying attention to you, and he says, "You look too good. That guy is staring at you—we're leaving," the meaning is very clear—danger! Danger! Major warning! Young girls can mistake possessiveness for love, and it's not. This negative attention is a sign of ownership, not love. Control is not love. What is missing inside of them that makes this feel like love?

I understand that when you're young and feeling your way, and don't quite yet know who you are, it can be very seductive to have a man give you what feels like a validation of your appeal. But that's exactly the reason you have to have self-validation first and not depend on someone else to give it to you. If you can only see yourself reflected in a man's eyes, you're in for a world of hurt. In my work with domestic violence, I have seen countless young women who tell the same sad stories. Everything started out lovey-dovey, the men adored them, blah, blah, blah. How did things go wrong? They can't see that things were wrong from the start. They ended up in abusive, controlling relationships because they mistook their boyfriends' behavior as loving and caring, protective. It's not. I've spoken with young women in physically violent relationships. Their boyfriends hit them, and they cover it up, hide the abuse from the world. But sometimes secretly they feel kind of proud that someone loves them enough to be driven to such rage. But love doesn't terrorize. It doesn't come with slaps and punches.

And why is this happening? I think it's because kids are having sex way too young. They're getting too intensely involved at too young an age. How many parents know that their fifteen-year-old daughters are having sex with their boyfriends? That they're drinking or doing drugs? That they're being slapped or talked down to or treated disrespectfully? That they're spending time in Internet chat rooms?

Here's the message, loud and clear: if a man doesn't treat you right, get out of it *now,* because he's giving you a list of the coming attractions, and it's not even complete yet.

Everybody's got problems. I look around and sometimes I laugh. I know so many people with so much money, and they're miserable. They're miserable. And I've said it to my children, I've said it to myself, if you can't find happiness in yourself, whether it's twelve o'clock in the afternoon or twelve o'clock at night, you can never be happy in a relationship.

Rule one in a relationship is to ask: Can I make it without this person? Can I see myself clearly as a separate individual? Even when the relationship is good, you have to ask that. And I'm not just talking about emotionally, because your emotions don't put food on the table. Ask yourself whether you've abdicated your financial independence. I recently talked to a woman who had lived with a guy for almost ten years. Never got married because her boyfriend said, "It's just a piece of paper." Let me tell you about that piece of paper. It ended up being pretty important when they broke up. The house was in his name. The cars were in his name. She had nothing. He kicked her to the curb. How did this happen? She believed in love, and she wanted to prove that she trusted him. Fine. But you have to be realistic and self-protective. You have to be responsible for 50 percent of the relationship, as well as 50 percent of its demise. Keep your own bank account. Get your name on the deed. Have a backup plan. Get a strip mall, not the diamonds. A lot of women have been tricked into thinking it's cynical to take those steps. But how many men do you know who would tolerate having nothing in their name?

5. Don't Buy the DVD

After *Pretty Woman* came out in 1990, twelve-year-old Margaux wanted a pair of high-heeled boots just like Julia Roberts wore in the movie. Now, Julia was playing a hooker. I went crazy, and I cursed the industry for putting Julia Roberts, America's sweetheart, in a role that had young girls aspiring to a warped Cinderella theme. *Pretty Woman* was a movie selling a fantasy—a gorgeous prostitute with the appearance and personal habits of a grand lady (she flosses, for Christ's sake!) who falls in love with a mogul (who happens to be Richard Gere), and he with her. So she gets a lot of really swell clothes and jewelry, and then they live happily ever after.

Oh, my girls loved Julia—who doesn't?—especially in that movie. But what was I supposed to tell them about their favorite role model? They didn't know what a prostitute was. They only knew that Julia was Pretty Miss Perfect, and ever so charming. But they *really* wanted those thigh-high boots.

Then there was the phenomenon that was Madonna. Like millions of other little girls, they wanted to tart themselves up, dress just like her, and belt out "Like a Virgin." And how many parents have watched their six- and seven-year-old daughters prance around singing Britney Spears' hit single "Oops, I Did it Again"?

You know, they get stuck on these market creations before they know who they are themselves. They're mesmerized. There is a huge amount of peer pressure—more than ever—to imitate the dolls of fame.

I have been driven to despair that these dolls of fame have become the role models for our daughters. We need to find a more substantial message for our children to emulate. Those in the entertainment industry only want to generate money. We need to be the watchdogs of our culture, to help our kids avoid the pitfalls of cultural popularity that lead them to do foolish things, spiraling downward to join the crowd instead of soaring above to blaze their own path. Individuality is very difficult. It is easy and false to grow up believing that tabloids, cheap TV, and scripted "reality" shows define you.

6. Accept Help

"Hope comes in many forms," says Dr. Melfi. Can you tell it's one of my favorite quotes from the show? It has become like a mantra to me. When you're depressed, you don't see it. It's dark outside all of the time. You don't think the dawn will ever come.

After I received an award from the American Psychoanalytic Association for my portrayal of Dr. Melfi, and spoke openly for the first time about my experiences with depression, several drug companies approached me about being a spokeswoman. Initially I said no, but then, years later, I started thinking about the enormous stigma associated with mental illness. I thought of all the fans who had come up to me, wanting to talk about their depression and the embarrassment they felt about being on medication. That's what finally pushed me to team up with Pfizer to educate the public about medical treatment for depression, and to launch the website DepressionHelp.com.

I hope my story encourages people to come forward and get the help they need. I want to help others to do what I did—to let go of the shame and the fear. The most important thing is to go to a doctor for help, whether it's for medication, talk therapy, or a combination of both.

Besides the stigma, the taboo, I think people are afraid to scratch the surface of their own inner selves. They can't stand the idea that they're weak, that some bigger force has a hold over them. We can talk about cancer—nothing to be ashamed of. We can talk about breaking a leg—nothing to be ashamed of. But depression? Shhhh! God forbid you should be depressed. That's terrible. You must have done something to deserve it. The thinking on this subject is downright Neanderthal sometimes.

When I was depressed, I wallowed in the idea that the best part of my life was over. I blew it. I took the wrong path, and this was what I got—what I *deserved*. I told myself, you made your bed, now you lie in it. Thank God I found help before I went too far down that road.

It was the best decision I ever made for myself. I know I sound like a broken record, but it really was. I'm still a very vibrant woman. Not too bad looking. I'm a smart girl. I'm funny. And to think I was willing to throw myself away. It gives me a chill. To think I was willing to give myself nothing, to let my problems eat away at me instead of having joy and following my dreams. It was a close call.

There's help. It's treatable. Getting treatment for depression was the best decision I ever made; going public about it was the second best. People ask me, "Were you embarrassed to tell the world about your depression?" I'm not going to sugarcoat it. It wasn't a walk in the park. It's difficult to let people in on the inner you, especially if it's not so pretty.

A couple of months after I started therapy, I drove over to my parents' house. There had been so much I hadn't wanted them to know. I was worried that they would be disappointed in me, and see my depression as a weakness. I was worried I was coming to them again, bearing not such good news, and they wouldn't be able to take it. I said to them, here's the story. And I told them what had been going on with me. That day, we began to talk about the past and the present, and secrets and disappointments we had never talked about before. It was healing. I wasn't afraid anymore.

I understand people being afraid to talk about their depression.

But don't be so sure that others won't want to listen, or will judge you harshly. It was a relief to put it on the table.

I think there are points in people's lives—being in the dying throes of a bad marriage, separation, divorce, children getting sick, parents dying—that propel them into a depression. Not everyone is able to just move on and everything is all right. Life just doesn't work that way. People get depressed, they grieve, they get sick themselves, they start having panic attacks, they can't get out of bed in the morning; their whole life just goes to shit. It happens, and it happens a lot. And it happens to all kinds of people, so it's a massive problem.

What do you think is going to be the result of the horror people in New Orleans experienced from Hurricane Katrina? There are tens of thousands of people traumatized, maybe hundreds of thousands of people in need of help. Think of all the children who watched as their parents lost everything. And they don't need just food and water, not just housing, clothing, and work, but more, much more. People's entire lives have been destroyed. I don't even know if we have enough mental-health professionals to help all of the people who are going to need it. People are going to be depressed and traumatized by all that has gone on. It may not be today, and it may not be tomorrow, but eventually a lot of these people will need extensive therapy and probably medication to help them get through this.

I never thought I'd see our nation brought so low, and not seem to have the means for the government to respond to such a massive disaster in an immediate way. It blows my mind. And it makes my point even more urgent—if you need help, get help. Don't hesitate. The life you save will not only be your own, but those of all of your family and friends. If one person has the courage to seek help, it acts as an example to many others to seek help, too. It snowballs, and a lot more people receive help than would have otherwise. So, if you're reading this, and you know that something is wrong, please get help. You are worth it. Don't be afraid. Don't hesitate. I wish I had not waited. Be brave and seek aid. I did, and it made all the difference.

I know that sometimes people feel trapped in relationships—maybe you're with an addict, or an abuser, or someone who doesn't have your best interests at heart. How do you look out for yourself? Where do you go if you don't have the resources or the connections, and you have a couple of kids to worry about? I've had women say to me, "I know I don't deserve this, but what am I supposed to do? Take my kids and live on the street?" I hear that. I know how it feels to be trapped. I made a big mistake when I was going through the horrible custody fight and the ensuing depression. I didn't reach out for a long time. When you can't reach out to the people who are closest to you—whether it's your friends or your family—and tell the truth about what you're feeling and experiencing, that's a sad place to be in. I believed that no one could really help me, and I was so wrong. So even if the situation seems impossible, take that first step of reaching out.

You don't have to suffer. It doesn't matter what people think. Get the help you need. I did.

7. Enjoy the Ride

"There is no cure for life." Well, sure, there's always death, but that's a zero sum game. The playwright Eugene O'Neill, in *The Great God Brown,* said, "Man is born broken. He lives by mending. The grace of God is glue." So maybe life isn't about finding a cure, but instead discovering what it takes to keep ourselves together, to mend ourselves, so we can go on and live life to the fullest. There is no cure for the pain and the suffering we experience as human beings. I have learned that it is how we choose to deal with that part of life's journey that defines our essence.

There are a lot of people who get stuck in their blame and anger, and they lose sight of how great life is. They become bitter and impoverished. How sad to live with a closed heart.

Beyond *The Sopranos* and my role as Dr. Melfi, I think I have a reputation as a woman who can hold her own and who finally speaks her mind, who refuses to be marginalized just because she's fifty.

I'm more interested in substance than stuff these days. You can't take it with you. That's what I know. I don't care so much about being with the big boys and having the big toys. None of my stuff is going to feed my soul. At the same time, making money and being independent mean freedom to me. I like to be free to make my own choices. And if I make a wrong choice, then *I* make it. Trust me, I'd rather kick myself in the ass than have somebody else do it for me.

I approach my fifties hungry for life, but it's a different kind of hunger than I had before. I'm not starving but I'm ambitious to devour life. I'm hungry for the simple, real pleasures. For good conversation over good food and wine. Toasting life and the pleasure of living. I love it when Dr. Melfi says to Tony, "When we're not constantly having to put out fires, we can really delve into who you are and what you're really after in your very brief time on this earth." Without the fear and anxiety and melodrama, I've opened up a clear space for self-discovery and growth. It's a great place to be.

Acknowledgments

Along the way, a lot of people told me to write a book. Well, shit happens. Here's the story: At a birthday party for Whoopi Goldberg, I found myself next to John Edward, a great pal and renowned psychic medium. I had just finished the Broadway run of *The Graduate*—he had sent me a big fluffy robe as a gift—funny, right?—and we were talking. Out of the blue, John said to me, "Write the book." How did he know that I had been approached about doing a book? "Sign it up," he insisted. "Do you need me to send you a pen?" Who in their right mind would ignore a psychic?

So, thanks to my literary agent, Jeanne Forte Dube (and little Dube), who wouldn't let me ignore her, and made this book happen. Catherine Whitney helped me to capture my spirit on the page. My publishers at Putnam not only kept their promises but fed me well. I am grateful for the endless patience of my editor, Chris Pepe. As for Ivan Held, let's just say that he's been a lot of fun.

In the middle of my chaos, my brother Sal told me, "The only advice I have for you, Lorraine, is that your success will be your best revenge." This book is a result of that struggle. John Hoving, Heather Reynolds, Lisa Davis, Ruthie Bergman, Peggy Moran: You each waited for me when I fell behind and I am so grateful to all of you.

David Chase, you gave me Melfi. Ilene "Moneybags" Landress, you are the true Melfi and more. Shout out to Momo.

Family really is everything. Mom, Dad, Sal and Lizzie, Jill, Aidan—I love you. My affection and love to Barbara King. Jason Cipolla, you have been such a gift to me. Margaux and Stella, you are the heart and soul of my life. And just remember, don't forget to bring a coat.

Resources

My Life Onscreen and Onstage

Film and Television Credits

Max and Grace (aka *My Suicidal Sweetheart*) (2005): directed by Michael Parness. Role: Sheila.

Law & Order: Trial by Jury, "Vigilante" episode (2005): TV, directed by Dwight H. Little. Role: Karla Grizano.

Death of a Dynasty (2003): directed by Damon Dash. Role: Enchante, R&B Singer No. 2.

Tangled (2001): directed by Jay Lowi. Role: Detective Anne Andersle.

Riding in Cars with Boys (2001): directed by Penny Marshall. Role: Mrs. Teresa Donofrio.

Custody of the Heart (2000): directed by David Hugh-Jones. Role: Claire Raphael.

The Sopranos (1999 to present): TV series created by David Chase. Role: Dr. Jennifer Melfi.

Ladies Room (1999): directed by Penelope Buitenhuis. Role: Gemma.

The Taking of Pelham One Two Three (1998): TV remake, directed by Félix Enríque Alcalá. Role: Detective Ray.

Silent Cradle (aka *Le Berceau Muet*) (1997): directed by Paul Ziller. Role: Helen Greg.

Lifeline (aka *Cap Danger*; aka *Reckoning*) (1996): TV, directed by Fred Gerber. Role: Kits Maitland.

Les Menteurs (aka *The Liars*) (1996): directed by Elie Chouraqui. Role: Helene Miller.
Hackers (1995): directed by Iain Softley. Role: Margo.
The Basketball Diaries (1995): directed by Scott Kalvert. Role: Jim's mother.
Getting Gotti (1994): TV, directed by Roger Young. Role: Diane Giacalone.
Even Cowgirls Get the Blues (1993): directed by Gus Van Sant. Role: Delores Del Ruby.
Scam (1993): TV, directed by John Flynn. Role: Maggie Rohrer.
Being Human (1993): directed by Bill Forsyth. Role: Anna.
Traces of Red (1992): directed by Andy Wolk. Role: Ellen Schofield.
Radio Flyer (1992): directed by Richard Donner. Role: Mary.
Medicine Man (1992): directed by John McTiernan. Role: Dr. Rae Crane.
Switch (1991): directed by Blake Edwards. Role: Sheila Faxton.
Talent for the Game (1991): directed by Robert M. Young. Role: Bobbie.
Goodfellas (1990): directed by Martin Scorsese. Role: Karen Hill.
Sea of Love (1989): directed by Harold Becker. Role: Denice Gruber (uncredited).
In una Notte di Chiaro di Luna (aka *As Long as It's Love*) (1989): directed by Lina Wertmüller. Role: Sheila.
The Dream Team (1989): directed by Howard Zieff. Role: Riley.
Sing (1989): directed by Richard J. Baskin. Role: Miss Lombardo.
Someone to Watch Over Me (1987): directed by Ridley Scott. Role: Ellie Keegan.
The Pick-up Artist (1987): directed by James Toback. Role: Carla.
Crime Story, "Hide and Go Thief" episode (1986): TV series created by Chuck Adamson and Gustave Reininger. Role: Hostage.
Un Complicato Intrigo di Donne, Vicoli e Delitti (aka *A Complex Plot About Women, Alleys, and Crimes;* aka *Camorra*) (1986): directed by Lina Wertmüller (uncredited).
Fais Gaffe à la Gaffe (1981): directed by Paul Boujenah. Role: Margaux.
Mais Qu'est-ce Que J'ai Fait au Bon Dieu pour Avoir une Femme Qui Boit dans les Cafés avec les Hommes? (aka *What Did I Ever Do to the Good Lord to Deserve a Wife Who Drinks in Cafes with Men?*) (1980): directed by Jan Saint-Hamont. Role: Barbara.
Duos sur Canapé (1979): directed by Marc Camoletti. Role: Bubble.

THEATER CREDITS

The Graduate, directed by Terry Johnson. Role: Mrs. Robinson. Broadway, November 19, 2002, through March 2, 2003. National tour, January 6, 2004, through March 13, 2004.
Goose and Tomtom, workshop directed by David Rabe. Role: Lulu. Mitzi Newhouse Theater, 1986.

My Favorite Causes

As you know, I believe that the best thing you can do for yourself is to give to others. We live in a very privileged society, so let's share some of that wealth of time, money, and spirit. Here are some of my favorite causes. I invite you to join me in lending a hand. To all the volunteers, who give of themselves for the betterment of those less fortunate, know that you are my true heroes.

COMMON GROUND
Common Ground Community is a nonprofit housing and community development organization whose mission is to solve homelessness. Common Ground provides a comprehensive support system of safe, affordable housing, medical care, and job placement designed to help people regain lives of stability and independence.
www.commonground.org
(212) 389-9300

CROHN'S AND COLITIS FOUNDATION OF AMERICA, INC. (CCFA) (GREATER NEW YORK CHAPTER)
The mission of the Crohn's and Colitis Foundation of America, Inc., is to prevent and cure Crohn's disease and ulcerative colitis through research, and to improve the quality of life of children and adults affected by these digestive diseases, through education and support. Known collectively as inflammatory bowel diseases (IBD), these painful, chronic illnesses affect approximately 1.4 million Americans, including some 140,000 children under the age of eighteen.
www.ccfa.org
(212) 679-1570

DRESS FOR SUCCESS
A nonprofit organization that gives free interview suits, confidence boosts, and career development to low-income women. Available in over seventy-five local communities. Go to the website for local help and information.
www.dressforsuccess.org

FRIENDS IN DEED
Since 1991, Friends in Deed has provided emotional support for anyone with a diagnosis of HIV/AIDS, cancer, or other life-threatening physical illness, along with their family, friends, and caregivers, as well as anyone dealing with grief and bereavement. They run a major HIV-prevention program for teens in New York City public schools.
www.friendsindeed.org
(212) 925-2009

Habitat for Humanity

A nonprofit, ecumenical housing organization that builds simple, decent, affordable housing in partnership with people in need.
121 Habitat St.
Americus, Georgia 31709
(229) 924-6935
www.habitatforhumanity.org

HELP USA

HELP USA is the nation's largest nonprofit builder, developer, and operator of transitional housing, with on-site human services for the homeless, serving more than 6,600 individuals every day.
www.helpusa.org
(212) 400-7000

Joe Torre Safe at Home Foundation

A foundation devoted to educational projects to end the cycle of domestic violence and save kids.
Grand Central Station
P.O. Box 3133
New York, NY 10163
(877) 878-4JOE
www.joetorre.org

Police Athletic League (PAL)

The Police Athletic League is New York City's largest nonprofit, independent youth organization. Founded in 1914, PAL serves 70,000 New York City boys and girls each year with recreational, educational, cultural, and social programs. PAL is the official youth agency of the New York Police Department.
www.palnyc.org
(212) 477-9450, x351

Riverkeeper

An organization that protects New York's great Hudson River and the future of our most important natural resources.
828 South Broadway
Tarrytown, NY 10591
(800) 21-RIVER
www.riverkeeper.org

Rockland Family Shelter

A grassroots organization dedicated to ending violence against women, children, and youth, providing community services and information.

2 Congers Rd.
New City, NY 10956
(845) 634-3391
24-hour hotline: (845)-634-3344
www.rocklandfamilyshelter.org

Safe Horizon
A victims-assistance organization that provides support, prevents violence, and promotes justice for victims of crime and abuse.
2 Lafayette St., 3rd Floor
New York, NY 10007
(212) 577-7700
Hotlines:
Domestic violence: (800) 661-HOPE
Crime victims: (866) 689-HELP
Rape, sexual assault: (212) 227-3000
www.safehorizon.org

United Network for Organ Sharing (UNOS)
UNOS brings together medicine, science, public policy, and technology to facilitate every organ transplant performed in the United States. Every day, UNOS assists transplant doctors, patients, and members of the public by helping to ensure that organs are procured and distributed in a fair and timely manner.
www.unos.org
(888) 894-6361

United Service Organizations (USO)
The USO's mission is to bolster morale and provide welfare- and recreation-type services to our men and women in uniform. The original intent of Congress—and enduring style of USO delivery—is to represent the American people by extending a touch of home to the military.
www.uso.org
(800) 876-7469

My Book List

When I was fighting depression, my therapist gave me some very good advice. She told me to use that time to learn and explore, to take an inner journey. I decided to feed my soul at the local bookstore. These are fifteen books that informed and nourished me during that time and to this day. Maybe you'll find help in them, or in your own choices. I'm living proof that reading can change a person for the better.

Mitch Albom, *Tuesdays with Morrie: An Old Man, a Young Man, and Life's Greatest Lesson*. New York: Doubleday, 1997.

Julia Cameron, *The Artist's Way: A Spiritual Path to Higher Creativity*. New York: Jeremy P. Tarcher, 2002.

Rachel Carson, *Silent Spring*. New York: Mariner Books edition, 2002.

Deepak Chopra, *The Seven Spiritual Laws of Success: A Practical Guide to the Fulfillment of Your Dreams*. San Rafael, CA: New World Library/Amber-Allen Publishing, 1995.

Karen Levin Coburn and Madge Lawrence Treeger, *Letting Go: A Parent's Guide to Understanding the College Years*. New York: Quill, 2003.

Gerald Corey, Cindy Corey, and Heidi Jo Corey, *Living and Learning*. Belmont, CA: Wadsworth Publishing, 1996.

His Holiness the Dalai Lama, and Howard C. Cutler, M.D., *The Art of Happiness: A Handbook for Living*. New York: Riverhead, 1998.

Kahlil Gibran, *The Prophet*. New York: Alfred A. Knopf, 1923.

Thich Nhat Hanh, *Anger: Wisdom for Cooling the Flames*. New York: Riverhead Books, 2001.

M. Scott Peck, *Further Along the Road Less Traveled: The Unending Journey Toward Spiritual Growth*. New York: Simon & Schuster, 1993.

M. Scott Peck, *The Road Less Traveled: A New Psychology of Love, Traditional Values, and Spiritual Growth*. New York: Simon & Schuster, 2002.

Sogyal Rinpoche, *The Tibetan Book of Living and Dying*. San Francisco: HarperSanFrancisco, 2002.

Eckhart Tolle, *The Power of Now: A Guide to Spiritual Enlightenment*. Novarto, CA: New World Library, 1999.

Marianne Williamson, *The Gift of Change: Spiritual Guidance for a Radically New Life*. San Francisco: HarperSanFrancisco, 2004.

Gary Zukav, *The Seat of the Soul*. New York: Simon & Schuster, 1989.

This checklist could help change your life or that of someone you care about.

Depression Checklist

If you think you might have depression symptoms, this checklist can help you talk about your concerns with your doctor.

Just answer the questions, and take the finished checklist to an appointment with a doctor or other healthcare professional. Your answers can help your doctor determine if you have depression.

Over the past two weeks,
how often have you been bothered by any of the following problems?

1. Little interest or pleasure in doing things
   - ☐ Not at all ☐ Several days
   - ☐ More than half the days ☐ Nearly every day

2. Feeling down, depressed or hopeless
   - ☐ Not at all ☐ Several days
   - ☐ More than half the days ☐ Nearly every day

3. Trouble falling or staying asleep, or sleeping too much
   - ☐ Not at all ☐ Several days
   - ☐ More than half the days ☐ Nearly every day

4. Feeling tired or having little energy
   - ☐ Not at all ☐ Several days
   - ☐ More than half the days ☐ Nearly every day

5. Poor appetite or overeating
   - ☐ Not at all ☐ Several days
   - ☐ More than half the days ☐ Nearly every day

6. Feeling bad about yourself, or feeling that you are a failure or have let yourself or your family down
   - ☐ Not at all ☐ Several days
   - ☐ More than half the days ☐ Nearly every day

7. Trouble concentrating on things such as reading the newspaper or watching television
   - ☐ Not at all ☐ Several days
   - ☐ More than half the days ☐ Nearly every day

8. Moving or speaking so slowly that other people notice. Or the opposite—being so fidgety or restless that you have been moving around a lot more than usual
   - ☐ Not at all
   - ☐ Several days
   - ☐ More than half the days
   - ☐ Nearly every day

9. Thinking that you would be better off dead or wanting to hurt yourself in some way
   - ☐ Not at all
   - ☐ Several days
   - ☐ More than half the days
   - ☐ Nearly every day